The Orbit of Meter

The Orbit of Meter

Writings on Poems and Prosody

by Robert Wallace

Edited by
James S. Baumlin and Anne Marie Baker

Foreword by
Christine Wallace

Springfield, Missouri
Missouri State University Libraries
2023

Published by the Ozarks Studies Institute, an initiative of the Missouri State University Libraries.
© 2023 Missouri State University. For inquiries, contact:
Duane G. Meyer Library
901 South National Avenue
Springfield, MO 65897
417.836.4525

Cover Photo | Herbert Ascherman, Jr. Photographer/Ascherman.net
Book Cover and Layout Design | Staci Stokes, Stokes Design Co.

Acknowledgments:
Wallace, Robert. "Meter in English." *Meter in English: A Critical Engagement*, edited by David Baker, pp. 3-42. Copyright 1996 by the University of Arkansas Press. Reprinted with the permission of the University of Arkansas Press, www.uapress.com.
Wallace, Robert. "On Not Teaching Poetry." *Moon City Review 2011*, edited by Marcus Cafagña and Joel Chaston, pp. 277-96. Copyright 2011 by Moon City Press, an imprint of the Department of English, Missouri State University. Reprinted with permission, http://moon-city-press.com.

Library of Congress Cataloging-in-Publication Data:

Names: Wallace, Robert, 1932-1999, author. | Baumlin, James S., editor. | Baker, Anne Marie, editor. | Wallace, Christine, writer of foreword.

Title: The orbit of meter : writings on poems and prosody / by Robert Wallace ; edited by James S. Baumlin and Anne Marie Baker ; foreword by Christine Wallace.

Description: Springfield, Missouri : The Ozarks Studies Institute, an initiative of the Missouri State University Libraries, 2023. | Includes bibliographical references.
Identifiers: ISBN 978-1-73796-16-3-5
Subjects: LCSH: Poetry—History and criticism. | English language—Versification. | Free verse—History and criticism. | LCGFT: Bibliographies. | Personal correspondence.

Classification: LCC PE1505 .W35 2022 | DDC 808.1—dc23

The **Ozarks Studies Institute (OSI)** of Missouri State University seeks to preserve the heritage of the Ozarks, its culture, environment, and history by fostering a comprehensive knowledge of Ozarks' peoples, places, characteristics, and dynamics. The Institute promotes a sense of place for residents and visitors alike and serves as an educational resource by collecting existing—and discovering new—knowledge about the Ozarks and by providing access to that knowledge. *The Orbit of Meter* is a part of the OSI publication series.

Contents

The Orbit of Meter

Foreword

This book fulfills a promise I made to my husband, Robert Wallace, twenty-two years ago. These essays are the work of Bob's final days on this earth, and the ideas he was trying to express occupied his days and nights to the end. His supreme effort to be precise and clear will be apparent in his words, even as he fought the ravages of disease and medication. The publication of *Free Verse and the Orbit of Meter* was his final request of me.

Immediately after Bob's death, I hesitated to publish *Orbit* without heavy editing, fearing that pain—and pain medication—prevented him from expressing himself clearly enough, and with scholarly composure. I did not wish to embarrass him by publishing something below his own very high standards. No poet or prosodist myself (I am a lawyer by trade), I participated in enough discussions about the fine points of *Orbit* to understand the elusive nature of its contents, but not enough to feel qualified to edit it myself.

Over time, however, I realized that no one was in a position to edit Bob's thoughts, so I finally feel compelled to allow the release of his analysis on its own terms, warts and all. If the text seems dated, a bit caustic, or unclear in any way, I humbly ask that you bear in mind the circumstances under which it was written, as well as my hesitation in publishing it.

Missouri State University is the repository of all of Bob's papers and books, as well as the owner of his copyrights. Bob hand-picked this vibrant university in his home town of Springfield, Missouri to sustain his memory and promote the poetry, prosody, publishing, and teaching that were so important to him. I must express my appreciation to Dean Thomas A. Peters of MSU's Duane G. Meyer Library, and Anne M. Baker, Head of Special Collections, for their support of this and many other efforts to promote awareness of the Wallace Collection. I would also like to thank Karl Schmidt of the MSU Foundation, who helped me to establish the Robert Wallace Poetry, Prosody, and Publishing Fund to continue support of these causes at Missouri State University well into the future.

Dr. James S. Baumlin has been at the heart of this book project, gently prodding me along, shaping the book into a workable form, and guiding it to publication. His intense familiarity with the Wallace Collection and its contents have led us to include in this volume "The Smoothest Typer Ever to Come Out of Springfield," Jim's descriptive tracing of Bob's life through the letters in the Collection. Bob's lecture, "On Not Teaching Poetry," which Jim found in his research, is included as well. If these provoke interest in the Wallace Collection, and perhaps prompt further research, they will have well served their purpose here. I am beyond grateful to Dr. Baumlin for his efforts.

This book begins with the essay, "Meter in English," to give the reader a full understand Bob's metrical analysis. Bob wrote "Meter in English" in 1993 to provoke debate among metrists—successfully I might add. The resulting collection of essays, *Meter in English: A Critical Engagement*, was edited by David Baker and published by the University of Arkansas Press in 1996. My thanks to University of Arkansas for allowing us to reprint Bob's original essay here.

Adjusting and refocusing the discussion begun in *Meter in English, Free Verse and the Orbit of Meter* attempts to unify the language with which we discuss the contents of *any* poetic line by defining and limiting the kinds of feet that can exist in English poetry. The complex interaction between foot and line, particularly in modern poetry, can then be discussed within a single system, allowing for a comprehensive understanding of the inner workings of a poem. As Bob says in his preface to *Orbit*, "The value, as always, lies in what we may discover about poems."

Be warned: *Orbit* casually incorporates ideas and authors and works from across several hundred years of English literature. These were all exceedingly familiar to the author, a lifelong poet and teacher. His analysis was intended for an audience already immersed in both prosody and poetry. It is not for the everyday reader. Still, I hope it will give insight and provoke lively debate among the poets, teachers, and lovers of language who are its intended audience.

– Christine Wallace
July 2022

Robert Wallace and the Wallace Collection

An Introduction

Anne Marie Baker and James S. Baumlin

More than craft, poetry was his vocation: in writing it, teaching it, editing it, publishing it, Robert Wallace (1932-1999) made strong contributions to American letters. In his final years, he turned to the theory of poetry itself, offering to systematize English prosody. Before him, discussions of metrics had made for a Babel of competing systems and vocabularies, whereas Wallace aimed to develop a single, flexible, teachable model. His essay, "Meter in English" (1996), argues for an iambic-anapestic metrical system bound to one prevailing verse-type—the accentual-syllabic, which had governed English poetry since its evolution from Anglo-Saxon. In between the publishing of "Meter" and the drafting of his unpublished *Free Verse and the Orbit of Meter,* Wallace added an additional foot-type, the bacchic, to his system. With the addition of this foot-type, Wallace would claim to have settled, once and for all, the noisy debate over prosody. The modern varieties of English poetry, including "free verse," all draw from an iambic-anapestic system made infinitely flexible by anacrusis and foot-substitutions (including the bacchic, previously under-appreciated).

Wallace believed in the importance of his last manuscript, and with good reason. For the work presents "nothing less than a paradigm shift in metrics, a potentially dramatic redirection of our study of meter and prosody," as Wallace's editor, David Baker, notes (*Meter in English* xvi). But he did not live to see it through to publication.

We will return to these texts shortly, for they are centerpieces of this present collection and deserve more readerly context. As we turn to the man and his biography, we wish to make one further point on Wallace's contribution to letters. To his successes as poet, teacher, editor, publisher, and prosodist, we should note his success in promoting the work and careers of fellow poets. For Wallace, it was not just the poem but the poet that mattered: The writings here gathered demonstrate his dedication to the community of poets and their appreciative readers. Poems that are not read—or, more importantly, read aloud—lose their lifeblood. As a teacher (particularly at Case Western Reserve in Cleveland), Wallace presided, as it were, over a network of fellow poets, drawn mainly from the American Midwest, who visited each others' schools and communities, giving poetry readings, lectures, interviews, workshops. The correspondence contained within the Robert Wallace Collection bears witness to "the Wallace circle" (as J. Baumlin terms it in an essay appended to this collection): More than fellow poets, Wallace's correspondents were friends, many of them lifelong. They are a testament to the man and to his dedication to the art, culture, economics, and community of poets.

Born January 10, 1932, Robert Wallace grew up in Springfield, Missouri, the only child of Roy Franklin and Tincy Stough Wallace. Roy operated a small factory that produced cherry and walnut furniture of his own design. Tincy was a homemaker.

Wallace showed an interest in poetry at a young age. "Bobby Wallace, a fifth-grader at Phelps school, likes to write poems, and he writes a lot of them. He has a whole notebook full. When he grows up, he wants to be a writer." So reads a local-interest column in the *Springfield Daily News* of February 23, 1942. In his reading, he was drawn to the American humorists. Ogden Nash (with whom he began an early correspondence) and Richard Armour were favorites. His first formal success came at sixteen when his poem, "Tee Hee," appeared in *The Rotarian* magazine. Based on his work as a golf caddy, the poem imitates Nash's wit and wordplay.[1] Wallace's love of light, humorous verse continued through his career, both in his own poetry and in the poems he edited and published through Bits Press. Two things his youthful experience taught him: that poetry belongs to children as much as to adults—hence his later collections, *Critters* (1978) and *Charlie Joins the Circus* (1981)—and that poetry, among its many therapeutic powers, can make us laugh.

In the fall of 1949, having graduated from Springfield High School (now Central High School), Wallace headed to Harvard, where he met his undergraduate housemate and lifelong friend, John Updike. There, he expanded his

---

[1] The brief poem reads: "He set the ball upon the tee / In manner oh-so-nice. / He said—this golf is pie for me— / And took another slice."

knowledge and appreciation of poetry. Nash and Armour gave way to new models: John Donne, W.B. Yeats, Robert Frost, and William Carlos Williams. He took literature and writing courses from noted authors, including the short story under Richard Wilbur. While at Harvard, several of his poems were published in *The Christian Science Monitor* and *The Lyric*. Graduating in 1953 with an A.B., summa cum laude, in English, Wallace received a Fulbright Scholarship to St. Catharine's College at Cambridge (1953-1955) and was made a Woodrow Wilson fellow (1953-1954). He completed his studies at Cambridge in 1955, earning the English Bachelor of Arts degree with honors (which became a Master of Arts in 1959).

In 1955 Wallace joined the military, where he served in the U.S. Army Counterintelligence Corps until his discharge in 1957. Professionally, 1957 was a halcyon year. His poetry continued to appear in numerous magazine publications and his first book, *This Various World and Other Poems*, was published by Scribner's. That year, he won the William Rose Benet Memorial Award from the Poetry Society of America, one of many awards he would win in his career. And he began his teaching career at Bryn Mawr College, where he was an instructor in English to 1961.

Following Bryn Mawr, Wallace spent two years teaching at Sweet Briar College (1961-1963), then two at Vassar College (1963-1965). In 1965, Wallace joined Case Western Reserve University in Cleveland, Ohio, as an associate professor of English. He stayed at Case Western Reserve for the rest of his academic career.

Professionally, 1965 was a second halcyon year: *Views from a Ferris Wheel*, a collection of poems, and *Poems on Poetry: The Mirror's Garland*, an anthology (co-edited with James G. Taaffe) were both published by Dutton. In 1968, Dutton published another book of poems, *Ungainly Things*. During the 1972-1973 academic year, a sabbatical allowed Wallace to spend a semester in Portugal, writing poems and learning the language. He returned to Ohio in the winter term as the George Elliston Visiting Lecturer at the University of Cincinnati. In 1972 he won the Emily Clark Balch Prize from the *Virginia Quarterly Review*. In 1974, he was promoted to full professor at Case Western Reserve.

In 1974, Wallace bought a tabletop letterpress and, adding to an already busy career, became a small-press publisher. Initially, he had planned to publish an anthology of poems from the Cleveland area. The response, however, was so enthusiastic that he widened the search to make it nationwide. With this, Bits Press and its literary magazine, *Bits,* was born. *Bits* was published semiannually from January of 1975 through January of 1980. Soon after the press was founded, Wallace developed a class that combined writing and printing poems (a commitment to print technology and to the "business" of small-press publishing, which was then a rarity in academia). This provided a unique learning experience for the students—and free labor for the press.

That student labor was a great help. Even as they expanded their publications list, Bits faced the same problem most small presses do: how to make enough profit in sales to cover costs. Wallace now owned a 12" by 18" Chandler and Price letterpress, enabling Bits to do all its printing inhouse. Given initially weak sales, they solved the problem of magazine subscriptions by giving copies away and covering expenses by small grants. (And, when these fell short, Wallace and other supporters reached into their own pockets to keep *Bits* magazine going.) In 1977, Bits Press published its first poetry chapbook, Peter Klappert's *Non Sequitur Connor*. This last publication proved pivotal, providing the press with a new business model. There was a collector's market for small print-runs of fine-art chapbooks (assuming sufficient name-recognition on the author's part). Thus, Bits Press turned to publishing fancy signed limited-edition chapbooks and broadsides. This business model succeeded in part because of Wallace's friendships and professional relationships with notable writers of the time. In 1978, Bits Press chapbooks included Mary Oliver's *The Night Traveler* (which was favorably reviewed by Joyce Carol Oates, contributing to Oliver's winning of a Pulitzer) and Peter Meinke's *The Rat Poems*. In 1985, Wallace's college friend, John Updike, published *Five Poems*: limited to 185 copies (with some printed on handmade paper), these were signed by Updike—which made *Five Poems* immediately collectible.

Bits magazine finished its run in 1980, but Bits Press continued. That year the press released seven chapbooks and a short journal of fiction, with another five chapbooks following in 1981. And Wallace was publishing some of his own work with Bits, including the children's book, *Charlie Joins the Circus*.

In 1982, Little, Brown, and Co. published the first edition of *Writing Poems*—a textbook for college poetry writing classes and easily the most widely known of Wallace's works. For the next forty years following, students of poetry learned their craft from Wallace and his co-editor (2nd ed. Scott Foresman, 1987; 3rd ed. HarperCollins, 1991; 4th ed. with Michelle Boisseau, HarperCollins, 1996; 5th ed. with Michelle Boisseau, Longman, 2000). In the meantime, Bits Press was gearing up for its next big publishing project.

Published in 1983, *Light Year '84* aimed to broaden the readership of poetry by stressing humor and lightening-up its subjects and approaches—making it more accessible, more "popular," like television and novels. In effect, Wallace was returning to his roots in American humor. Recalling the onetime popularity of humorists Ogden Nash and Richard Armour, he embarked on a personal campaign to revive poetry through light verse and market it to people who didn't think they liked poetry.

Meanwhile, Wallace was taking a page from the literary habits of his famous friend, Updike, who wove personal relationships (if somewhat thinly disguised) into his novels. In 1984, Wallace's eighth book, *Girlfriends and Wives*, was published by Carnegie–Mellon. It was a collection of poems based on his experiences with women. Wallace was in his fourth marriage at the time, having been married to Emily Mitchell, herself an English scholar from Springfield (m. 1954); Janeen Ann (Jan) Weaver, a painter and philosopher of science (m. 1965); and Sharon Lillevig, a technical writer and editor (m. 1977). In 1982, Wallace married Christine M. (Tina) Seidler, an attorney to whom he was married until his death.

Having negotiated a new contract with Case Western Reserve, Wallace saw his teaching duties cut in half, which relieved some of his workload. Still, as the 1980s progressed, Wallace continued to juggle multiple projects in publishing and writing. In 1986, Bits Press published *The Gavin Ewart Show*, a selection of poems by the British poet, Gavin Ewart. Wallace helped publicize the book by arranging for readings across the U.S. In the meantime, interest in *Light Year* was waning; in 1989, Wallace told supporters that the publication was coming to a close. Bits Press continued to publish several chapbooks yearly, with the last chapbook coming out in 1993. Perhaps Wallace's most challenging chapbook, Gary Adamson's *Studios* centered on woodblock prints carved by the author.

With the shuttering of Bits Press, Wallace headed full-steam into his last major project: a reexamination of English meter—the subject of this present collection. He had published several articles on the subject, and his essay, "Meter in English," formed the centerpiece of David Baker's edited collection, *Meter in English: A Critical Engagement*, published in 1996 by the University of Arkansas Press.

Robert Wallace passed away on April 9th, 1999. At the time of his passing, he was working on the fifth edition of *Writing Poems* and readying his manuscript, *Free Verse and the Orbit of Meter*, for press review.

Robert Wallace's life and work is preserved in his papers at Missouri State University. Wallace did not have a direct tie to the university: he neither attended nor taught at MSU. But he had friends among the English faculty,

Springfield was his hometown, and the university recognized the value of his papers. In the spring of 1985, Wallace came to MSU and gave a reading at an event co-sponsored by the English Department and the Friends of the Librar- ies. After some negotiation, English faculty members and fellow poets Robert Henigan, Michael Burns, and Clark Closser co-wrote a grant proposal to the MSU Foundation, which orchestrated the acquisition of the materials. With that support in place, the transfer of Robert Wallace's papers began.

It was agreed that Wallace would send papers as they were no longer need- ed and would include anything published by Bits Press. Through the years following, Wallace regularly sent additions to Missouri State University. After his death, Christine Wallace, his widow, arranged for the remaining archival materials to come to Springfield. Today there are more than thirty boxes— thirty-plus linear feet—of archival materials, making the Wallace Collection a substantial prize of the University Archives and Special Collections. Visitors to Missouri State University's Meyer Library can open a box and find let- ters from John Updike and other luminaries, explore a poem's development through an author's hand-written drafts (with Wallace's running comments in the margins), and study the art as well as the "business" of small-press pub- lishing. All reflect Wallace's impact on American letters from the mid-to-late 20th century.

The three pieces printed here deserve more detailed comment. First, for the essay, "Meter in English" (1996). David Baker—a poet, teacher, and poetry editor (for the distinguished *Kenyon Review*) in his own right—worked with Miller Williams, founder and first editor of the University of Arkansas Press, in soliciting a collection of essays "all based on issues of meter in English and all based, more particularly, on Wallace's primary article."[2] It's a distinguished collection, indeed: In addition to Wallace's "ambitious essay, which serves as part 1 of this book and the impetus for the rest of it" (Baker, xii), essay-re- sponses came from poets, prosodists, and teachers the likes of Eavan Boland, Annie Finch, Dana Gioia, Rachel Hadas, Charles O. Hartman, Robert Hass, Margaret Holley, John Frederick Nims, David J. Rothman, Timothy Steele, Lewis Putnam Turco, Barry Weller, Richard Wilbur, and Susanne Woods— fourteen in all. Baker elaborates:

---

[2] David Baker, "Introduction," *Meter in English: A Critical Engagement* (1996), xii. The pas- sages following are taken from this text (ix-xxii).

Part 2 of *Meter in English* opens up the critical engagement which gives this book its subtitle and its unique character. We wanted to offer a rich, diverse articulation of the state of metrical analysis today. Each contributor to part 2 received a copy of Robert Wallace's "Meter in English," along with two guidelines: that each contribution specifically address, in full or in brief, all ten of Wallace's main propositions and that any more general discussion of meter should still remain focused on Wallace's concerns. (xiii)

"The final section, part 3, is once again Robert Wallace's work" (xiv), as Baker notes:

> It seemed right—in fact necessary—to end where we began, with the congruity of his single perspective, as a debate returns to the affirmative for its rebuttal. Indeed, Wallace's afterword, "Completing the Circle," is more extensive an argument than his "Meter in English." Here he is able himself to engage and assess the specific and often adverse opinions of his respondents in their analyses of his ten propositions; he focuses sharply the lively issues of this discussion which, we hope, will continue beyond these pages. Here too he widens the scope, surveying what he sees as a crisis, "the incoherence of the present understanding of meter." (xiv)

Wallace's task of responding to the "often adverse opinions of his respondents" grew from the afterword abovementioned into the monograph, *Orbit of Meter* (1998), which we print posthumously. The significance of *Meter in English* holds for its sequel, *Orbit of Meter*. As Baker describes it, "one of the most hotly debated issues in *Meter in English: A Critical Engagement* is Wallace's contention that the accentual-syllabic method constitutes the only viable or true meter in our language" (xv). Baker continues:

> Fully half of his initial proposals, and much of the ensuing discussion in part 2, probe the reasons for and implications of this assertion. Wallace does not want to discard syllabics as an important compositional method, but he wishes to exclude both it and accentuals from the category of real meters. Meter, to Wallace, must be auditory, and hereby he argues that one cannot hear any consistent or predictable pattern in an accentual arrangement of words in a line, much less a syllabic one. (xv)

We have already quoted Baker's estimation of the originality and potential lurking in Wallace's metrical system. Here's Baker's discussion in full:

> Wallace further extends his prosodic strategy by proposing that iambic rhythm is the exclusive basis of his one meter, accentual-syllabic…. [T]aken with his proposals about the singularity of accentual-syllabic meter, Wallace's conviction about iambics describes nothing less than a paradigm shift in metrics, a potentially dramatic redirection of our study of meter and prosody. This stance elicits some of the book's most inflamed but educative debate. In defining anapestic, trochaic, and dactylic rhythms as useful metrical feet within the iambic accentual-syllabic norm, but not as meters in their own rights, Wallace both clarifies and simplifies the system. Some of his respondents are adamant to maintain the fuller range of equal meters. Some too disagree with Wallace's proposal that a two-degree system of stresses in scansion is sufficient, indeed is preferable to a three- or four-value system. The reader will find everywhere the search for the line dividing valuable simplification and over-simplified reduction. (xvi)

Readers of the posthumous *Orbit of Meter* are asked to join in this same search for clarity.

The third piece included here, "On Not Teaching Poetry," is an invited lecture, undated and apparently unpublished in Wallace's lifetime. Internal references place this playfully "anti-establishment" text in 1966. The year prior, Wallace had joined the faculty at Case Western Reserve and published his own book of poems as well as the edited collection, *Poems on Poetry*. We assume that this formal lecture acknowledges Wallace's growing prominence as a poet and teacher.

In the spirit of Susan Sontag's *Against Interpretation* (1966), Wallace's lecture serves as a reminder to today's teachers and students: freedom and pleasure rest at the center of aesthetic experience, which poetry gives in abundance. "The job," as Wallace's lecture declares, "is to get poetry out of the schools and back under the bedsheet." He elaborates:

> Any work of art requires what I shall call *the necessary ignorance*—which is a little more than "willing suspension of disbelief," but not much more. We must submit ourselves to the poem or painting, ignorant as barbarians, willing to go the way it takes us, unable to go any other way; prepared to feel first and, if necessary, to think later.

Acknowledgments

With minor corrections, we follow the text of "On Not Teaching Poetry" as published in *Moon City Review 2011*. We thank the MSU English Department's Moon City Press for permission to reprint. We thank the University of Arkansas Press for permission to reprint "Meter in English." In preparing this essay for a new printing and audience, we have made several interpolations and abridgements; in each case, these are marked by brackets (and explained in footnotes). In addition, the essay's citations have been silently edited to conform to current MLA style. We present the typescript of *Free Verse and the Orbit of Meter* in its entirety and without significant intervention beyond the correction and regularizing of critical citations. These, combined with citations from "Meter" and "On Not Teaching Poetry," have been gathered into the appendix, "A Wallace Bibliography." Meticulous in his scholarship, Wallace would surely have kept his own Works Cited pages. But, as we have been unable to find the same, we have sought to fill in his critical references. We are pleased to acknowledge the assistance of Katherine Coulter, an undergraduate English major whose critical spadework has been incorporated into "A Wallace Bibliography." Eric Knickerbocker, a graduate student in the MSU English Department, worked on the original typescript of *Free Verse and the Orbit of Meter*, adding scansion markings and checking the text. We thank Ross Payton, an alumnus of the English graduate program, for his help in researching an early draft of the appended essay, "'The Smoothest Typer Ever to Come Out of Springfield': A Treasury of Letters from The Robert Wallace Collection."

We thank Christine Wallace for so enthusiastically supporting this project. We thank MSU Dean of Libraries, Thomas A. Peters, for featuring this collection in the Ozarks Studies Institute's Publications Series. We thank Kathy Harris for her ongoing support of Special Collections. Mrs. Harris's contributions have allowed the MSU Libraries to enhance its rare books holdings and now help with making *Orbit of Meter* a successful new publication. And we thank our colleagues in MSU Special Collections and University Archives, Tracie D. Gieselman-France, Jeffrey L. Lawson, and

Shannon N. Mawhiney. They helped with searches, aiding in our navigation through boxes, folders, files.

Our aim in compiling, editing, and publishing this book is to bring attention to an important work by an important writer whose archival remains are made accessible in an important regional collection, one capable of generating original scholarship and of teaching future generations of students how to write, read, and appreciate poetry.

Meter in English (1996)

In English, the poetry makes the rules, not the rules the poetry.
—George Saintsbury, *A History of English Prosody*

An outsider would be startled at the lack of consensus among poets and metrists about the nature of metrical verse in English. Those of us interested in meter have perhaps grown accustomed to the confusion, and therefore careless. The poetry matters, after all, not the theory. But it cannot be argued safely that our understanding is irrelevant to our practice nor, I hope, that our teaching is irrelevant to the future of poems written in meter.

My aim, therefore, is to question our assumptions and differences of opinion. To make a beginning, I will go over what seems safe and familiar ground.

It is the unit of line that distinguishes verse from prose or speech. Line introduces into the sentences of verse a further set of breaks or pauses complementary to those already present in the syntactical organization. When line-ends coincide with and so reinforce them, these syntactical breaks are in effect promoted, while others are in effect demoted. We call such effects, respectively, end-stopped lines and caesuras. Line-ends may also occur where there are no syntactical breaks or only very slight ones, thus in effect creating breaks or pauses. Such effects we call run-on lines. Together, these modulations control the special character of verse. How far such effects of line-end are aural (affecting pauses in performance) or merely visual (that is, perceptual) depends on individual practice.

In free verse, the units of line are, or appear to be, arbitrary; that is, relatively unpredictable. In metered verse, the units of line are relatively regular or predictable, measured (metered) by the counting of some quality or qualities of the language that seem natural for this purpose. In English, for instance, a normative line is

When I | consid | er how | my light | is spent.

By convention, following the terminology of classical prosody, this line is rationalized as pentameter ("five-measure"), each unit of measure being a "foot," here specifically an iambic foot or iamb: an unstressed syllable followed by a stressed one. There may also be tetrameter ("four-measure") lines, and so on.

Two things should be noticed. Greek and Latin meters were based on vowel duration (long/short) rather than on accent (stress/unstress), and the adaptation of classical terms to cover English practice thus introduced the possibility of confusion in terminology. Entities may seem to exist in English (e.g., the cretic foot: $-\cup-$), when they do not in actuality, or, to put it differently, when they might be rationalized in a different or simpler way. The pyrrhic foot ($\cup\cup$) is puzzling. Lacking any stress, it makes little sense in a language where we count or hear primarily stresses. Probably it does not exist in English, except in one isolated configuration. I will return to this point in Section 3, "Coming to Terms."

Metrical counting in English is binary. Despite the wide range of levels of stress occurring in speech, syllables are counted as either stressed or unstressed. That determination is made relative to the stress of neighboring syllables; that is, by comparison, and not absolutely, as was the case in determining long/short duration in classical prosody. In the line,

$$\cup \quad \diagup \quad \cup \,(\diagup) \quad \cup \quad \diagup \quad \cup \quad \diagup \quad \cup \quad \diagup$$
Nor ser | vices | to do | till you | require

the third syllable of "services," which is almost unaccented in speech, counts fully, so that the line is regular iambic. If we are scanning merely to determine the meter (aha, this line is pentameter), there will be little difficulty. But when we scan—as we do more often—to inspect the rhythm of a line or passage, there is enormous room for difference of opinion or, less charitably, for confusion.

Three further conventions complete the metrical system: An unstressed syllable at the end of a line, as in

$$\cup \quad \diagup \quad \cup \quad \diagup \quad \cup \quad \diagup \quad \cup \quad \diagup \quad \cup \quad \diagup \quad \cup$$
And yet | it may | be said | I loved | her dear | *ly*

is metrically uncounted. That is, the line remains regularly iambic. We need a fresh term for this, and I suggest that **(1) Instead of the term "feminine ending," we should say simply extra-syllable ending,** which may be abbreviated as e-s ending. (Equally, we may speak of extra-syllable or e-s rhymes.)

Conversely, an unstressed syllable at the beginning of a line may be omitted without changing the normative scansion, as in

$$x \quad / \quad \cup \quad / \qquad \cup \quad / \quad \cup \quad /$$
Fif | ty springs | are lit | tle room

The first foot here is counted as if it were an iamb rather than an irregular or "lame" foot, which elsewhere in a line would mark a noteworthy rhythmic interruption. A common variation, this omission of an initial syllable appears in the seventeenth century:

$$x \quad / \qquad \cup \quad / \quad \cup \quad / \quad \cup \quad /$$
Come, | and trip | it as | ye go

as in the fourteenth century:

$$x \quad / \qquad \cup \quad / \qquad \cup \quad / \qquad \cup \quad / \qquad \cup \quad /$$
Twen | ty book | es, clad | in blak | or reed

Several terms for this convention are current, among them acephalous line (from Greek, meaning "headless"), decapitation, and initial truncation (from the Latin verb meaning "to shorten by cutting off, as limbs from trunk or torso; to maim or mutilate"). As these terms both overstate and seem pejorative, I suggest that **(2) For an omitted first syllable of a line, we should use the term anacrusis** (from Greek, meaning "the striking up of a tune") which Saintsbury allows in this sense (1: 64, 78, 170).

The third convention is the substitution, for an iamb in the normative line, of any of several other feet: trochee ($/ \cup$), pyrrhic ($\cup \cup$), spondee ($//$), anapest ($\cup \cup /$), or dactyl ($/ \cup \cup$). The point is to accommodate in the metrical norm certain other frequent rhythmic patterns of English, as well as to avoid metronomic rigidity.

$$/ \quad \cup \quad \cup \quad / \quad \cup \quad \cup \quad / \quad / \quad \cup \quad /$$
When to | the ses | sions of | sweet si | lent thought.

Despite substitutions of trochee, pyrrhic, and spondee in the first, third, and fourth places, the line remains iambic pentameter.

There has been, and remains now, some prejudice against the legitimacy of trisyllabic substitutions, that is, anapests and dactyls. Historically, however, as Saintsbury argues (1: 402), the anapest made its appearance "practically at once" in English meter, and has persisted with enough frequency for him to conclude that it is "omnipresent." An example from about 1500 is

$$\breve{}\ /\quad \breve{}\ \breve{}\ /\quad \breve{}\ /$$
And I | in my bed | again

The musical notation in the manuscript makes the foot unmistakable. Instances exist even in the verse of poets as syllabically rigorous as Pope. The naturalness of the anapest derives, if for no other reason, from the structure of simple prepositional phrases. That structure can also be accommodated by allowing the meter to point up a light stress on syllables that would be virtually unaccented in speech, as in

$$\breve{}\ (/)\quad \breve{}\ (/)\quad \breve{}\ /\quad \breve{}\ /\quad \breve{}\ /$$
That on | the ash | es of | his youth | doth lie

or by contriving a trochaic substitution to fit, as in the first two feet of

$$/\ \breve{}\quad \breve{}\ /\quad \breve{}\ /\quad \breve{}\ /\quad \breve{}\ /$$
But, of | the two, | less dang | 'rous is | th' offence

But it is plainly simpler, and entirely natural, to use an anapest as the anonymous poet does in "And I in my bed again," or as appears in

$$\breve{}\ /\quad \breve{}\ /\quad \breve{}\ \breve{}\ /\quad \breve{}\ /$$
Two roads | diverged | in a yel | low wood

The convention of trisyllabic substitution replaces another convention, which no one would now wish to revive, practiced most notably in those periods when anapestic substitution was least in favor. I mean elision, as in

$$\breve{} \quad \diagup \qquad \breve{} \quad \diagup \quad \breve{} \qquad \diagup \quad \breve{} \quad \diagup \quad \breve{} \qquad \diagup$$

And moan | th' expense | of man | y a van | ished sight

In order to maintain the regularity of syllables, one is required to mouth or imagine such barbarous, artificial syllables as "th' ex-" and "-y a." Similarly, in the Pope, "th' of-" avoids "the offence." The anapest is a good, and frequent, foot in English verse.

Meter is thus a system of measurement, conventional but natural to the language, which makes the rhythmic units of line more or less predictable to a reader or hearer of verse.

What meter measures is speech. We tend to speak in clothesline-looping phrases, with one primary stress per phrase, the other syllables (secondary stresses or unstressed) being spoken rapidly so that normally we scarcely distinguish among them. Playing over the metrical expectation, this speech-run produces what we may call poetic rhythm. The process may be figured

$$\frac{\text{speech-run}}{\text{meter}} = \text{rhythm}$$

We read a poem neither as we would say its sentences in speech nor by the rigid te TUM te TUM of meter, but in a way somewhere in between the two. The speech-run is slowed, made more distinct—so that, for instance, we may hear the light stresses on "on" and "of" in the line "That on the ashes of his youth doth lie." Subtleties we may be unaware of in speech are thus magnified into perception. Conversely, the rigidity of meter (an inch is an inch) is given a more flexible embodiment. No two lines of iambic pentameter, therefore, can ever be quite the same.

In reading metered verse, we hear its rhythmic approximation of the underlying metrical pattern. Divergences that are conventional are felt as regularities. Reading unmetered verse, by contrast, we are not aware of any fixed or predictable underlying pattern. In free verse, there will of course be natural patterns and probably significant repetitions of them, but we have no consistent sense of predictability or expectation. (An oddity is, as free verse has claim to having become the predominant verse form in the twentieth century, how little curiosity there has been to sort out the different kinds of it or the variety of patterns and conventions that operate in it.)

In thinking about poetic rhythm in meter, we may be aware of two sorts of effect. The subtler occurs in the relative levels of unstress and stress in the paradigmatic iambs of a line. In Shakespeare's "And yet it may be said I loved her dearly," though all the feet are clearly iambic, the unstressed syllables "I" and "her" carry somewhat more accent than the other unstressed syllables, making the line seem to slow or become more emphatic at the end. This sort of effect may be very expressive, as in Wilbur's "A ball will bounce, but less and less." A more obvious sort of rhythmic effect occurs when, in whatever form, substitution displaces the paradigmatic iamb, by adding a syllable as the anapest does in "*in a yellow* wood," by reversing the expected unstress/stress as the trochee does in "*But, of* the two," or by replacing an unstressed syllable with a stressed, as the spondee does in "*sweet sil*ent thought."

Both sorts of effect contribute to what we may feel as expressive or imitative rhythms, as in

$$\breve{\ }\ /\ \breve{\ }\ /\ (/)\ /\ \ /\ /\ \ \breve{\ }\ /$$
When A | jax strives | some rock's | vast weight | to throw

The two spondees suggest heaviness. An impression of difficulty or strain, though, has already begun to register in the relatively heavy or hard-to-enunciate unstressed syllables of the iambs in the first two feet, "When" and "-jax." The line, thus, builds to the release in the final iamb, "to throw," where the distinct contrast between the unstressed syllable and the stressed one seems to let us feel the physical gesture. This extremely clever line depends of course on the inversion. If we restore "to throw" to its place in normal word order, Ajax is left standing there with the rock sagging in his grip:

$$\breve{\ }\ /\ \breve{\ }\ /\ \breve{\ }\ /\ \ /\ /\ \ /\ /$$
When A | jax strives | to throw | some rock's | vast weight

The particular value of the spondee is that it can damp or modulate the regular alternations in the flow of a passage. Its effects may be of lightness or stasis as well as of weight, as in Keats's third line here:

No stir of air was there,
Not so much life as on a summer's day

$$/\ /\ /\ /\ /\ \breve{\ }\ \ \breve{\ }\ /\ \ \breve{\ }\ /$$
Robs not | one light | seed from | the feath | ered grass

The suggestion is, in the unruffled evenness of the five level stresses, an absence of such breeze as might dislodge even a single poised bit of dandelion fluff. The metrical stress—the counting stress—is made to fall on "not" and "light," thus muting an emphasis we are perhaps readier to hear. Consider this clumsy alternative scansion:

$$x \quad / \quad (/) \quad / \quad (/) \quad / \quad \smile \quad \smile \quad / \quad \smile \quad /$$

Robs | not one | light seed | from the feath | ered grass

Keats plays masterfully on the foot-structure of the line. His spondees resist the natural flow, as if debating within themselves whether to accept it; and that slight indecisiveness of stress makes the line's rhythm expressive. The little tug of quickness in "from the feathered grass" cannot overcome it.

Meter is useful for its predictability, which keeps reader or hearer tuned to even fine variations of rhythm. Actual lines are interesting for their approach to, as well as their divergence from, the iambic norm.

I have been discussing what is called accentual-syllabic meter, because in theory both stresses and syllables are counted. As to both, however, the counting may be rather flexible in practice. A pentameter with anacrusis will have nine syllables. A pentameter with e-s ending will have eleven syllables—or perhaps with an anapest or two as many as thirteen syllables or so. The number of stresses carried by a line is even more variable. With spondees, we may count as many as nine stresses in

$$/ \quad / \quad / \quad / \quad / \quad / \quad \smile \quad (/) \quad / \quad /$$

Slow, slow, | fresh fount, | keep time | with my | salt tears

or as few as three speech stresses in

$$/ \qquad / \qquad /$$

Advantage on the kingdom of the shore

Timothy Steele ("On Meter" 298) points out a pentameter with only two speech stresses:

$$/ \qquad /$$

In our competitive humility

In such cases, by fine-tuning our response, meter supplies the light stresses that fill out the pattern; expectation in effect makes up the lack. Nor is any contrivance needed to somehow reduce Jonson's spondees to iambs for us to sense the line's pattern properly.

This meter, accentual-syllabic, as described, is English meter. There is no other.

It evolved from the accentual-alliterative meter of Old English, influenced probably by changes taking place in the language itself, by the syllabic meter of French, and by efforts to adapt classical prosody to the vernacular. Historical puzzles remain—if it was Chaucer's meter, for instance, why were there uncertainties about it for another century and a half? But, unquestionably, sometime just before 1600 English meter as we understand it was fully in place.

II. ONE METER

My purpose in this essay is to clarify our understanding of meter in English. So far, I have tried to lay out the system succinctly; and except for the two minor propositions about terminology (e-s ending and anacrusis), there is no novelty in that outline, though it will have provoked disagreement about this or that. I must turn now to those areas of disagreement—or to what I see as the confusions and unexamined contradictions in the various accounts of English meter at present, in which those of us who are interested often seem to be talking past one another. In arguing for the propositions embedded in this and the next two sections, I will be as quick and frugal as I can, although the discussion must be specific and exacting.

Recent authoritative accounts, such as Paul Fussell's in *Poetic Meter and Poetic Form* (1965), hold that there are four meters in English: syllabic, accentual, accentual-syllabic, and quantitative. Most critics seem agreed to put aside the last as unworkable, or primarily of historical interest, though there have been attempts (as late as Robert Bridges's) to imitate in English the counting of duration from Greek and Latin. The problem is that the strong accents of English tend to override, for all but the most classically trained readers, the pattern of vowel-lengths. As X.J. Kennedy remarks (*An Introduction to Poetry* 166), "Campion's 'Rose-Cheeked Laura, Come' was an attempt to demonstrate [quantitative meter] in English, but probably we enjoy the rhythm of the poem's well-placed stresses whether or not we notice its vowel sounds." As the poem is scannable as accentual-syllabic, no metrical question arises:

Rose-cheeked Laura, come,
Sing thou smoothly with thy beauty's
Silent music, either other
    Sweetly gracing.

Sidney's "O sweet woods, the delight of solitariness," also recommended as a lovely poem in quantitative meter, is a harder case. Except for a line or two (like "Such wisdom, that in her lives speculation"), it would be regularly scannable only with great awkwardness:

Nought disturbs thy quiet, all to thy service yield,
Each sight draws on a thought, thought mother of science,
Sweet birds kindly do grant harmony unto thee,
Fair trees' shade is enough fortification,
Nor danger to thy self if be not in thy self.

As William A. Ringler, Jr. (editor of *The Poems of Sir Philip Sidney*) notes, the poem is one of only thirteen "experiments" in quantitative verse by Sidney; and "the meter is exceedingly imperfect, for the rules of quantity are broken in one or more places in 16 of the 42 lines" (404). More generally, Ringler says (392), Sidney's "application [of quantities] results in patterns of scansion that continually clash with Elizabethan pronunciation. Since Sidney measures his lines by artificial rules that are divorced from phonetic actualities, [a passage] may have the appearance of, but cannot be read aloud to sound like verse."

Such experiments, especially in the period of the founding of English meter, are both understandable and admirable. But as they hardly amount to a body of work in quantitative meter, or prove its workability in English, it will be economical and clarifying to drop the term from our list. **(3) Quantities are not a basis for meter in English.** Odd cases can be valued as odd cases. Even successful imitations of sapphics or alcaics needn't be seen as establishing a meter in English.

Fussell also has misgivings about syllabics, noting that "syllabism is not a natural measuring system in a language so Germanic and thus so accentual as English." Given contemporary poems in the form, especially by Marianne Moore, however, textbooks and other accounts continue unquestioningly to include it.

Let's be firmer. **(4) Syllabics is not a meter in English.** We do not *hear* the count of syllables. By itself, and taking no account of where accents occur, a line's number of syllables in no significant way determines its rhythm. There is no interplay or tension between sentences and a pattern of sound, no predictability—any syllables, stressed or unstressed, in any order will do. Syllabics is a kind of free verse. For the poet constructing lines by syllable-count, it is only a trellis, like shaped stanzas, William Carlos Williams's variable-foot indentings, or (say) the counting of the number of *letters* as the basis for line. The actual rhythm is determined freely, line by line, according to whatever mixtures of stressed and unstressed syllables may be natural in speech, as in other free verse. Variations in such syllabic norms, as in Moore's "Critics and Connoisseurs" or "Poetry," cannot be rhythmically meaningful in themselves. Even locating variations is painstaking and usually without point.

The two poems by Moore are good, if not exactly fair, examples. "Poetry" has claim to be the most famous poem in syllabics in English—if it is in syllabics at all, which is a question open to a good deal of doubt.

Both poems were written, as appears to have been Moore's practice, in stanzas of which the corresponding lines have an exactly identical number of syllables. The first line in each stanza of "Critics and Connoisseurs," for instance, has fourteen syllables, the second line in each has eight syllables, and so on. In revising the poems between appearances in print, however, Moore made excisions in several lines *without bothering to re-regularize the syllable-count.* So, technically, in the versions we are likely to be familiar with, neither poem is in syllabic meter. However useful Moore found syllablecount in composition, it is clear at least that she placed no very great formal value on it in the finished poem.

Although there is some merit in that debating-point, my reason for calling it to your attention is to make you uncertain, when I quote corresponding lines from the four stanzas of "Critics and Connoisseurs," whether they are syllabically exact or inexact. Please read the lines and, before you count on your fingers, decide whether they are syllabically identical or not:

similar determination to make a pup

proclivity to more fully appraise such bits

itself, struck out from the flower-bed into the lawn

in proving that one has had the experience

If you are still not sure after having counted on your fingers, you will see the difficulty of treating syllabics as a meter. Whatever the French are able to do, it is plain that in English we cannot really hear syllable-count; and that there is no perceptible, or discussable, rhythmic similarity in syllabically equal lines.

I invite any reader still unconvinced to spend an hour studying the texts of these two poems in two or three printed versions, including those in the 1951 *Collected Poems* and the 1967 *Complete Poems* (and, for "Poetry," in Moore's 1921 version, which may be found in *Marianne Moore: An Introduction to the Poetry,* by George W. Nitchie [37-38]). Given printers' difficulties with the longer lines, it is not easy even to decide, or to keep in mind, how many *lines* the stanzas have. In one of the very best books about Moore, a fine critic says that "Poetry" in its most familiar version is a poem of thirty-eight lines when in fact it has only twenty-nine lines; and that Moore's final, very abbreviated version has four lines, when in fact it has only three.

The claim that, in English, syllabics is a meter rests in quicksand. Accentual meter is, alas, even more problematic. In the obvious sense, like syllabics, it does not exist; that is, it is not a meter. As I will argue, counting only stresses offers no meaningful predictability and is, ultimately, hopelessly subjective. Moreover, the accounts invariably describe one thing but mean something else entirely, causing terminological confusion. Moreover again, that something else turns out to be only accentual-syllabic meter *allowing trisyllabic substitution.* Consider:

> [Accentual meter] maintains a more or less regular number of stresses within the line; there is no fixed number of unstressed syllables. This is the *strong-stress meter* of Old English poetry. (Harvey Gross, *Sound and Form in Modern Poetry* 24)

> While in syllabic meter only the syllables are counted, in accentual meter only the accents are. Syllables may vary in number per line, it being assumed that three or four short syllables can be uttered in the same time that one or two long ones can. (Fussell 9)

> [In accentual meter] the poet does not write in feet (as in other meters) but instead counts accents (stresses). The idea is to have the same number of stresses in every line. The poet may place them anywhere in the line and

may include practically any number of unstressed syllables, which do not count. (Kennedy 157)

Noting that what is described is *not* Old English meter (lacking both the alliteration and the strong medial caesuras), let's begin with the obvious sense of these definitions. Only Gross and John Frederick Nims (in *Western Wind* [1983]) discuss examples that reflect this obvious sense of the term. Gross (37-38, 187) cites the opening eighteen lines of "The Waste Land" as four-beat accentual meter. As "even in Old English verse we encounter lines of three or four stresses" (25),[3] Gross notes, the line

> ／　　　　　／　／
> Memory with desire, stirring

Is an acceptable variation in the four-stress norm.
Even so, at its most regular, we are required to hear as *metrically identical*

> ／　／　　　／　／
> Dull roots with spring rain

and

> ／　　　　／　　　　／　　　　／
> I read, much of the night, and go south in the winter.

Nims (258) cites

> rough roads, rock-strewn

and "the unlikely but possible"

> due to the *ru*thlessness of the *ru*morings, due to the Per*u*vians' incommunica*bi*lity ...

---

[3] More accurately, Gross and McDowell write, "we encounter lines of three or five stresses" (23), their point being that the four-stress line remains normative. (Wallace's transcription error is thus negligible.) *-Eds.*

There are clearly two problems with accentual meter in this sense. It may be plausible enough, given the metrical norm TUM TUM TUM TUM, to accept TUM TUM te TUM TUM ("Dull roots with spring rain") as a rhythmic variation. But it seems exceedingly implausible to take as also metrically *equal*: te TUM te te te TUM te te TUM te te TUM te ("I read, much of the night") or: te te te TUM te te te te TUM te te te te te te TUM te te te te te te te TUM te te (the line about the Peruvians). On the face of it, this meter offers no predictability at all; and I do not see how we might even begin to discuss the rhythm of such lines if "the number of syllables does not matter" (Nims 291) and we do not count the unaccented syllables or notice where they occur.

The second problem is that what we may count as a stress seems extremely subjective. Nothing in theory prevents that determination from being arbitrary. The very existence in speech of any number of levels of stress makes it impossible to tell exactly which stresses should count as the *metrical* stresses. Why, for instance, in

／   ／   ／   ／ ／   ／

I read, | much of | the night, | and go | south in | the winter

do we not find six stresses? (The line is scannable iambic hexameter with trochees as the second and fifth feet?) In the line about the Peruvians, why don't we also hear as stresses "Due," "due," and—as necessary to the meaning—the first syllable of "incommunicability"? Whereas accentual-syllabic meter has evolved a roughly workable way of bringing the wide variety of stress-levels in speech into its binary counting, accentual meter offers no way at all. Anything that might seem a stress in speech might equally be a stress in accentual meter—*or not*. Hence, of course, the need for the *defining* alliteration and caesuras of Old English meter.

I do not see how a poet, setting out to write in this meter, would be guided in any useful way; or how a reader, suspecting the meter, could ever be sure it was operating. There is, obviously, no body of work written in this supposed meter. Like syllabics, accentuals in this sense is not a meter but a form of free verse. (Gross's otherwise elegant analysis of Eliot's verse, and Robert Hass's "Listening and Making" in *Twentieth Century Pleasures*, however, show the usefulness of studying free verse by examining its accentual patterning.)

As I said, what Fussell, Kennedy, and Nims and Gross elsewhere—along with others, such as Miller Williams in *Patterns of Poetry: An Encyclopedia of Forms* and Timothy Steele in *Missing Measures*—mean by the term accentual verse is accentual-syllabic meter that allows trisyllabic—dactyls being rare, anapestic—substitution. We can arrive at this understanding, however, only by inference from the poems they offer as exemplary of accentual meter, since the descriptions seem almost deliberately misleading.

In the illustrative poems or passages, there is scarcely any irregularity, other than anapests, that we might not expect to encounter in Robert Herrick. The student will search in vain for the strings of three or four unstressed syllables suggested by Fussell's comment or, for that matter, for stressed syllables clumped or otherwise not regularly spaced by unstressed ones. The poems are all written in metrical feet. [...]⁴

[T]ake as an example Meredith's "About Opera." Williams comments that the lines all have five stresses, and he confirms my marking of "on" as stressed in line 12. (Line 3 might optionally be scanned with anapest and iamb in the third and fourth places.)

<pre>
     ‿ /   ‿   /   ‿   /   ‿ / ‿ /   ‿
It's not | the tunes, | although | as I | get old | er
x / ‿ (/)   ‿   /   ‿ /   ‿   /   ‿
A | rias | are what | I hum | and whis | tle.
     ‿   /   ‿   /   /   ‿   / ‿ ‿ ‿ /   ‿
It's not | the plots | —they con | tinue to | bewild | er
   ‿ ‿   /   ‿ /   ‿ ‿ /   ‿ ‿ /   ‿ / ‿
In the tongue | I speak | and in sev | eral that | I wrestle.

     ‿   /   ‿ ‿ ‿/   ‿ ‿ (/)   ‿   /   ‿/
An im | age of artic | ulateness | is what | it is:
   / ‿   ‿   /   ‿   /   ‿   /   ‿ /
Isn't | this how | we've al | ways longed | to talk?
    /   ‿   ‿   /   ‿   /   ‿ /   ‿   /   ‿
Words as | they fall | are mon | otone | and blood | less
    ‿   ‿   /   ‿   /   ‿   /   ‿   /   ‿ /
But they yearn | to take | the risk | these nois | es take.

         ‿   /   ‿ / ‿ ‿   /   ‿ /   ‿ /
What danc | ing is | to the slight | ly spas | tic way
</pre>

---

⁴ This passage, including "a tabulation of substitutions and variations" ("Meter" 17), has been abridged. -*Eds.*

```
  /    ᴗ    ᴗ    /    ᴗ    /      ᴗ    /    ᴗᴗ   /
Most of | us teet | er through | our bod | ily life
  ᴗ     ᴗ    /    ᴗ    /    ᴗ  ᴗ   /    ᴗ    /     ᴗ   /
Are these meas | ured cries | to the clum | sy things | we say,
  ᴗ   ᴗ   /     ᴗ  /   ᴗ (/)    /     /      ᴗ   /
In the heart's | dures | ses, on | the heart's | behalf.
```

[…] The poem remains, I think, plainly scannable with trisyllabic substitution.
    One other of the examples merits comment, the anonymous "I Have La-
bored Sore" from the fifteenth century:

```
   ᴗ   ᴗ    /    ᴗ    /    ᴗ    /    ᴗ     /
 I have la | bored sore | and suf | fered death,
    ᴗ   /    ᴗ  /    ᴗ    /    ᴗ    /
 and now | I rest | and draw | my breath;
    ᴗ  /    ᴗ    /    ᴗ   /    ᴗ    /
 but I | shall come | and call | right soon
    /  ᴗ     ᴗ    /    ᴗ    /    ᴗ    /
 heaven | and earth | and hell | to doom;
    ᴗ   /    ᴗ    /    ᴗ    /   ᴗ ᴗ   /
 and then | shall know | both dev | il and man,
  x  /    ᴗ /    ᴗ   /    ᴗ /
 what | I was | and what | I am.
```

Routinely scannable, it nonetheless retains clear signs of the Old English me-
ter—the spaced, distinct medial caesuras and residual indications of formal
alliteration, although the rhyme belongs to the new accentual-syllabic metric.
The poem thus seems to illustrate the transformation of the old meter into the
new. The Old English accentual meter did not disappear, only to burst forth
again several centuries later, as we have been told (Burton Raffel, *From Stress
to Stress* [1992]). It long ago *changed* into the tetrameter and pentameter of
accentual-syllabics, a meter far more flexible and adaptable to the variety of
the language.
    In *all* of the examples, iambs predominate, though only narrowly in the
stanza of "Neutral Tones." Steele notes:

A metrician might say that the rhythm of the poem is "iambic anapestic";
or since the iambs outnumber the anapests by a slight margin, he or she

might call the rhythm "iambic with frequent anapestic substitutions." But such terms do not entirely suit a poem like Hardy's, which approaches the condition of a sort of rhymed accentual verse. (23)

It seems clear here that accentual meter is only an *alternative term* to be used instead of accentual-syllabic meter in *some cases*, those where trisyllabic substitution appears. Fussell (49), distinguishing between scanning Pope and scanning Browning, notes that "by the nineteenth century trisyllabic substitution had become a metrical convention," though he does not explain why he nonetheless attributes accentual meter to Yeats and Auden. But of course, despite the definitions with their guff about all those unstressed syllables we needn't count, accentual meter in this sense isn't a separate meter at all.

I don't see the advantage of having two different systems for describing the same thing, especially if they are presented as describing two different things. Nor do I see the greater precision of saying that Hardy's stanza "approaches the condition of a sort of rhymed accentual verse" as against saying that it is "iambic with frequent anapestic substitutions." It isn't even clear how a student might be expected to recognize a poem in accentual meter. At the appearance of one anapest, as Fussell's example from Yeats implies? Or with something more than "frequent anapestic substitutions," as Steele's "approaches" seems to suggest? Nor is there anywhere in the accounts even a hint as to how, having determined that a poem is in accentual meter, we might then insightfully discuss its rhythm—not bothering of course with the unaccented syllables.

Far from aiding in understanding, the attribution of accentual meter to such a poem appears likely to plunge us into confusion ... from which we can rescue ourselves only by returning to accentual-syllabic scansion, recognizing trisyllabic feet. We may as well do so openly, thus regaining the simplicity and elegance of the evolved metrical system in English, strict or loose iambic, in Frost's phrase. Trisyllabic substitution may be more or less frequent, as well as more or less to our taste, but the fact cannot be blinked away, whether quarantined out of some snobbish purism or promoted, as Coleridge claimed, as "a new principle."

The source of all the confusion about "accentual meter" is of course Coleridge's brief, grossly inaccurate note about the meter of "Christabel":

I have only to add that the metre of the Christabel is not, properly speaking, irregular, though it may seem so from its being founded on a new principle; namely, that of counting in each line the accents, not the syllables. Though the latter may vary from seven to twelve, yet in each line the accents will be found to be only four. Nevertheless, this occasional variation in number of syllables is not introduced wantonly, or for the mere ends of convenience, but in correspondence with some transition in the nature of the imagery or passion.[5]

This, in its entirety, is the seed from which both of the kudzu-like notions hiding in the term "accentual meter" have grown. No new principle at all is involved in the poem's practice; Saintsbury tartly remarks (3: 56) that it is "inconceivable" that Coleridge thought there was. The poem scans regularly, without anomaly, having among its 2665 feet: 2210 iambs (83 percent), 201 anapests and one dactyl (7.8 percent), 174 spondees, 46 trochees, and 33 lines with anacrusis. In that, then, is the source of the idea that trisyllabic substitution somehow means a separate meter.

As to the other sense of the term, the unaccented syllables in "Christabel" are all unquestionably counted, and they space the metrical accents with undeviating regularity. There is nothing about "practically any number of unstressed syllables," whether few or many, nor about nearly innumerable silent Peruvians. That is merely gossip, changing as it gets passed along. Nor is it even true that Coleridge counted only speech accents. As Robert Bridges points out (*Milton's Prosody* 73): "Now the primary law of pure stressed verse is, that there shall never be a conventional or imaginary stress: that is, the verse cannot make the stress, because it is the stress that makes the verse." "Christabel" is littered with such light accents, like that in

$$\smile \; / \quad \smile \; / \quad \smile \; (/) \quad \smile \; /$$
The gems | entang | led in | her hair

As to what's left, Saintsbury remarks (3: 55): "Now, there is no piece of Coleridge's celebrated 'f-f-f-f-fun' which is more complicatedly and dangerously funny than this." The muddle of our textbooks demonstrates how dangerous.

Let's put "accentual meter" into the dustbin. The term has no legitimacy even in regard to Old English verse (or to contemporary imitations such as Pound's "*The Seafarer*" and Wilbur's "*Junk*"), as stress is only one of its

---

[5] Quoted from Coleridge's Preface of 1816. See Lincoln R. Gibbs, *Selections from Coleridge* (82). -*Eds.*

essential characteristics. The more common terms "alliterative meter" or "Old English meter" will do.

(5) In modern English, accentual meter does not exist. The term, for prosody, like the breath-measure of Charles Olson, is denotatively empty.

(6) Anapests and dactyls are legitimate substitutions in the iambic norm of English meter.

There is one meter in English: accentual-syllabic, and its base is always iambic.

III. COMING TO TERMS

Our prosody has all along been pestered by the terminology of classical prosody. The metrical system in English verse, as it has developed, is in fact simple, elegant, and comprehensive. Our descriptions of it, however, and in some measure our understanding of it, have been continually thwarted by error and obfuscation brought over from classical prosody. We need, for instance, as Fussell notes (21), only six feet to account for everything that occurs in English verse, but he then adds, "it does no harm to be acquainted with the following ..." and lists in tabular format: amphibrach; antispast; bacchic; choriamb; cretic; first, second, third, and fourth epitrite; ionic a majore; ionic a minore; first, second, third, and fourth paeon; molossus; and tribrach.

The harm is in intimidation and in a sort of general obfuscation, as if someone might figure out something to do with these Greek terms. And of course someones do. In *The Public Poet* (53), Lewis Turco scans a line by Dana Gioia, "The flickering lights reflected from the city," as ending in an amphibrach (∪ ⁄ ∪), rather than in an iamb and extra-syllable ending.

The notion that, as none of our watches goes just alike, we may each keep time as we please, fails Saintsbury's great touchstone: "The only safe and philosophical rule in prosody, as in other things, is not to multiply your entities" (1: 403). Until someone offers a convincing, totally new account of English meter (which probably will dispense with the classical concept of feet altogether), those of us interested in the future of meter must take care to be precise and frugal in our terms. It is risky to make meter seem, to our students, more complex, cumbersome, or esoteric than need be.

If Turco's attribution of an amphibrach is merely gratuitous, a serious claim has been made for that foot's advantage in scanning Auden's "'O where are you going?' said reader to rider," the suggestion being that it forms the basis for the poem's meter. I will scan the poem here in that way, though it seems to me a sufficient difficulty that the poem is obviously and entirely scannable in the traditional way with anapests (35), iambs (27), trochees (2), and extra-syllable endings. Most readers, even most very experienced ones, will read the poem in that way. So the question perhaps is whether a metrical expectation can significantly influence the way we hear the identical poem. Italics show those places where the amphibrachic norm fails.

ᵕ ⁄ ᵕ ᵕ ⁄ ᵕ ᵕ ⁄ ᵕ ᵕ ⁄ ᵕ
"O where are | you going?" | said reader | to rider,
   ᵕ ⁄ ᵕ ᵕ ⁄ ᵕ ᵕ ⁄ ᵕ ᵕ ⁄ x
"That valley | is fatal | when furna | *ces* burn,
x ⁄ ᵕ ᵕ ⁄ ᵕ ᵕ ⁄ ᵕ ᵕ ⁄ ᵕ
Yonder's | the midden | whose odours | will madden,
   ᵕ ⁄ ᵕ ᵕ ᵕ ⁄ ᵕ ⁄ ᵕ ᵕ x
That gap is | the grave where | the tall re | *turn.*"
   ᵕ ⁄ ᵕ ᵕ ⁄ ᵕ ᵕ ⁄ ᵕ ᵕ ⁄ ᵕ
"O do you | imagine," | said fearer | to farer,
   ᵕ ⁄ ᵕ ᵕ ⁄ ᵕ ᵕ ⁄ ᵕ ᵕ ⁄ x
"That dusk will | delay on | your path to | *the pass,*
   ᵕ ⁄ᵕ ᵕ ⁄ ᵕ ᵕ ⁄ ᵕ ᵕ ⁄ ᵕ
Your dili | gent looking | discover | the lacking,
   ᵕ ⁄ (ᵕ) ⁄ ᵕ ⁄ ᵕ ᵕ ⁄ x
Your footsteps | *feel* | from granite | *to grass?*"
   ᵕ ⁄ ᵕ ᵕ ⁄ ᵕ ⁄ ᵕ ᵕ ⁄ ᵕ
"O what was | *that bird,*" | said horror | to hearer,
   ᵕ ⁄ (ᵕ) ᵕ ⁄ ᵕ ᵕ ⁄ ᵕ ⁄ x
"*Did you see* | that shape in | the twisted | *trees?*
   ᵕ ⁄ ᵕ ⁄ ᵕ ᵕ ⁄ ᵕ ᵕ ⁄ ᵕ
Behind you | *swiftly* | the figure | comes softly,
   ᵕ ⁄ ᵕ ᵕ ⁄ ᵕ ᵕ ⁄ ᵕ ᵕ ⁄
The spot on | your skin is | a shocking | *disease.*"
x ⁄ ᵕ ᵕ ⁄ ᵕ ⁄ ᵕ ᵕ ⁄ ᵕ
"*Out of this house*" | said rider | to reader,
x ᵕ ⁄ ᵕ ⁄ ᵕ ⁄ᵕ ᵕ ⁄ ᵕ
"Yours never | *will*" | —said farer | to fearer,
   ᵕ ⁄ ᵕ ᵕ ⁄ ᵕ ⁄ ᵕ ᵕ ⁄ ᵕ
"They're looking | *for you*" | —said hearer | to horror,

∪ ∕ (∪)　∪　∕　∪ ∕ (∪)　∪　∕　　x
As he left | them there, | as he left | them there.

Lines 1, 5, and 7 are regular; and with only the minor variations of anacrusis or omitted final syllable, 2, 3, 6, and 12 are nearly so. Omission of a syllable at the caesura isn't disturbing in lines 9 and 15, nor in 13 where (with anacrusis as well) the syllabic tightening is felt but seems suitably emphatic. The trochee "swiftly" in line 11, far from disrupting, helps make it the sleekest line in the poem.

Five lines, however, seem problematic. Monosyllabic feet—"-turn" in 4, "feel" in 8, and "will" in 14—are rhythmic jolts, for which I sense no expressive purpose. Nearest to working is "feel," but after the rattling amphibrachs of the preceding lines, it seems almost bathos to focus so intently on blind feet seeking the softer grass. In all three instances, an iambic reading would be superior; and in the last two, the possibility of spondees would allow a useful rhythmic modulation. The three nearly equal stresses in

∪　∕　(∪) ∕　∪　∕　∪ ∪ ∕
Your foot | steps feel | from gran | ite to grass

would give the line a subtler expressive gesture. So, too, in

∕　∕　∪　∕　　∪ ∕ ∪　∪ ∕ ∪
"Yours ne | ver will" | —said farer | to fearer

I take it that the first three lines in stanza 4 are responding to the questions and statements in the first three stanzas respectively. That is, "'Out of this house'" answers "'O where are you going?'" If then "'Yours never will'" answers "'O do you imagine ... That ... Your diligent looking [will] discover,'" and so on, the strong rhetorical emphasis should be on "'Yours.'" My looking may not discover, but *yours* never will, because you do not search at all. Perhaps it is only that we are so unaccustomed to reading amphibrachs that we inevitably miss the subtlety. Nonetheless, the monosyllabic emphasis on "will" appears quite unhelpful.

The two remaining lines, read with amphibrachs, involve distortions of speech stress. Line 10 is doubly troubling, showing yet another jolting monosyllabic foot, "trees." But the main problem is the false amphibrach—

‿ ╱ (‿)
"Did you see …"

—needed to keep the meter. Only the need for a very strong rhetorical stress on "you" could justify this reading, but it seems clear that the meaning focuses at least equally on the *seeing*, noticing, being aware of the shape. A traditional scansion causes no real loss:

‿ ‿ ╱ ‿ ╱ ‿ ‿ ╱ ‿ ╱
"Did you see | that shape | in the twist | ed trees …"

Nor can I justify the distorting "As he left" in line 16. As Anthony Hecht correctly argues (*The Hidden Law* 455), Auden is fudging with the pronoun "he," uniting the trio of rider, farer, and hearer into a single figure. But marking "he" for special stress in no way clarifies the matter; and in any case, the adventurous leaving is at least equally important to the meaning. The traditional scansion, with its slightly less strong stress on "there," gives a rhythm that, rising, then falling—repeated in the second half of the line—seems cogently plaintive:

‿ ‿ ╱ ‿ ╱ ‿ ‿ ╱ ‿ ╱
As he left | them there, | as he left | them there

Tempting as it may seem for the poem's first line, an amphibrachic scansion is not advantageous.

In general, the difficulty with trisyllabic feet, anapests or amphibrachs, is that they cannot really carry stress on more than one of the three syllables[6]. A forced muting of a speech stress, as here in "Did you see" or as in Browning's

‿ ╱ ‿ ‿ ╱ ‿ ‿ ╱ ‿ (‿) ╱
I turned | in my sad | dle and made | *its girths tight*

will invariably seem a flaw—for which the term "false anapest" seems handy. A poet may risk false anapests if, say, a galloping rhythm seems worth overriding sense for; and they may be acceptable in comic forms like the limerick. Otherwise, however, they are blemishes.

---

[6] This difficulty may be overcome by acceptance of the bacchic (‿╱╱), as Wallace argues in *Free Verse and the Orbit of Meter*. -Eds.

Conceivably, somewhere, a poem will show a foot-pattern ◡/◡ that can't be avoided as a substitution. If so, such a case will be rare; and we needn't preserve the term amphibrach to refer to it. We will do as well to call it an anomalous foot, as I did of the pattern ◡ ◡ ◡ / in "About Opera." Strictly, that could be called a "fourth paeon," but I see no wisdom in being able to invoke that term.

We can, therefore, accept Fussell's limitation to six feet for scanning English meter, with one modification. **(7) We should drop the pyrrhic foot (◡ ◡) and accept in its place the double-iamb (◡ ◡ //), as one of the six foot-terms necessary: iamb, trochee, anapest, dactyl, spondee, double-iamb.**

This change was suggested by John Crowe Ransom in "The Strange Music of English Verse" (471). He noted its utility in scanning, for example,

◡ ◡ / /

the mar*riage of true minds*

"I have computed hastily," he says, "that there is an average of more than one [such] foot in the Shakespearian sonnet, and at least as good an average (of one in each fourteen lines) in the pentameter verse of Milton, Shelley, Keats, Tennyson, and many other poets." Ransom uses the Greek term "ionic foot," but plain English seems preferable, carrying with it a reminder that a *double-iamb* counts as two feet, and having the advantage (*double-iamb*) of suggesting that this pattern is quite normal to the iambic base. A traditional scansion of Marvell's line would show *four* substitutions (two pyrrhics, two spondees):

◡ ◡ / / ◡ ◡ / /

To a | green thought | in a | green shade

The line in context, however, seems smooth and we will be closer to the character of the language in thinking of it as two doubleiambs and so fairly regular.

Having the double-iamb at hand, I believe, will also give us a reliable scansion of the much discussed first line of Yeats's "After Long Silence":

x / ◡◡ / / ◡ (/) ◡ /

Speech | after long si | lence; it | is right

Anacrusis (followed by two unstressed syllables) accounts for the sense of abruptness we feel in the rhythm; and the caesura dividing the fourth foot registers the sense of awkward stopping and starting up again. The line is really much more regular than some have supposed.

Other than in the double-iamb sequence, I believe, the pyrrhic foot will always be scannable as iamb or trochee, taking a stress, however light, on one or the other syllable, as in "Nor ser*vices* to do till you require." For example, consider in this line by Keats the foot scanned as pyrrhic by W. Jackson Bate and David Perkins (*British and American Poets* 996):

$$\smile \diagup \mid \smile \diagup \mid \smile \smile \mid \smile \diagup \mid \smile \diagup$$
The hare | limped trem | *bling through* | the froz | en grass

No difficulty occurs if we accept the foot as iambic. Indeed, iambic seems, as to performance, more accurate.

I said earlier that sometimes in scanning there may be differences of opinion or confusion. It is, I think, confusion when the interpretation results from different assumptions about the way meter works. Not one of the four feet of Marvell's line as scanned above is scanned in the same way by Donald Hall (*The Pleasures of Poetry* 38):

$$\diagup \smile \mid \smile \diagup \mid \diagup \smile \mid \smile \diagup$$
To a | green thought | in a | green shade

Hall's logic seems impeccable but is not:

> No one could deny that "green" is louder than "To"; but the difference is metrically irrelevant. What is metrically relevant is that each group of two syllables contains one syllable that is louder than the other.

It is dubious to assume that, since the meter is iambic, relative stress is to be weighed exclusively as to "each group of *two* syllables." We do parse stressed/unstressed syllables relative to those adjacent (I would prefer to say "neighboring," to allow more flexibility when a line's pattern isn't obvious at once). But "green" is also adjacent; and the anapestic possibility ($\smile \smile \diagup$) ought to keep the interpretation open. Suppose the line turned out to go, "To a green*est* thought ...."

Hall, albeit grudgingly, accepts anapestic substitution; so he might equally hear

$$\smile \smile \diagup$$
To a green ...

or

> /⠀ ᴗ⠀ ᴗ
> To a green ...

As to "To a" (/ ᴗ) and "To a" (ᴗ ᴗ), there is precious little difference in their levels of unstress; and meter can supply the lack in the right context:

> (/) ᴗ⠀⠀ ᴗ /⠀⠀⠀ ᴗ /⠀⠀ ᴗ /
> Into | my hands | themselves | do reach

What is startling in Hall's view, then, is the divergent reading of "green" and "green,"
to which he seems forced by his assumption in contexts only slightly different.

The explanation perhaps lies in his holding that meter and rhythm are "wholly different things" (30):

> Rhythm is a large, loose, and inclusive word. Rhythm is things like fast and slow, staccato and smooth.... Meter, on the other hand, is a repeated number of something.... Meter indicates a form of arithmetic; we add something, and we find the same number of it in another line.

Excluding pyrrhics and spondees as feet in English (45-46), he adds, "In English, these effects are rhythmic and not metrical." So—if I understand Hall's view—the *meter* of "To a green thought" is / ᴗ ᴗ /, but the *rhythm* could be ᴗ ᴗ | / /. Speaking of a substituted anapest, however, he says (36), "It is a common metrical variation, which makes us take a little rhythmic quick step in saying the line. "Saying that, though, seems to void the distinction between meter and rhythm as "wholly different." I am puzzled.

Scansion, it seems to me, does two things. It shows a line's sufficient *approximation* of the metrical norm; and, more important, it shows those *divergences* from the norm (as in Hall's comment about the anapest) that let us begin to discuss the line's characteristic rhythm, its musical qualities, which of course also include such effects as alliteration, assonance, or syntactical balance/imbalance. Hall's assumption about each group of two syllables arises because he is discussing iambic meter. He suggests (31-32) that there are other meters in English, and means at least anapestic, trochaic, and dactylic. To these we may now turn.

Testing again with Saintsbury's touchstone, I conclude that **(8) Anapestic, trochaic, and dactylic meters do not exist in English.** In theory, I suppose, though I have never seen it stated this way, these are (along with iambic meter) *sub*-meters of accentual-syllabic meter. Even with the sub-meter distinction carefully made, however, these seem to be multiplied entities that may be confusing. Poems in accentual-syllabics are overwhelmingly iambic, so it makes sense to see iambic as the metrical base; and, given substitution, the other so-called sub-meters obviously all lie somewhere along a *continuous* spectrum of variations. At some point iambic meter with anapestic substitutions turns into anapestic meter with iambic substitutions-and the distinction is, thus, needless. One could hardly claim, to any purpose, if the balance in the stanza of Hardy's "Neutral Tones" shifted from eight iambs/seven anapests to seven iambs/eight anapests, that the *meter* had changed. It seems clear that when we are tempted by terms like "anapestic meter," what is involved is not meter (the system) but variations in rhythm. These we can discuss usefully by speaking of "frequent anapestic substitutions" or, if we want to be precise, by quantifying the proportion of anapests (or whatever) to iambs in any poem or passage. (I count the first stanza of "How They Brought the Good News from Ghent to Aix" as comprising eighteen anapests, four iambs, two spondees. So, "heavily anapestic.")

I hope we agree that, properly, meter refers to *poems*, not lines *per se*. We do not, for instance, if we find three spondees and perhaps only one iamb in "And with old woes new wail my dear time's waste," conclude that the line is spondaic.

So-called trochaic meter is merely a mirror image of iambic, so this is another case of having two quite different ways of describing the same thing:

```
x    /   |  ᴜ   /|ᴜ /|ᴜ  /        [as iambic]
     Come, and trip it as ye go
       /     ᴜ |/  ᴜ|/ ᴜ|/   x    [as trochaic]
```

Often, as here, the iambic reading is faithful to the pattern of the wording. Buckets of ink and spittle might have been spared over "L'Allegro" alone, which has fully iambic lines like "To live with her, and live with thee." Whatever we may want to say of the syncopation of rhythm in such lines as "Come, and trip it as ye go" in Milton, or in Larkin's "First Sight," or in Herrick's "Here she lies, a pretty bud, / Lately made of flesh and blood"-which ends, "The earth, that lightly covers her"—the *meter* is iambic tetrameter. Poems do not change meter from line to line; and Milton's "Then to come in spite of sorrow," even in a poem entirely of such lines that is, with no lines ending in a stressed sylla-ble-would remain iambic, scannable with anacrusis and extra-syllable ending; as it would seem odd to say that a line can be in iambic meter in one poem and in trochaic meter in another. Also, we cannot be consistent about extra-syllable endings if, in trochaic meter, we do count the syllable as belonging to a foot.

What I am urging in this proposition is of course fully implicit in Frost's comment about strict and loose iambic. Our loss, in having multiplied entities, is the failure to see clearly how splendidly unitary English meter is.

IV. TWO LEVELS OF STRESS

In our century, in an illusion of greater precision, linguistics has multiplied entities for prosody. In 1900 ("Notes on Metre," reprinted in *The Structure of Verse*, ed. Harvey Gross [1966]), Otto Jespersen first applied *four* levels of stress to English verse, rather than the conventional two levels. Marked numerical-ly, they are: 4 = "strong," 3 = "half-strong," 2 = "half-weak," 1 = "weak." He comments (115) that "in reality there are infinite gradations of stress ... but it will be sufficient to recognize four degrees." In 1951, in *An Outline of English Structure*, George L. Trager and Henry Lee Smith, Jr., offered a comparable system of four levels of stress ("primary" = /, "secondary" = ^, "tertiary" = \, and "weak" = ◡), which has been employed by metrists Harold Whitehall, Seymour Chatman, and others.

Useful as linguistic analysis may be in other ways, let me be emphatic: **(9) We should never use four degrees of speech stress for scanning.** It will be sufficient for prosody to recognize two degrees of stress, as Shake-speare, Pope, Keats, and Frost have done. As to poetry, persons in white lab coats will bring not help, but confusion. The term *isochronic*, for instance, is merest jargon. It is simply not true that meter (or English, for that matter) is stress-timed, each foot taking exactly the same time to articulate (so that we hurry the unaccented syllables of an anapest to make them fit). If we are then told that, although this may not be true in fact, it is nonetheless true perceptually, we are only back where we started: a foot is a foot. So never mind isochronism.

The use of Trager-Smith stress-levels is meant to complement regular binary foot-scansion; that is, as Seymour Chatman says ("Robert Frost's 'Mowing'" 422), "to account for the phonological complexity of verse by envisaging a tension between *two* systems: the abstract metrical pattern ... and the ordinary stress-pitch-juncture system of spoken English." Harold Whitehall ("From Linguistics to Criticism" 418) speaks of an "orchestration" of the meter and the varied stress-levels of speech. This formulation is essentially what I described as the interrelationship of speech-run and meter that produces the individual rhythm of a line or passage of verse. The implicit claim is that using *four* levels of stress will produce a finer discrimination of the rhythm than is possible conventionally.

On the evidence of the model applications by Chatman and Whitehall, however, the claim is untrue. On the contrary, if we occasionally have difficulty ascribing unstress or stress in a two-valued system, the four-valued system almost predictably results in further disagreement and still more elaborate confusion. Moreover, Chatman and Whitehall seem to see the linguistic rules that apply to speech as *overriding any* special character meter may have; and so their accounts in fact fail to explore the special relationship (tension or orchestration) it was their intention to examine.

Whitehall (418-19) marks only two lines to exemplify the Trager-Smith scoring (the vertical lines are phrase markers); I have added a regular scansion below the lines:

$$\breve{} \quad / \quad \backslash \qquad \wedge \quad \breve{} \quad / \quad \backslash \quad \wedge \quad \breve{} \qquad \breve{}$$

The curfew | tolls the knell | of parting day

$$\breve{} \quad / \; | \; \breve{} \qquad / \; | \; \breve{} \qquad / \; | \; \breve{} \quad / | \breve{} \qquad /$$

and

$$\breve{} \quad \backslash \quad \breve{} \qquad / \qquad \backslash \qquad \wedge \quad \breve{} \quad \backslash \quad \breve{} \qquad /$$

The lowing herd | winds slowly | o'er the lea ||

$$\breve{} \quad / \; | \breve{} \qquad / \; | \qquad / \qquad / | \breve{} \qquad / \; | \quad \breve{} \quad /$$

The Trager-Smith scoring of the iambically regular first line is unobjectionable though one may wonder what insight we can draw from the "orchestration" shown in ascribing secondary stresses to "tolls" and "part-" or tertiary stresses to "-few" and "of." The information doesn't seem very helpful.

The other line, however, is a calamity. I assume that Whitehall has correctly performed whatever linguistics operations give this result, but the result is unacceptable for scanning English meter. That "low-" and "winds" (the verb!) get only tertiary stresses like that on "o'er" and (in the other line) "of" is clearly disputable. I *hear* no such major difference from the stresses on "herd," "slow-," and "lea." The stresses of "winds slow-"seem virtually level and the foot is a spondee. Predictably, Whitehall's discussion focuses, not on the indicated rhythm or orchestration and what it may tell us about Gray's moo-cows, but on the way the English language works. [...][7]

Turn[ing] now to the use of Jespersen's four levels of stress, the ride will be similarly bumpy, albeit with a difference. As to the difficulty of having four sorts of choice we can make, instead of just two, Jespersen himself comments (116):

> It is not always easy to apply these numbers to actually occurring syllables and it is particularly difficult in many instances to distinguish between 3 and 2. Unfortunately, we have no means of measuring stress objectively by instruments.

(That was 1900. By now, I fancy, electronics could at low cost equip us, our students, and poetry readers everywhere with elegant, portable Metermeters.)

The difference I mentioned is important. Jespersen's purpose in introducing four levels of stress, recall, is to *replace* foot-scansion—which he concludes is absurd—by a new system (118) involving the regular alternation of "an upward and a downward movement, a rise and a fall, an ascent and a descent, at fixed places," that is, from each syllable to the next. A pentameter is figured in this way, with *a* and *b* representing syllables and the slashes representing the required ascent (/) or descent (\):

a / b \ a / b \ a / b \ a / b \ a / b \ a / b

The *relationship* of each stressed syllable *(b)* to the next unstressed syllable *(a)* is fully as important as the relationship between an unstressed and a stressed— hence, the irrelevance of feet.

This isn't the place for a full critique of Jespersen's system. However interesting, it is complicated, and plausible only up to a point. It is also incomplete, making no provision whatever for trisyllabic substitutions (or meter). And it is finally a mess, collapsing in the face of actual lines Jespersen is at a loss to explain without great contrivance and some deliberate misreading of levels of

---

[7] Wallace's critique of Seymour Chatman's *Theory of Meter* ("Meter" 32-34) has been excised. -*Eds.*

speech stress. As he confesses (123), "In spite of all this there will remain some instances in which the second syllable cannot easily be made stronger than the third. Metrics is no exact science aimed at finding out natural laws that are valid everywhere." Whatever may be others' view of Jespersen's system, no recent metrist has chosen to adopt it.

The difficulty with using Jespersen's four stresses for scanning, then, is that there is nowhere to go with the result *except back to the conventional system of feet*, and so, by translating, skewing the wonderfully adaptive system of binary unstress/stress. Consider a scansion of Marvell's line with Jespersen stress-scoring, to which I have added below the line the resulting foot-relationships marked conventionally:

2 1 3   4   2 1 3   4
To a green thought in a green shade
╱ ∪| ∪   ╱ |╱ ∪| ∪   ╱

The binary result, coincidentally, is the same as Hall's scansion (27)[.][8]

Given that we will encounter in reality far more actual levels of stress than four, assigning Jespersen's levels of stress will often be even more arbitrary than in a binary system. "To" is perhaps more strongly stressed that "a," though not by much; neither is anywhere near the adjective and noun that follow. Why might we not scan "To a" as 1 1? Further, to my ear "green," which is the surprising word and is, moreover, surprisingly repeated, rings at least as strong as either the expected "thought" or "shade." Why not, then, 1 1 4 4 1 1 4 4 or, conceivably, 1 1 4 3 1 1 4 3? The answer, if we are following Jespersen, will turn out to be *not* that we are listening very carefully and accurately, but that a mistaken theory is afoot.

Consider a line of Frost cited by Steele (*Missing Measures* 61), which he scans elsewhere by Jespersen stresses:

3   4 1 2   3   4 1 4   2 4
Snow falling and night falling fast, oh, fast

Here is the line again, with above it the Jespersen stresses translated into breve and ictus, and below it a commonsense scansion (with double-iamb):

---

[8] This and the next paragraph have been abridged. *-Eds.*

```
  ∪  ╱ | ∪  ╱ |  ∪  ╱ | ∪  ╱ | ∪  ╱
```
Snow falling and night falling fast, oh, fast
```
╱  ╱ | ∪  ∪   ╱  ╱ | ∪  ╱ |(╱) ╱
```

The Jespersen-based translation (above the line) shows it as being entirely iambs, and has lost the subtlety registered in the numerical and traditional scansions. Steele would affirm the iambic reading here, I think. In "On Meter" (298-99), [Steele] cites a number of lines including the following which, he says, "appears to have seven notable speech stresses" (his italics):

Kind pity chokes my *spleen; brave scorn* for*bids*

I would agree so far, seeing spondees as the first and fourth feet. Steele, however, sums up:

> Despite their rhythmical differences, all the lines quoted above are metrically identical. All the lines conform in one way or another to the lighter-to-heavier movement. All the feet in the lines are iambic, in that the second syllable is more emphatic than the first.

The puzzle is, what is *gained by* thus insisting on the absolute iambic regularity? There is at least a risk of loss, or of being misunderstood.

An issue lurking in much of the foregoing must now be focused on: the spondee. It seems odd that we need to discuss at this late date whether there is or is not a spondee in English meter; and our students—or a physicist who happened into our classrooms—might well be puzzled at the disorder about something so basic. But, as some authoritative accounts firmly declare that the spondee doesn't exist in English (Hall, 45) or that it is extremely rare (Yvor Winters, "The Audible Reading of Poetry," in *The Function of Criticism* [1957] 90), let me assert **(10) The spondee is a good, and fairly frequent, foot in English.**

Insofar as rejection of the spondee may depend on the TragerSmith schema, I have suggested that we not worry about snowflakes. Let's pursue the question as to the Jespersen system.

Steele ("On Meter" 305-6) is among those who consider "true" spondees rare in English verse. Discussing a line of Keats, scanned by Bate and Perkins as having an iamb and a spondee as the first two feet—

$$\breve{} \diagup \quad \diagup \quad \breve{} \quad \breve{} \quad \breve{} \quad \breve{} \diagup \quad \breve{} \diagup$$
The hare | limped tremb | ling through | the froz | en grass

—Steele offers instead this Jespersen-stress reading:

1   2 / 3   4
The hare limped trembling ...

Steele's slash shows foot-division, the feet being iambs of course.

In following the trail here back to Jespersen, let me go the long way around. Steele's reading of "hare" as a 2 is astonishing. Without question, Jespersen would have scored the Keats fragment as 1 4 3 4, or 1 4 2 4, rather than as 1 2 3 4, on the model of his reading of "*The still sad music* of humanity" (116)—a reading that would preserve the normal "descent" from the second to the third syllable.

Steele's 2 for "hare" is not a typo, however. He introduces his reading of the fragment by saying that "we appear to have, in these two feet, one of those cases of four successive syllables representing four rising degrees of stress." Just before (301) he has mentioned this as a "special case." "From time to time, in iambic English verse, one will encounter two adjacent feet whose four syllables represent four rising degrees of stress," and he cites the beginning of Sidney's line:

1   2 / 3 4
With how sad steps O moon thou climbst the skies

This points us correctly to the place in "Notes on Metre" (125), where Jespersen is struggling unsuccessfully to reconcile to his system a number of lines such as "*In the sweet pangs* of it remember me." Of this pattern Jespersen then comments

I incline to read it with 1 2 3 4 and thus to say that the ascent is normal between the first and the second as well as between the third and the fourth syllable, so that there is only the one small anomaly of a slight ascent instead of a descent between the second and the third syllable. It is worth noting how frequently this figure contains an adjective (stressed 3) before a substantive (stressed 4).

With startling nonchalance—"I incline to read it"—Jespersen chooses to ignore actual speech stress to favor his theory, as he also does on page 122 to deal with another difficulty.

Steele's 1 2 3 4 for "The hare limped trembling," we see, then, is an attempt (albeit mistaken) to follow a doctrine. And here, in Jespersen, we see the doctrine being created. He needs a 1 2 for "In the"—as he does for "And the," "But the," and even "are the"—in order to make the lines he is considering even *almost* fit his system. A reading of 2 1, as in Hall's reading of "To a green thought," would of course be more like what we hear; or a 1 1. But Jespersen is not listening, he is making dogma.

Here, too, is the doctrine of 3 4 for "sweet pangs"—or for "green thought," "brave scorn," "Snow falling," or "limped trembling," no matter what we may hear. Requiring alternating ascent/descent for his system, Jespersen will not admit a 4 4; and those who scan by Jespersen-scoring will not admit a spondee.

But there is no necessity about this. Go back to what Jespersen has said (116) just before he outlines the system:

> Verse rhythm is based on the same alternation between stronger and weaker syllables as that found in natural everyday speech. Even in the most prosaic speech, which is in no way dictated by artistic feeling, this alternation is not completely irregular: everywhere we observe a natural tendency towards making a weak syllable follow after a strong one and inversely.

In speech, two equal or virtually equal stresses may occur together; so a spondee is plainly possible in meter. The refusal to accept it is mere dogma, borrowed from the failed theory of Jespersen's system. Even Winters, in his striptease about the extremely rare "truly spondaic foot" (139), one of which he ultimately uncovers in Barnabe Googe, is following the dogma, as his comment about "When to the *sessions of sweet* silent thought" suggests (94): "we have in effect a series of four degrees of accent within two successive feet." The point of talking mysteriously about "true" spondees has always been one-upsmanship. Meter cannot depend on discriminations too fine for ordinary mortals, poets or readers, to make out pretty easily.

Meter is not a seismograph, but a binary system of conventional *approximations* of the language's rapid and complex levels of stress. We know, from "To a," that "green thought" counts as two stresses; as we know, from "green thought," that "To a" counts as a pair of unstressed syllables. The binary nature of English meter, which requires that we resolve everything into its two values, means that we must be at once flexible and precise.

In scanning, a simple method of noting possibly ambiguous cases is to show the breve or ictus in parentheses, as I have often done in this paper. In marking

> ‿ ╱ ‿ ╱ (╱) ╱ ╱ ╱ ‿ ╱
> When A | jax strives | some rock's | vast weight | to throw

I mark "some rock's" as spondee, for instance, but suggest that hearing it as an iamb is also plausible. In this way, we can moot some disagreements as well as make our scanning somewhat more finely responsive. The device will give us, in effect, a way to register an intermediate level of stress when, occasionally, that may aid in interpretation.

In scanning, we often show such tact rather than rigor. For instance, we allow as stressed a syllable that in speech is virtually unaccented, as in Frost's

> ‿ ╱ ‿ (╱) ‿ ╱ ‿ ╱ ‿ ╱
> That gath | ers on | the pane | in emp | ty rooms

As Miller Williams says deftly, "Any set of three unaccented syllables will nearly always be read with a perceptibly greater force on the middle one." But-notice-we ignore this effect in other cases, as in Housman's

> ╱ ‿‿ ‿ ╱ ‿ ╱ ‿ ╱
> Loveliest | of trees, | the cher | ry now

where, I think, the tetrameter context of the line determines what we register as metrically relevant. In a passage of pentameters, however, we might properly hear:

> x ╱ ‿(╱) ‿ ╱ ‿ ╱ ‿ ╱
> Love | liest | of trees, | the cher | ry now

Underlying tact is what might be called the LCD rule (lowest common denominator). In scanning, when more than one interpretation of a line is possible, we should usually opt for the simpler or closer to the metrical norm. "Loveliest of trees" might be read as either dactyl/iamb or trochee/anapest, but the former is preferable, as showing only one substitution. Similarly, a less than preferable reading of the Yeats line, which is scannable as anacrusis/double-iamb/iamb/iamb (26), would be

$$/ \quad \cup \quad \cup \quad / \quad \quad / \quad \cup \quad x(/) \; / \quad \cup$$
Speech af | ter long | silence; | it | is right

which shows two trochaic substitutions and a lame foot. Equally awkward would be reading "it is right" as an anapest, thus giving the line only four feet though the poem is clearly otherwise pentameter. Any of these alternative interpretations can be rationalized as emphasizing expressive effects, but none seems necessary for that purpose. Turco's amphibrach (22) violates the LCD rule.

A scansion in a textbook, cited by Steele—

$$\cup \;\; \cup \;\; / \quad\quad / \;\; \cup \;\; /\cup \;\; \cup \;\; \cup \quad\quad / \;\; /$$
To the land | vaguely | rea | lizing | westward

—manages to read a pentameter with no iambs at all, though it is in fact fairly regular:

$$\cup \;\; \cup \;\; / \quad / \quad\quad \cup \;\; / \quad \cup(/) \;\; \cup \;\; / \quad\quad \cup$$
To the land vague | ly re | aliz | ing west | ward

An anapestic reading of "To the land" would be correct if the next syllable was unstressed,

$$\cup \;\; \cup \;\; / \quad\quad \cup \;\; / \quad\quad \cup$$
To the land | *that* vague | ly ...

But it is incorrect for the line as it reads. That error leads to the mistaken attribution of trochees in the next places, and so to a mishearing of the plain secondary stress on "-liz-" and to a false stress on "-ward."

My aim in all of the foregoing has been to urge that we simplify our accounts of meter in English. Hereafter, we should expect that any new or revised account will be simpler than what we have. Hoping for and confidently predicting such a "synthesis" in 1907, T.S. Omond (*English Metrists* 240) noted, "When it does come, I suspect it will be found less and not more complex than its many predecessors."

Unworkable complexity, I think, defeats both Jespersen and the theory offered by Morris Halle and Samuel Jay Keyser (*English Stress* 139-46, 164-80). I am unaware that anyone on the literary side has adopted Halle and Keyser's account, but it appears still to have currency on the linguistics side, so a comment seems in order. Their process of scansion strikes me as hugely cumbersome. We might, I suppose, grow accustomed to that. But consider the results produced. This line by Keats—

How many bards gild the lapses of time

—is judged (171) "unmetrical since it has a stress maximum in the fourth W position in violation of the last alternative of (52bii)."[9] But the following (invented) line would, by their system, be metrical, scanning as iambic pentameter (178):

Billows, billows, serene mirror of the marine boroughs, remote willow

Smokey Stover, thou shouldst be living at this hour!

Perhaps Omond's expectation is doomed to be forlorn. If, however, a truly new synthesis appears, we will know it by the ease and clarity with which it accounts for the roughly regular use of unstressed syllables (and sometimes stressed ones, as in spondees) as spacers between countable stresses. It will be simpler than the system of native footnotes wild we have now. Meanwhile, let us carefully strip away the inessentials from this homemade prosody and make do. It is, I think, seen properly, both simple and elegant.

Going by recent authoritative accounts, however, the situation hasn't improved since 1907, when Omond concluded

This, for certain, that we have as yet no established system of prosody.... It is a strange fact so late in the history of our literature; Greek metrists would have viewed it with surprise.

---

[9] Halle and Keyser outline a series of linguistic rules presumably governing the alternation of W (weak) and S (strong) syllables in verse. Their rule 52bi states, "when a fully stressed syllable occurs between two unstressed syllables … within a line of verse, this syllable is called a 'stress maximum.'" Cited in the passage above, rule 52bii states, "Fully stressed syllables occur in S positions only and in all S positions OR Fully stressed syllables occur in S positions only but not in all S positions" (Levin 606)—this last being the "alternative" Keats is accused of violating. -*Eds.*

Free Verse and the Orbit
of Meter (1999)

Preface

These essays sketch a fresh understanding of English meter that incorporates free verse. My argument centers on two propositions, both presented in Section 1, "The Free Verse Myth": that the bacchic (◡ ⁄ ⁄) is one of the six indispensable feet in our meter; and that, when we scan with bacchics, all verse turns out to be metrical, that is, measurable within the same system. I am indebted to Charles O. Hartman for insisting in *Meter in English* ("Some Responses" 113) that we credit bacchics in scanning poems like Browning's "How They Brought the Good News from Ghent to Aix," a point I accepted ("Completing" 339)—and extended to include poems in iambic meter, since I can only assume that we must credit such feet wherever we find them.

The full significance of bacchics hadn't occurred to me when *Meter in English* went to press.[10] With them, however, we can scan "free" verse and so study its rhythms in detail just as we do those of verse in meter. This will be a major advance in an area still troublingly beyond our skills. Relative regularity/irregularity will replace, with new precisions, the generally vague and unhelpful distinction metrical/nonmetrical.

Sections 2 ("On Justice on Stevens, with Asides") and 3 ("Dragons in the Verse Patch") pursue the taxonomy of free verse and meter, first with regard to accentual and syllabic meters, then with regard to conventional accentual-syllabic meter, all of which we can readily simplify. Neither accentuals nor syllabics really functions as a meter, as I argued in *Meter in English*; so we may discard these null classifications. (Syllabics may nonetheless be useful to poets as a resistance in composition.) So-called trochaic, anapestic, and dactylic meters are also needless and obfuscatory terms. They try to make distinctions that were never very precise and that seem now merely arbitrary. Other than nonce "double-dactyls," I doubt there is a single poem in full dactylic meter, that is,

---

[10] In 1993. *-Eds.*

not suffering catalexis and even double-catalexis. So, as "meters," they too may be dropped—although, I hasten to add, the terms anapestic and trochaic may occasionally be useful to describe the rhythm of runs of these feet in particular poems; as we might speak of the rhythm of Browning's poem, "How They Brought the Good News," as strongly anapestic.

These clarifications are timely, in light of the rapidly spreading prosodic muddle of the last half-century. As several of the following essays document, confusion is now turning into sometimes almost comic license, even in new textbooks, manuals, and guides being offered round with great praise.

Section 4 ("Mr. Pinsky Sets a Problem") continues to exemplify the metricality of free verse. Since most of these further examples were not chosen by me, I hope they will be persuasive in encouraging fuller, careful exploration of the formerly white areas on our prosodical maps. The value, as always, lies in what we may discover about poems.

R.W.

I. The Free Verse Myth

In America there is little to be observed except natural curiosities. The new world must have many vegetables and animals with which philosophers are but little acquainted. I hope you will furnish yourself with some books of natural history, and some glasses and other instruments of observation. Trust as little as you can to report; examine all you can by your own senses.
—Samuel Johnson, "Letter to Dr. Staunton" (1762)

Oddly, since it is said to have become the dominant form of the century, free verse remains largely a white area on the prosodical maps. The terms themselves—"free," "open," "fluid," "organic"—resist the notion of anything systematic or countable, and the variety of kinds of verse referred to by the terms has no doubt discouraged analysis. One purpose of my essays in *Meter in English* was, by clarifying what we mean by meter, to sharpen the possibility of understanding the nonmetrical, that "slippery non-class" ("Completing" 343).

Poetic meter is always based on properties of a language that can be systematized and counted. We would therefore expect to find, and do find, occurring naturally in speech and in prose what we may call metrical cadences. Without our intending or noticing them, for instance, strings of iambs show up in speech, especially in passionate speech.

Metrical cadences also show up naturally in poems written in free verse. It would be startling if they did not.

Here, however, they create something of a conundrum, since free verse is defined primarily with reference to meter, as *not* metrical. When I began this inquiry, my view was the common one, I think: that so long as metrical cadences in free verse remain below the level of notice, they are of no special concern. Poets writing in free verse would aim to keep it this way—that is, to avoid such cadences or at least to evade the reader's noticing them, although poets could also use them deliberately, exploiting them for local purposes, as Whitman does in "When I Heard the Learn'd Astronomer":

When I heard the learn'd astronomer,
When the proofs, the figures, were ranged in columns before me,

> When I was shown the charts and diagrams, to add, divide, and measure them,
> When I sitting heard the astronomer where he lectured with much applause
>   in the lecture room,
> How soon unaccountable I became tired and sick,
> Till rising and gliding out I wander'd off by myself,
> In the mystical moist night-air, and from time to time,
> Look'd up in perfect silence at the stars.

The last line is unmistakably iambic pentameter. After the convoluted and te-
dious syntax that describes the lecture, the music of the familiar pentameter
evokes, paradoxically, what is natural and lacking in artifice, the unmediated
experience of standing out beneath the stars themselves.

I am not alone in noticing metrical lines in poems we take to be free verse.
Henry Taylor notes that some of Louis Simpson's poems "suggest ... that free
verse can be rewardingly varied by the occasional use of meter" (46). In *Meter
in English*, Robert Hass makes a similar observation about a passage of Ken-
neth Rexroth's "The Signature of All Things" ("Prosody" 148–49): "To account
for the rhythms of Rexroth's lines, one would have to examine the pacing of
the stresses and notice what we have been noticing, the way it hovers about and
sometimes coincides with metrical stress," the last line of the passage being, for
instance, "a firm, slightly skipping iambic trimeter": "The meadow is bright as
snow." Robert Pinsky notes in Ginsberg's "Howl" passages of "striking single
pentameters buried in the free-verse context" (*Sounds* 72–73).

More often than a casual reader might suspect, poems in free verse climax
or end in metrical cadences or lines. These are the rough equivalent to bringing
up the music at the end of a movie. Whitman does it often:

> [of the Muse]
> Smiling and pleas'd with palpable intent to stay,
> She's here, install'd amid the kitchen-ware.

> There in the fragrant pines and the cedars dusk and dim.

> As fill'd with friendship, love complete, the Elder Brother found,
> The Younger melts in fondness in his arms.
> Thy trills of shrieks by rocks and hills return'd,
> Launch'd o'er the prairies wide, across the lakes,
> To the free skies unpent and glad and strong.

Nor is Whitman alone among free verse poets in being drawn to the metrical. In order to make the metrical cadences clearer, I have rearranged the lineation of three familiar passages:

Unconfusion submits its confusion to proof
it's not a Herod's oath that cannot change.

It is difficult to get the news from poems
yet men die miserably every day
for lack of what is found there. Hear me out
for I too am concerned and every man
who wants to die at peace in his bed besides.

Ah, dear father, graybeard, lonely old courage-teacher,
what America did you have when Charon quit poling his ferry
and you got out on a smoking bank and stood
watching the boat disappear on the black waters of Lethe?

In various ways, Marianne Moore, William Carlos Williams, and Allen Ginsberg, disguising the metrical cadences which underlie the lines of their poems, successfully evade the reader's noticing. Gary Snyder seems not to bother with evasion at all in the opening and closing lines of "Riprap":

Lay down these words
Before your mind like rocks.
ants and pebbles
In the thin loam, each rock a word
a creek-washed stone

Granite: ingrained
with torment of fire and weight
Crystal and sediment linked hot
all change, in thoughts,
As well as things.

The iambic base is equally clear in the last stanza of Adrienne Rich's "Diving into the Wreck":

> We are, I am, you are
> by cowardice or courage
> the one who find our way
> back to this scene
> carrying a knife, a camera
> a book of myths
> in which
> our names do not appear

We need not look far for pentameters: "I came to see the damage that was done," "the wreck and not the story of the wreck," or

> And I am here, the mermaid whose dark hair
> streams black, the merman in his armored body

There is something puzzling about all these metrical cadences where we don't expect to find them. Looking at poetry journals, we find that much free verse these days is mostly metrical. What sounds right, what clicks into place for the poet, are metrical cadences.

Perplexity becomes public confusion when poems entirely or substantially metrical are asserted to be free verse, or rather *assumed* to be, as often are T.S. Eliot's "The Love Song of J. Alfred Prufrock" or W.H. Auden's "Musée des Beaux Arts." So Stephen Dobyns doesn't even argue the claim as to Williams's "To Mark Anthony in Heaven," Philip Larkin's "Coming," Donald Justice's "Absences," or Michael Ryan's "When I Was Conceived," though all these might be accounted for as metrical. So Jack Myers and Michael Simms cite Larkin's "The Poetry of Departures," quoting the first stanza to exemplify free verse because it is "structured on semiformal speech rhythms" (123–25). But the poem is unmistakably in meter:

> Sometimes | you hear, | fifth-hand,
>
> As ep | itaph:
>
> He chucked | up ev | erything
>
> And just | cleared off

⏑ / ⏑ ⏑ / ⏑ /
And al | ways the voice | will sound

x / ⏑ / ⏑ /
Cer | tain you | approve

⏑ ⏑ / ⏑ / ⏑⏑ /
This auda | cious, pur | ify | ing,

x / ⏑ / ⏑ /
El | emen | tal move.

Iambic trimeters, with dimeters at lines 2 and 4? Line 7 might be construed as tetrameter if performance wants a stress on "This." The very least we can conclude is that, for a very large number of contemporary poems, we just can't be sure whether they are in free verse or in meter. The distinction is not nearly as clear as we might have thought.

The most bizarre claim that poems, apparently metrical, are free verse is made by H.T. Kirby-Smith, who argues that free verse "appeared in English for the first time about 1590" (44). Earlier practitioners included Barnabe Barnes, George Herbert, John Milton, Abraham Cowley, John Dryden, and later, William Blake, Robert Southey, Matthew Arnold, Coventry Patmore, William Ernest Henley, and T.S. Eliot (in "Prufrock" of course). Kirby-Smith's criterion is simply any arbitrary variation in line length. For instance, with lines varying from monometer to pentameter, "The Collar" is adjudged "completely irregular and unpredictable," and so not metrical (50). "Lycidas," given fourteen trimeters like "And all their echoes mourn" among its 193 lines, all otherwise pentameters, is also free verse—despite the poem's conclusion in a verse paragraph that is a firmly wrought ottava rima, invoking a tradition that includes Boccaccio, Tasso, and Spenser. Happy to punch below the belt, Kirby-Smith even argues that Milton's writing free verse "is quite in keeping with his advocacy of divorce, his defense of free speech, his belief in free will, and his general cantankerousness" (74–75).

Moreover, since in Kirby-Smith's account we must abandon the idea that a free verse line "is constructed of subsidiary units—whether syllables, accents, or feet" (54), and so must assume that the unpredictable "line itself becomes the atomic unit of the prosody" (73), there would appear to be no way of even discussing such verse. As he remarks (43), "scansion of free verse is impossible." Iambs we were counting in "Lycidas" only a moment ago to determine the pentameters and trimeters have (in a critical poof) vanished along with, it seems, even syllables.

Regular line length is no more a necessary and inviolable convention of English meter than is, say, exact regularity of foot-type; one could argue as plausibly that substitution (or enjambment and caesural variation) makes the lines of any poem "completely irregular and unpredictable." In short, Kirby-Smith errs, mistaking part of the freedom of meter for free verse. In "Out, Out—," when Frost substitutes a tetrameter at a telling moment—

$$/ \quad / \quad \cup \quad / \quad \cup \quad / \quad \cup / \quad \cup$$
So. But | the hand | was gone | alread | y

—he is working within, not outside, the metrical system.

Other efforts at providing a theoretical basis for free verse turn up equally empty.

Meter is about counting. So free verse must involve what is *not* metrically countable. That appears to be something like Charles O. Hartman's definition in *Free Verse: An Essay on Prosody* (24–25): "*the prosody of free verse is rhythmic organization by other than numeric modes*" (his italics). One mode, Hartman says, is "symmetry," and he gives as example two versions of a line:

Shivering in their beds in November's wind.
Shiver in their beds in November's wind.

Of the one, he says that "ordinary metrical compensations keep control.... We read the line as iambic pentameter." Of the other, that

> although the line can conceivably be regularized, a pattern is generated that is nonmetrical.... The best conventional scansion would come close enough to breaking the iambic norm so that the natural speech rhythm of the words takes over instead.... The line could end a free-verse poem, but not a sonnet.

The problem with this is that *both* lines are metrical, insofar as one can say anything without a context. I agree with Hartman about the first:

$$/ \cup \quad \cup \; (/) \quad \cup \quad / \quad \cup \quad \cup \; / \quad \cup \quad /$$
Shiver | ing in | their beds | in Novem | ber's wind.

But the second is equally plausible:

$$x \quad / \quad \cup (/) \quad \cup \quad / \quad \cup \quad \cup / \quad \cup \quad /$$

Shiv | er in | their beds | in Novem | ber's wind.

It is even arguable that anacrusis (the convention of omitted initial syllable) keeps the line closer to the iambic alternation of stress than does the trochaic inversion, and also compensates for the syllable added by the anapest later in the line. Both versions of the line are countable. The more symmetrical one, with its extra unstressed syllable, isn't really symmetrical; and even if it were as symmetrical as Prospero's "Twelve | year since, | Miran | da, twelve | year since," it would be metrically countable: iambic pentameter. Symmetricality can't be the point anyway, since then Blake's "The Tyger" or Jonson's "Epitaph on Elizabeth, L.H." would probably be accounted free verse.

A peculiar variant of the theoretical confusion is the notion that there is hidden in free verse some regular meter from which the poem is supposed to have diverged inexplicably. (The notion is a misreading of a paragraph in Eliot's cryptic "Reflections on *Vers Libre*.") So Paul Fussell sees the last line of "When I Heard the Learn'd Astronomer" as disclosing "the ghost meter which the poem has been concealing all along" (86). Fussell doesn't of course show us the ghost meter concealed in the poem's earlier lines, which may be scanned as tetrameter, pentameter, octameter (and so on), or explain how it is *concealed* in them. The claim remains presupposition.

Graham Hough has a go at demonstrating the hidden meter (91–93). Citing the first 22 lines of "The Love Song of J. Alfred Prufrock," he says—implausibly, given the incessant rhyming—"The experience of reading this passage, I suggest, is very much that of reading blank verse." It is the longer lines that trouble Hough, as "we are never much surprised by short lines in blank verse, partly because we are so accustomed to the broken lines at the ends of speeches in dramatic verse, and partly because the short lines in Virgil give them a sort of classical precedent." Then Hough sees, if he *relines* the heptameters—

The yellow fog that rubs its back upon the window-panes
The yellow smoke that rubs its muzzle on the window-panes
Licked its tongue into the corner of the evening.

—in this way:

The yellow fog that rubs its back upon
The window-panes, the yellow smoke that rubs

Its muzzle on the window-panes, licked
Its tongue into the corner of the evening.

that Eliot's lines "*contain* blank verse, though they do not so appear on the page." The poem, he concludes triumphantly, "is in fact *vers libéré* rather than *vers libre.*"

Now there is no such thing as *vers libéré* in English. Otherwise, given substitution, extra-syllable endings, and so on, we would have to say that English verse has always been *libéré*. In French, the term has to do mainly with loosening the strict caesural segmentation of the alexandrine; and Hough drags it in, only because he intends to conclude that free verse is prose. And he wants to save Eliot's poem, which he likes, but which (like Kirby-Smith) he thinks must be free verse, since its lines are irregular in length. He could have spared a lot of fuss if he had only thought of Donne's "A Valediction: Of Weeping," whose lines range from two to seven feet, Arnold's "Dover Beach," whose lines range from two to five feet, or Frost's "After Apple-Picking," whose lines range from one to six feet. In fact, Hough appears to change his mind anyway, noting that "we do not need a new principle at all. We are simply confronted with an extension of the liberties that have been normal in English verse over a great deal of its history" (102).

Hartman buys into Hough's French term but remembers "Dover Beach," so he tries to do some fast footwork. Noting that "there are two logical ways to extend or loosen the iambic meters, by varying either the kinds of feet or their number," he takes Arnold's poem, "which may indeed have been an important model for Eliot," as an instance of "clearly metrical poems whose lines vary in length." "But," he goes on,

> though Arnold varies the number of iambs in the line (from two to five), he replaces the iambs with other feet only according to familiar principles of substitution, which he applies conservatively. However flexible the accentual-syllabic meter may be, it will not accept both kinds of variation at once in the degree to which Eliot employs them. The concept of the foot has meaning only metrically—that is, within a numerically regular system. When feet vary ad hoc in both number and kind, they lose metrical significance. (*Free Verse* 117)

And we are back to a merely subjective judgment about regularity. Moreover, the implication that in "Prufrock" Eliot violates the "familiar principles of substitution" is quite wrong. Eliot's substitution is in fact more conservative than Arnold's. In only one line of "Prufrock" do other feet outnumber iambs:

/ ∪ ∪ / / ∪ ∪ / / /
Combing | the white | hair of | the waves | blown back,

to which we may compare Arnold's line, which leaves only one iamb of the paradigm intact:

∪ ∪ / / / ∪ / / ∪ /
Of the | night wind | down the | vast edg | es drear.

It is true that Eliot's line lengths vary more than Arnold's—three of the 131 lines of "Prufrock" exceed the heptameters about the yellow fog. Two of these are essentially iambic:

x / ∪ / ∪ / ∪ / ∪ / ∪ / ∪ / ∪ (/)
But | as if | a mag | ic lan | tern threw | the nerves | in pat | terns on
∪ /
| a screen
∪ / ∪ / ∪ / / / ∪ / / /
Though I | have seen | my head | (grown slight | ly bald) | brought in
∪ / ∪ / ∪
| upon | a plat | ter.

The other uses trochaic inversion and two anapests, but concludes in a firm iambic pace:

/ ∪ ∪ / ∪ / ∪ ∪ / ∪ ∪ / ∪ / ∪
After | the nov | els, af | ter the tea | cups, af | ter the skirts | that trail
/ ∪ /
| along | the floor.

I am not sure how far a poet can go before he or she is no longer substituting "conservatively," or how many line-lengths are allowable in a metrical poem, but Hartman's generalization strikes me as self-shredding. It attempts to legislate taste. The countability of "Prufrock" is not in question, just as the countability of "The Collar" or "Musée des Beaux Arts" is not in question, although the last apparently has a line of nine or perhaps ten feet. If our purpose is to *describe* (or discuss) the verse of these poems, rather than to approve or disapprove or to construct theories, we will find it practical to conclude that this verse is *measurable* by the same system as more regular verse: that is, that it is metrical. Irregularity (of feet, of line-length) is standard in English metrical verse. It is a rare poem indeed, if any exist at all, that preserves the paradigm intact.

Usually the hidden issue in discussions of free verse is regularity, not (as it should be) countability. Irregularity = free verse. It is this shift in meaning that creates the confusion. "Prufrock" and "Musée des Beaux Arts" are entirely countable (measurable, metrical) but are also quite irregular. So the disagreement is merely about how much or what kind of irregularity is *acceptable*—and that is a matter of opinion. For prosodists, the issue can never be "Where *should* we draw the line? but only where, in fact, metrical countability vanishes. "In English," as George Saintsbury says, "the poetry makes the rules, not the rules the poetry" (1: 307).

The virtual omnipresence of metrical cadences in what is taken to be free verse and the difficulty of our giving a clear, coherent account of the form lead to a reasonable suspicion that free verse does not exist in English. Perhaps, all along, it has been a myth; useful, enabling, but nonetheless a myth.

I do not know why Eliot did not reprint "Reflections on *Vers Libre*," which appeared in the *New Statesman* in 1917, until he allowed it into what turned out to be the posthumous volume, *To Criticize the Critic* (1964). The essay is enigmatic and quirky, certainly, and it probably wears too obviously the politics of its moment in literary criticism. Eliot may not have continued to believe what he once said. Whatever his reservations, the essay has rarely been taken seriously, though it is often cited for the remark "that the ghost of some simple metre should lurk behind the arras in even the 'freest' verse; to advance menacingly as we doze, and withdraw as we rouse" (187). (One recalls, with Prufrockian puzzlement, that it was Polonius lurking behind the arras.) Authority of course proves nothing, but we might do well to listen again to a passage seldom quoted (183-84):

> It is assumed that *vers libre* exists. It is assumed that *vers libre* is a school; that it consists of certain theories; that its group or groups of theorists will either revolutionize or demoralize poetry if their attack upon the iambic pentameter meets with any success. *Vers libre* does not exist, and it is time that this preposterous fiction followed the *élan vital* and the eighty thousand Russians into oblivion.

When a theory of art passes it is usually found that a groat's worth of art has been bought with a million of advertisement. The theory which sold the wares may be quite false, or it may be confused and incapable of elucidation, or it may never have existed. A mythical revolution will have taken place and produced a few works of art which perhaps would be even better if still less of the revolutionary theories clung to them....

 Vers libre has not even the excuse of a polemic; it is a battle-cry of freedom, and there is no freedom in art. And as the so-called *vers libre* is anything but 'free', it can better be defended under some other label....

Recovering the Genetic Code of English Verse

Until raised in *Meter in English*, the question "What are the *English* feet?" had not been really open since George Puttenham's *Arte of English Poesie* in 1589. The usual consensus—iamb (◡ ´), trochee (´ ◡), spondee (´ ´), anapest (◡ ◡ ´), dactyl (´ ◡ ◡), and pyrrhic (◡ ◡)—has often been muddled by also listing, as in Paul Fussell's *Poetic Meter and Poetic Form* (21), all of the Greek and Latin feet. Recent metrists haven't been able to keep their hands out of that cookie jar or to resist ever goofier views of the conventions of our meter. Hartman's *Free Verse* (106–07), for instance, invokes a palimbacchic (´ ´ ◡) and amphibrachs (◡ ´ ◡) to scan two fairly ordinary pentameters of Philip Larkin's "Church Going":

<pre>
     ´ ◡   ◡ ´ ◡ ´   ◡   ´   ´   ´ ◡
Up at | the hol | y end; | the small | neat organ
     ◡ ◡ ´   ´   ◡ ´   ◡ ´ ◡   ◡ ´ ◡
And a tense, must | y, un | ignorab | le silence
</pre>

Using these feet is unnecessary and plainly manipulative, however, since the first line may be scanned simply as ending in a spondee and an extra-syllable (or feminine) ending, while the second scans as an iamb, anapest, and (again) e-s ending.

 Kirby-Smith engages in similar obfuscations, finding needless amphibrachs, amphimacers (´ ◡ ´), choriambs (´ ◡ ◡ ´), and an Adonic (´ ◡ ◡ ´ ´)—as well as what he calls (199) "a strange foot" (◡ ◡ ´ ◡) in the last four syllables of a line in Eliot's "The Love Song of J. Alfred Prufrock": "Like a patient etherized *upon a table*." In Greek or Latin verse the foot would be termed a third paeon, as Kirby-Smith could have found out wherever he had found the choriambs and Adonics. In English verse, the end of a line might simply be an anapest and e-s ending. But, here, the resolution is simpler even than that:

$$\breve{} \ \breve{} \ / \quad \breve{} \ / \quad \breve{} \ / \quad \breve{} / \quad \breve{} / \quad \breve{}$$

Like a pa | tient eth | erized | upon | a ta | ble

Kirby-Smith saw this possibility along the way, but cleverly talked himself out of it. As he reports, "'upon' is, by itself, a natural iamb that tends (as I hear it) to be speeded up here so as to lose its stress," though why he ends up with the strange foot still isn't clear. Demoting speech stresses—never a convention of English verse—was pioneered by Annie Finch (*Ghost of Meter* 29), who often hears dactyls and thus creatively transforms a simple Dickinson iambic trimeter—

$$/ \ \breve{} \quad \breve{} \ / \quad \breve{} \ /$$

This is | the Hour | of Lead

—into a dactylic dimeter:

$$/ \ \breve{} \ \breve{} \quad / \ \breve{} \ \breve{}$$

This is the | Hour of Lead

Kirby-Smith's innovation is imagining only the feet he wants to find in a line and ignoring the other syllables. Eliot's "Dull roots with spring rain," for instance, can then be described as "two spondees linked with a weak syllable" (206). Similarly, in his scansion, Pound's line in "The Return"—

$$* \quad / \ * \quad * \quad * \quad / \quad * \quad * \quad * \quad / \quad *$$

The trouble in the pace and the uncertain

—"gives us," he notes, "a line in which amphibrachs (* ⁄ *)—in English, the most indefinite of any nameable trisyllabic foot—are further blurred by intervening unstressed syllables" (240). The sense, it seems, calls for amphibrachs, though in a passage of blank verse the line would scan readily as a pentameter:

$$\breve{} \ / \quad \breve{} \ (/) \quad \breve{} \ / \quad \breve{} \ \breve{} \quad \breve{} \ / \quad \breve{}$$

The trou | ble in | the pace | and the | uncer | tain
Although Alfred Corn avoids the Greek and Latin cookie jar in *The Poem's*

Heartbeat, he scans with three levels of stress, marked numerically 1, 2, 3, "from weakest to strongest" (30), and so positions himself to transform speech stresses into metrically unstressed syllables, and syllables unstressed in speech into metrical stresses. The rationale for doing so is that "[t]wo consecutive syllables that at first glance might seem to bear equal stress turn out not to do so, on closer inspection" (25), since "the linguistic tendency is always to put more stress on the second of two otherwise equal syllables" (32). Thus, to correct what may be an imperceptible difference in stress, he can change a conventional binary scansion of a line from Sonnet 30—

$$/ \quad \cup \quad \cup \quad / \quad \cup \quad \cup \quad / \quad / \quad \cup \quad /$$
When to | the ses | sions of | sweet si | lent thought

—into

$$3 \quad 1 \quad 1 \quad 3 \quad 1 \quad 2 \quad 2 \quad 3 \quad 1 \quad 3$$
When to | the ses | sions of | sweet si | lent thought

turning both the pyrrhic "-sions of" and the spondee "sweet si-" into iambs (55). But note that, in the process, the syllables "of" and "sweet"—unstressed and stressed, respectively, in speech—have become *equal*, both 2's, quite implausibly. Moreover, Corn seems unaware that these also adjacent syllables are now in violation of the always-tendency rule—as are numerous others in his scansions, as in that of Wyatt's line from "Stand Whoso List" (41):

$$1 \quad 2 \quad 2 \quad 3 \quad 1 \quad 3 \quad 3 \quad 1 \quad 1 \quad 3$$
For him | death grip | peth right | hard by | the crop.

Here Corn makes "death grip-" 2–3 (an iamb) in accordance with the rule; but "right hard" is okay as 3–3, as are "him death" as 2–2 and "by the" as 1–1, though all violate the rule (which applies, apparently, only when one is manipulating feet).

Corn is also untroubled by violating the rule whenever he scans anapests as 1–1–3 and dactyls as 3–1–1, but his really interesting versions of these feet assign *three* levels of stress, as in making a dactyl 3–1–2 (46), or an anapest 1–2–3, as in this line of Dana Gioia's "California Hills in August" (62–63):

```
    1   3      1  2b    3      1  2a    1   3
```
And hate | the bright still | ness of | the noon.

Since "[a]ny sensitive ear will notice ... that 'bright' receives more stress than 'of,'" Corn thoughtfully distinguishes these further levels of stress by the notations 2a and 2b.

Corn already has 1–2, 1–3, and 2–3 iambs and discusses rhythmic modulations based on their "stress level differentials" (58–64) and later indicates, though he doesn't explain, certain restrictions on 1–2 and 2–3 iambs, which "make for doubtful scansion in 'free verse'" (127). So one can imagine his deploying six levels of stress: 1a, 1b, 2a, 2b, 3a, 3b and thus the exponential growth of foot-types—1a–3b or 2a–3a iambs, for instance, or even 2a–1–2b anapests, and so on. But it is just as well that he steps back from the abyss, if his scansion of a line of Elise Paschen's "My Father's Gun" is any indication:

```
    1   3     1   3      1  2      2a  2b    1   3
```
a wake | of rings | within | rings with | in rings.

where he seems not to notice that, stressing "within" on its *first* syllable, he is no longer reading English.

One further bit of Corn's foot-magic is worth observing—the anapest that's really an iamb in Shelley's

```
  1  1  3     1   3      1   3      1   3     1   3
```
Of the dy | ing year, | to which | this clos | ing night

"Notice," Corn says, "that the opening foot is indistinguishable from anapestic. Even so, we consider the foot iambic" (47). The phenomenon results from invoking a convention of classical prosody that we never need for English verse—"initial hypercatalexis" (added syllable at line-beginning). Even if by 1819 anapestic substitution were not ordinary enough and Shelley himself not one of the freest of those employing it, initial hypercatalexis would explain nothing that simply showing the anapest doesn't.

The confusion about meter shows even in these prosodists' preferring over the more conventional breve (◡) and ictus (╱) a numerical notation (Corn), x's (Hartman), and asterisks (Kirby-Smith). There are reasons for these choices—the breve and ictus, for instance, don't appear on most keyboards, though slash can substitute for the latter. The result is nonetheless idiosyncratic. The project of *Meter in English*, to clarify our metrical terms and conventions, remains timely; and as to the question of the *English* feet, one result—the recovery of the bacchic—turns out to be of startling importance.

At the risk of getting a little ahead of my discussion, let me lay out the essential English feet, modifying my conclusion in *Meter in English*:

iamb (◡ ⁄)
trochee (⁄ ◡)
anapest (◡ ◡ ⁄)
bacchic (◡ ⁄ ⁄)
spondee (⁄ ⁄)
pyrrhic (◡ ◡)

As a unit in a metrical system based on stress, the pyrrhic continues to seem problematic and probably should be regarded as enclitic, that is, as an extender of whatever foot follows it in a line. So, in a phrase like "ses | *sions of* | *sweet si* | lent thought," the pyrrhic may be regarded as forming a unit with the following spondee (what I have called double-iamb). In a phrase like "it is | a star," if we do not elect promotion, the pyrrhic may be regarded as forming a unit with the following iamb. The Pound line above offers a good instance of the pyrrhic | iamb unit:

◡ ⁄ ◡ (⁄) ◡ ⁄ ◡ ◡ ◡ ⁄ ◡
The trou | ble in | the pace | and the | uncer | tain

The second article "the," in a metrical stress position, won't quite bear promotion in the usual way (as "in" does, for instance), and that momentary faltering in the pace—appropriate to the meaning—registers in scanning pyrrhic | iamb. We may find both pyrrhic | iamb and pyrrhic | spondee in this line from Pope's "Rape of the Lock":

◡ ⁄ ◡ ◡ ◡ ⁄ ◡ ◡ ⁄ ⁄
This Nymph, | to the | destruct | tion of | mankind

Pyrrhic | iamb also provides an option, especially in longer or more colloquial lines, where registering a promotion, though possible, might seem prissy—as in Auden's heptameter:

˘　　／　　˘　　／　　˘˘　　˘／　　˘　　˘　／　˘　˘　　／　　˘／
In Breu | ghel's *Ic* | *arus*, | for in | stance: how ev | rything turns | away

Though probably very rare, the pyrrhic | bacchic and pyrrhic | anapest combinations may occur. The first appears plainly enough in Stevens's "To an Old Philosopher in Rome":

˘　　／　˘˘　　˘　／　　／　　˘　　／　　˘　／
How eas | ily | the blown ban | ners change | to wings

The second, if not simply my resisting a promotion of "as" that seems awkward, shows up in Stevens's "The World as Meditation":

˘　　／　˘　　˘　　／　　˘˘　˘　˘／　　˘　／　　˘／
The trees | had been mend | ed as | an essen | tial ex | ercise

Since the pyrrhic has usually figured among the English feet—it is one of Fussell's six feet needed (21)—we need not linger over these combinations. The real surprise is the recovery of the bacchic.

The bacchic arrives having slipped in (as it were) under all of the prosodists' radar. It isn't even mentioned by Brooks and Warren, Deutsch, Shapiro and Beum, Turco, Finch, Kennedy and Gioia, or Gross and McDowell. It shows up without special notice among the Greek feet in Fussell, Nims, Miller Williams, Myers and Simms, and *The New Princeton Encyclopedia*. Only Nims cites examples in English (in Byron, Swinburne, and Langston Hughes), though he shies away from naming these bacchics, referring instead to "mutant triple feet" (*Harper Anthology* 800)—very much as I had called them "false" or token anapests. Hartman calls these "bacchius" ("Prosody" 113), but he and Finch ("Metrical" 64) argue only from Browning's galloping or Clement Moore's jolly anapestics, and Hartman's intention is merely to allow bacchics as a substitution in triple meters. But if an anapest can substitute in an iambic line, it would have been unnatural for bacchics not to follow. In the twentieth century, they have done so unchecked. The foot Corn scans 1–2b–3 in Gioia's line is a clear instance:

˘　　／　　˘　　／　　／　　˘　(／)　˘　　／
And hate | the bright still | ness of | the noon.

The context in which all this must be understood is the mid-sixteenth-century consensus to limit English verse to disyllabic feet, to which George Gascoigne ruefully assented in 1575. Anapests reappear almost at once (in Shakespeare, for instance), but mainly by subterfuge before the nineteenth century; and though equally potential in the language, bacchics remained unacknowledged. Early examples seem merely eccentric, like Webster's

$$\text{/ ∪ \quad ∪ / \quad ∪ / \quad / ∪ / \quad / / }$$

Cover | her face; | mine eyes daz | zle; she | died young

or Middleton's

$$\text{∪ ∪ \quad / \quad / ∪ / \quad ∪ / \quad ∪ / /}$$

As the | parched earth | of mois | ture when | the clouds weep

—which George Wright explains lamely as an extra-syllable ending, albeit on "a secondary stress" (163–64), as, I assume, he might also justify a line in *The Tempest* (1.2.140):

$$\text{∪ / \quad ∪ / \quad ∪ / \quad ∪ \quad / \quad ∪ / /}$$

My tale | provokes | that ques | tion. Dear, | they durst not

No doubt there is a rationalization, too, for the line in Shakespeare's Sonnet 29:

$$\text{∪ / \quad ∪ / / \quad ∪ / \quad ∪ / \quad ∪ /}$$

And trou | ble deaf heav | en with | my boot | less cries

Donne of course is known to be rough or careless, as in "Satyre III":

$$\text{∪ / \quad ∪ / / \quad ∪ / \quad ∪ / \quad / /}$$

And what | the hill's sud | denness | resists, | win so

But there's also Milton, as in *Samson Agonistes*:

$$\text{∪ / ∪ / \quad ∪ / / \quad ∪ /}$$

In slav | ish hab | it, ill-fit | ted weeds

Though relatively shameless about using anapests on the stage, Shakespeare may be observed (in one instance at least) of going to some trouble to avoid seeming to use a bacchic. In the second scene of *The Tempest*, Miranda says:

> / ᴜ ᴜ / ᴜ / ᴜ / ᴜ / ᴜ
> If by | your art, | my dear | est fath | er, you | have
> / ᴜ / / ᴜ / ᴜ / ᴜ / ᴜ
> Put the | wild wat | ers in | this roar, | allay | them.

Following his normal practice, he would have put "have" on the line below, as in the passage just down the page:

> Had I been any god of power, I would
> Have sunk the sea within the earth or ere
> It should the good ship so have swallowed and
> The fraughting souls within her.

But that would give him a bacchic:

> ᴜ / ᴜ / / ᴜ / ᴜ /
> Have put | the wild wat | ers in | this roar

So he fudges "have" back up as a somewhat unusual e-s ending in order to keep the bacchic without seeming to do so.

Perhaps even Pope nods (*Odyssey*, Book X):

> / ᴜ ᴜ / / ᴜ / ᴜ / ᴜ /
> Where on | the all-bear | ing earth | unmark'd | it grew ...

> / ᴜ /ᴜ ᴜ / / ᴜ / ᴜ /
> Where the | Phlege | thon's loud tor | rents, rush | ing down

Perhaps Keats, in a context of pentameters, simply miscounted:

> ᴜ / / / ᴜ / / ᴜ /
> While barred | clouds bloom | the soft-dy | ing day

Either that, or he intended the awful

    ˘   ⁄   ˘   ⁄   ⁄   ˘   ⁄   ⁄   ˘   ⁄   ˘
While bar | red clouds | bloom the | soft-dy | ing day

Aside from such eccentric cases, bacchics mostly occur in songs or ballads in triple-meter, where they are almost surely masquerading as anapests:

    ˘   ⁄   ˘   ⁄   ⁄   ˘   ˘   ⁄   ˘   ⁄   ⁄
To kiss | the fair maids, | and possess | the rich Fleece
(Prior, 1715)

    ˘   ˘   ⁄   ˘   ⁄   ⁄   ˘   ⁄
And the jol | ly swain laughs | his fill
(Blake, 1783)

    ˘   ⁄   ˘   ⁄   ˘   ⁄   ˘   ⁄   ⁄
On ev | ery flower | that shuts | its sweet eyes
(Blake, 1783)

    ⁄   ⁄   ˘   ⁄   ⁄   ˘   ⁄   ⁄
Flow gent | ly, sweet Af | ton, among | thy green braes
(Burns, 1789)

    ˘   ⁄   ⁄   ˘   ˘   ⁄   ˘   ˘   ⁄   ˘   ⁄   ⁄   ˘
What care I | for the wreaths | that can on | ly give glor | y
(Bryon, 1821)

    ˘   ⁄   ˘   ⁄   ⁄   ˘   ˘   ⁄   ˘   ⁄   ⁄
And see | the rogues flour | ish and hon | est folk drown
(Browning, 1842)

    ˘ ˘   ⁄   ˘   ⁄   ⁄   ˘   ⁄   ˘ ˘   ⁄   ˘   ⁄   ˘ ˘   ⁄
Is it peace | or war? Civ | il war, | as I think, | and that | of a kind
(Tennyson, 1855)

Donald Justice (200) calls attention to bacchics, without naming them, in two lines of Shelley's "The Sensitive Plant" (1820):

    ˘   ⁄   ⁄   ˘   ⁄   ˘   ⁄   ⁄   ⁄
And each flower | and herb | on Earth's | dark breast ...

    ˘   ⁄   ⁄   ˘   ˘   ⁄   ˘   ⁄   ⁄   ⁄
Like young lov | ers whom youth | and love | make dear ...

There are a number of others in the poem, including

∪ / /   ∪ /   ∪ / ∪/

The snowdrop, | and then | the vi | olet ...

∪ / ∪ /   / ∪ / ∪ /

She sprin | kled bright wat | er from | the stream

Justice fudges a little in describing the meter as "*basically a sort* of anapestic tetrameter" (my italics). Iambs more than hold their own, as in the lines quoted above; but the rhythm is certainly such that one can't be sure Shelley intends more than anapestic ebullience.

    When genuine bacchics appear—valued for the weight of both stresses—is therefore difficult to say, though I think we find them in Browning's ballad-like "Soliloquy of the Spanish Cloister" (1842),

∪ / / ∪ ∪ / /

On grey pap | er with | blunt type

and in Swinburne's "Atalanta in Calydon" (1865):

∪ / ∪ / ∪ ∪ ∪ / /   ∪ /

But far | from danc | es and | the back-blow | ing torch

After 1900, bacchics continue to appear, frequent but seemingly unnoticed, as among the tetrameters of Edward Thomas's "A Cat":

∪ / ∪ / / ∪ / ∪ /

And birds | of bright voice | and plume | and flight,

or in the third line of this quatrain from his "Interval":

The wood is black,
With a misty steam.
Above, the cloud pack
Breaks for one gleam.

And no one would have thought to notice bacchics in what seemed free verse:

```
 /     /    ᴗ    /    /
Dull roots | with spring rain
 ᴗ  ᴗ   /    ᴗ    /   ᴗ   /   /
In the moun | tains, there | you feel free.
 ᴗ /    /    ᴗ ᴗ  /     ᴗ /   /    ᴗ ᴗ /   ᴗ
I read, much | of the night, | and go south | in the win | ter
```

Justice astutely notes that this "unusual version of the trisyllabic foot" appears early in Wallace Stevens's blank verse and "becomes a small stroke in his signature" (200):

```
 ᴗ  / /   ᴗ  ᴗ/   ᴗ   /    ᴗ  ᴗ     / /
A blue pig | eon it is, | that cir | cles the | blue sky
```

We may note the foot in other lines:

```
  /   /  ᴗ  ᴗ   /    ᴗ   /    ᴗ  /   /    ᴗ  /
Long af | ter the plant | er's death. | A few limes | remained ...
  /  ᴗ ᴗ  /   ᴗ /   ᴗ   /    /    ᴗ  /   ᴗ  /
One is | a child | again. | The gold beards | of wat | erfalls ...
 ᴗ  /    ᴗ  ᴗ   /   ᴗ  ᴗ   /   ᴗ  /   /
The fresh | ness of night | has been fresh | a long time ...
```

Bacchics also appear in Stevens poems sometimes considered free verse:

```
 ᴗ  (/)   ᴗ   /    ᴗ  /   /
And have | been cold | a long time ...
 ᴗ   /   ᴗ  /    /   ᴗ   /   ᴗ  /   ᴗ
Are twen | ty men cross | ing twen | ty bridg | es ...
x /   ᴗ  /   ᴗ   /    ᴗ  /   /   ᴗ
On | ly here | and there, | an old sail | or
```

After mid-century, bacchics began to appear, frequent but unnoticed, in the loosened meter of poets like James Wright, James Dickey, Philip Levine, and Louise Glück. I have often puzzled over poems by Levine that hover *near* meter but that would have been poorly explained as syllabics or accentuals. Consider, however, using bacchics in the opening, mostly tetrameters, of "Ask for Nothing":

    ᵕ ╱   ╱   ᵕ╱ ᵕ ᵕ ╱   ᵕ
Instead walk | alone | in the eve | ning
x   ╱ ᵕ ╱ ᵕ ╱   ╱   ᵕ ᵕ
  head | ing out | of town | toward the fields
    ᵕ╱   ╱ᵕ ᵕ ╱ ᵕ ᵕ ╱
asleep | under | a dar | kening sky;
    ᵕ ╱ ╱ ᵕ ╱   ᵕ ╱ ᵕ ╱
the dust ris | en from | your steps | transforms
    ᵕ╱ ᵕ ᵕ ᵕ ╱ ᵕ ╱ ╱ ᵕ
itself | into | a gold | en rain fall | en
    ╱ ᵕ ᵕ ᵕ ╱ ᵕ ╱ ╱ ╱
earthward | as a gift | from no | known god.
    ᵕ ╱ ╱ ᵕ╱ ᵕ ᵕ ᵕ ╱ ╱
The plane trees | along | the can | al bank,
    ᵕ ╱ ╱ ᵕ ╱ ᵕ ╱ ᵕ ╱
the few val | ley pop | lars, hold | their breath ...

We might almost call bacchics "the free verse foot," since acknowledging it among the English feet emptied my initial project of surveying poems that avoid or evade or disengage from metrical cadences. There aren't any. Consider the first five lines of a passage of Rexroth's "The Signature of All Things," cited by Robert Hass ("Prosody" 147–48) as free verse. I agreed. Without bacchics, the passage would exemplify the successful evasion of metrical cadences—lines 2–4 being scannable only with severe contortions. With bacchics, however, it becomes just five metrical lines:

    x ╱   ᵕ ╱   ᵕ ᵕ ᵕ ╱
Deer | are stamp | ing in | the glades,
    ╱ ᵕ ᵕ ╱ ᵕ╱ ╱
Under | the full | July moon.
    ᵕ ᵕ ᵕ ╱ ᵕ ╱ ╱
There is | a smell | of dry grass
    ᵕ ᵕ ╱ ᵕ ╱ ╱ ᵕ
In the air, | and more faint | ly,
    ᵕ ╱ ᵕ ᵕ ╱ ╱ ╱
The scent | of a far | off skunk.

As a further test, try Stevens's "Valley Candle" which Hartman offers (*Free Verse* 81–87) as an example of free verse using organic form or (the term he coins) "discovered form."

```
 ⏑  /   ⏑   /    ⏑/   ⏑ ⏑  ⏑   /  /   ⏑
My can | dle burns | alone | in an | immense val | ley.
  /    ⏑  ⏑   /   /    ⏑  /    ⏑/  ⏑
Beams of | the huge night | converged | upon | it,
 ⏑/   ⏑   /   /
Until | the wind blew.
   ⏑     /    ⏑ ⏑   /   /
Then beams | of the | huge night
  ⏑    /     ⏑/   ⏑ /    ⏑
Converged | upon | its im | age,
 ⏑/   ⏑   /   /
Until | the wind blew.
```

The poem is metrical, though very irregular. Hartman sees the poem as free verse structured "by massive repetition. Of the poem's entire second half, only 'Then' and 'its image' are not repeated from the first half." Hartman's discussion is illuminating, but his conclusion is not: that the poem's "*prosody* is one of counterpoint between syntax and lineation" (*Free Verse* 102, my italics). Counterpoint between syntax and lineation holds in all verse, however metrically regular. And there can be no reason to forego precise *metrical* information about "Valley Candle": the pattern of pentameter / tetrameter / dimeter / trimeter / trimeter / dimeter, for instance, or the poem's invariable linking of the *other*—valley, night, wind—in feet with paired stresses.

The bacchic is a hitherto missing bit of the genetic code of English verse. Arguably present from the beginning, the bacchic is indispensable for scansion in the twentieth century if we are to take account of the hidden evolution which no doubt continued "the relaxation of iambic pentameter [that] has been going on at least since Wordsworth," as Hartman puts it (*Free Verse* 108).

Moreover, it begins to be clear that free verse does not exist. All verse in English is metrical and belongs to a single system. With bacchics, we can virtually scan the language.

Perhaps, then, if poets writing freely write in meter, free verse has won out.

Free Verse and the Orbit of Meter

As I argued in "The Free Verse Myth," there are good reasons to suspect that free verse does not exist in English. Metrical cadences turn up everywhere in what is usually taken to be free verse; and accounts of free verse as a form, when they are not mere impressionism like Charles Olson's "composition by field" or the notion of breath-as-line, mistake some metrical irregularity—of line-length or foot-type—as demonstrating, not a difference of *degree* but, rather, a difference in *kind*.[11] Invariably, this is a matter of judgment and an effort to legislate taste.

The hypothesis that all verse in English is metrical—measurable and count-able within a single system—depends on an accurate understanding of the conventions of our prosody. George Puttenham saw as long ago as 1589 that we need to determine which of the myriad Greek and Latin feet belong to our meter—and "which feete we have not, nor as yet never went about to frame (the nature of our language and wordes not permitting it)" (22). In an effort to sort out quantity and stress, he declares, "we may at this day very well receive the auncient feete metricall of the Greeks and Latines saving those that be superflous as be all the feete above the trissillable...." (130). Despite the com-promise of 1557 that limited our verse to disyllabic feet, Puttenham recalls the earlier use of trisyllabic feet, noting that "we in our vulgar finde many of the like, and specially in the rimes of Sir Thomas Wiat" (142).[12] Puttenham cites, among others, Wyatt's line,

$$\cup \quad \cup \diagup$$

So is | my paine | full life | the bur | den of ire ...

and comments that "we must thinke he did it of purpose, by the odde sillable to

---

[11] "The breath," Olson argues, "should be a poet's central concern, rather than rhyme, meter, and sense" (Poetry Foundation). We quote from the Poetry Foundation's web "Introduction" to Olson's 1950 essay, "Projective Verse": The essay introduces his ideas of "composition by field" through projective or open verse, which is a continuation of the ideas of poets Ezra Pound, who asked poets to "compose in the sequence of the musical phrase, not in sequence of a metronome," and William Carlos Williams, who proposed in 1948 that a poem be approached as a "field of action." ... To listen closely to the breath "is to engage speech where it is least careless—and least logical." Olson notes, further, that "the syllable and the line are the two units led by, respectively, the ear and the breath." -*Eds.*

[12] A reference to Tottel's *Miscellany* (1557), which established Wyatt's fame as lyric poet of the Tudor age. In English, words of Germanic origin tend to be mono- or disyllabic; trisyllabic words are largely of Latinate origin. -*Eds.*

give greater grace to his meetre, and we finde in our old rimes, this odde sillable, sometime placed in the beginning and sometimes in the middle of a verse" (142).

Not for two centuries, however, would trisyllabic substitution begin to be freely allowed again; and only now, I believe—two centuries further along— can we truly answer the question, what are the *English* feet? With the surprising addition of the bacchic, we may at last fix certainly on these: iamb (ᴗ ╱), trochee (╱ ᴗ), spondee (╱╱), anapest (ᴗ ᴗ ╱), bacchic (ᴗ ╱╱), and pyrrhic (ᴗ ᴗ). In a stress-language, the pyrrhic may be regarded as an enclitic foot and counted as extending the foot that follows it—which means that it will not appear as the last foot in a line. In such cases, as in Cordelia's speech from *King Lear*—

>   ᴗ   ╱   ᴗ   ╱
> I can | not heave
>   ᴗ   ╱   ╱ᴗ   ᴗ   ╱   ᴗ ╱   ᴗ   ╱   ᴗ(╱)
> My heart | into | my mouth. | I love | your Maj | esty
>   ᴗ ╱   ᴗ   ᴗ   ᴗ   ╱
> Accord | ing to | my bond

—we should scan a promotion.

Readers tempted by the hypothesis that all verse in English is metrical will seek out more than the few examples I can provide here. Beyond the simplicity of the proposition and the problems that it resolves, its value will appear in significantly more detailed metrical information about poems hitherto barred from scrutiny by being designated as "free."

We are accustomed to thinking of free verse mainly in terms of longer lines (as in Whitman) or shorter lines (as in Williams). The reason is that the spectrum of regular verse in English centers on tetrameters and pentameters. Trimeters and hexameters are also quite workable. Beyond these, however, the metrical line weakens or tends to dissolve. Partly, we just aren't used to heptameters and so on. Even minimal substitution or variation can make it difficult to track these fragile meters, especially when syntax is complicated or when line-length varies, as in Whitman. Line always remains the determinant, and I suppose we can track

>   ᴗ   ╱   ᴗ   ╱   ╱   ᴗ   ╱   ╱   ᴗ   ᴗ   ᴗ   ╱
> The sniff | of green leaves | and dry leaves, | and of | the shore

ᵕ ╱ ╱ ᵕ ╱ ╱   ᵕ ᵕ ╱ ᵕ ᵕ ╱
and dark-col | or'd sea-rocks, | and of hay | in the barn,

which, surprisingly, has only nine feet. Tracking as we read is made easy by the simple, parallel syntax. But we get no such help in the fourteen feet of another line in "Song of Myself":

ᵕ ᵕ ╱   ╱   ᵕ ╱ ᵕ ᵕ ᵕ ╱ ╱ ᵕ ᵕ ╱ ᵕ
On a | bank lounged | the trap | per, he | was drest most | ly in skins, | his
ᵕ╱ ᵕ ᵕ ╱ ᵕ ╱ ᵕ ╱ ᵕ ᵕ ╱ ᵕ ╱
luxur | iant beard | and curls | protect | ed his neck, | he held
ᵕ ╱ ᵕ ᵕ ╱
| his bride | by the hand,

nor in

ᵕ ╱ ᵕ ╱ ╱ ᵕ ╱ ᵕ ᵕ ╱ ᵕ ╱ ᵕ ╱
The hair | y wild-bee | that mur | murs and hank | ers up | and down,
ᵕ ╱ ᵕ ╱ ╱ ╱ ᵕ ╱ ᵕ ╱ ᵕ╱
| that gripes | the full- | grown lad | y-flow | er, curves | upon
ᵕ ᵕ ╱ ᵕ ᵕ ╱ ╱ ╱ ᵕ ╱ ᵕ ╱ ᵕ
| her with am | orous firm | legs, takes | his will | of her, | and
╱ ᵕ ╱ ╱ ᵕ ᵕ ᵕ ╱ ᵕ ╱ ᵕ ╱ ᵕ╱
holds | himself | tremulous | and tight | till he | is sat | isfied

Counting has long since become pointless at 24 feet, although the line is nonetheless metrical and, if we wish to discuss its rhythm, we may scan it. Notably, the line that precedes it in "Spontaneous Me" is a pentameter:

╱ ╱ ᵕ ╱ ᵕ ╱ ᵕ ᵕ ╱ ╱
Soft fore | noon airs | that blow | from the | south-west

and the one that follows, a tetrameter:

ᵕ ╱ ᵕ ╱   ᵕ ᵕ ╱ ᵕ ╱
The wet | of woods | through the ear | ly hours …

The poem is a catalog of mingling/alternating sexual and natural images—a single sentence that runs through 45 lines that (excepting semi-colons at lines 17 and 34) include no punctuation stronger than commas. We can learn a great deal about the poem's pacing, I think, when we look in context at the lines just scanned:

> Earth of chaste love, life that is only life after love,
> The body of my love, the body of the woman I love, the body of
>   the man, the body of the earth,
> Soft forenoon airs that blow from the south-west,
> The hairy wild-bee that murmurs and hankers up and down, that
>   gripes the full-grown lady-flower, curves upon her with amorous
>   firm legs, takes his will of her, and holds himself tremulous and
>   tight till he is satisfied;
> The wet of woods through the early hours,
> Two sleepers at night lying close together as they sleep, one with an
>   arm slanting down across and below the waist of the other,
> The smell of apples, aromas from crush'd sage-plant, mint, birch-bark …

Whitman controls the poem's flow, carefully loosening and returning to regularity. Easily countable, the familiar pentameter and tetrameter both reassure us as we read and measure the agitation or excitement of the fairly untrackable, very long line.

We may observe a similar loosening and returning in the first section of "Song of Myself":

> ‿╱ ‿(╱) ‿ ╱   ‿ ╱   ‿ ╱
> I cel | ebrate | myself, | and sing | myself,
>   ‿   ‿ ╱ ‿ ╱   ╱ ‿   ‿ ╱
> And what I | assume | you shall | assume,
>   ‿ ╱   ‿ ╱ ‿ ‿ ╱   ‿ ‿ ╱ ‿ ╱   ‿ ╱ ‿ ╱
> For ev | ery at | om belong | ing to me | as good | belongs | to you.

> ‿ ╱   ‿ ‿ ╱   ‿ ╱
> I loafe | and invite | my soul,
> ‿╱   ‿ ╱   ‿ ‿ ╱   ‿ ╱   ‿ ‿ ╱ ‿ ╱ ‿ ╱
> I lean | and loafe | at my ease | observ | ing a spear | of sum | mer grass.

‿ /   / ‿/ ‿ ‿ ‿ /   /   ‿   ‿ / ‿ /
My tongue, ev | ery at | om of | my blood, | form'd from | this soil, | this air,

/   / ‿ /   ‿   /   /   ‿ / ‿ ‿ /   ‿ ‿ /
Born here | of par | ents born here | from par | ents the same, | and their par

‿ ‿ /
| ents the same,

x /   ‿ ‿ /   ‿ /   ‿ /   /   ‿ /   ‿   /   ‿/
I, | now thir | ty-sev | en years old | in per | fect health | begin,

/ ‿   ‿ /   /   ‿ /
Hoping | to cease not | till death.

x   /   ‿   /   ‿ ‿ /   ‿
Creeds | and schools | in abey | ance,

‿/ ‿ /   ‿ /   ‿ / ‿ /   ‿ / ‿ / ‿ ‿ / ‿
Retir | ing back | a while | sufficed | at what | they are | but nev | er forgot | ten,

‿ /   ‿ ‿ /   ‿ /   ‿ ‿ /   ‿   /   ‿ /   ‿ / ‿
I har | bor for good | or bad, | I permit | to speak | at ev | ery haz | ard,

/ ‿   ‿ ‿   /   ‿   ‿/ ‿ ‿ /   ‿ (/)
Nature | without check | with orig | inal en | ergy.

I count: 45 iambs, 15 anapests, 4 trochees, 1 spondee, 1 pyrrhic, and 5 bacchics. Iambs are a little over 60% (and in stanzas 1 and 2 are 75%) of the total feet. All five bacchics occur in the four-line stanza 3, and focus most of the poem's rhythmic complexity—appropriately, since the drama of turning from ease to action appears in that stanza: "I loafe" gives way to "I ... begin." Expressive, too, is the notably irregular last line where the pace of the trochee and string of anapests seems unblocked by the final, muted iamb. The section opens and closes with quite interestingly different pentameters.

Lines range from three to eight feet, which is equivalent to Donne's two to seven feet in "A Valediction: Of Weeping" or Frost's one to six feet in "After Apple-Picking." Six lines are heptameters, so that is something like a norm. In stanzas 1 and 2, the more confident and relaxed stanzas, shorter lines come to a poise in heptameters. Stanza 3 reverses the pattern; and stanza 4 may be thought of as balancing—beginning and then also ending with shorter lines.

Balance is, moreover, a rhetorical theme of the section. A system of parallels begins with *celebrate myself / sing myself, I assume / you shall assume, belonging to me / belongs to you,* continues in *loafe / lean and loafe, tongue, blood / soil, air,* and in the interlocking *Born here / parents born here and from parents the same / their parents the same.* It is perhaps recalled in the parallel clauses in line 12 and in the balancing, inclusive echo *with-* / *with* in line 13: "Nature without check with original energy."

Meter is far from being the only constituent of poetic rhythm, but it is an important one. Scansion enables us to notice not only line-length with precision but also, for instance, the relative limpidity of lines 4–5 (reflecting the simplicity of iambs and anapests), or to observe that the single anapest in each of these lines' three phrases shifts position slightly. Seeing the poem as metrical increases immeasurably our perception of how its verse works.

In a primarily oral poetry, meter determines the lines; that is, we recognize lines by hearing a consistently repeated metrical pattern—and we could be thrown off by a line shorter than the norm or irregular in pacing. Alliteration and medial caesuras, fixed beats, rhyme, and regular end-stopping belong to such verse. But with the advent of printing, it began also to be possible for the lines to determine the meter; that is, *we see* the lines and can, from them, identify the way they are measured. Meter may work then, not only by prediction—to use Dana Gioia's term in *Meter in English* ("Meter-Making" 85–86), but also by justification, after the fact (as I suppose our apprehension of the form of free verse was supposed to do). Historically, then, and in various ways, verse could draw ever closer to, could draw more upon, speech. And it seems that English meter loosened until it colonized the language—or was colonized by the language—so that we now write metrical verse under the illusion it is free, much like we take walks without computing the steps or distance. Even quite regular metrical cadences are hardly surprising with poets trained or experienced in regular meter, like William Carlos Williams or Adrienne Rich.

If there is no findable line between free verse and meter, then there is just *verse* in English, a continuous and measurable variety that runs from prose, where the metrical marker of line doesn't operate to perfect formality (that is, to the regularity of foot-type and line-length). One prosodical system does for all.

Turning to free verse written in short lines, we may distinguish two sorts. In the early Imagist period, following almost literally Pound's injunction "to compose in the sequence of the musical phrase, not in sequence of a metronome," poets divided lines at phrase- or clause-boundaries. Consider the opening of Williams's "Pastoral" (1917):

When I was younger
it was plain to me
I must make something of myself

Older now
I walk back streets
admiring the houses
of the very poor:

Lines might have been broken differently—"admiring / the houses of the very poor," for instance, or "admiring / the houses / of the very poor." But the practice allows few options, lending some credibility to the objection that such verse is stacked prose, since the lines merely follow syntactical joints already in the sentences. The passage is more like restacked verse, however:

When I was younger it was plain to me
I must make something of myself.
Older now I walk back streets
admiring the houses of the very poor.

What no doubt made the phrases "musical" to poet or reader are the metrical cadences of these underlying pentameters and tetrameters. Williams's comment on the poem in the 1950s (*Collected Poems I*) isn't revealing: "Unconsciously I was playing with the form of the line, and getting into the American idiom" (481).

The poem is metrical throughout, as we'll see, but the interesting question is what gave the initial illusion of freedom. The constant choice of slightly varying ways to divide phrases into lines—to emphasize "admiring" by isolating it, or not, for instance—produces a somewhat novel sort of rhetorical control, but another key must be an inherent volatility at the short-line end of the metrical spectrum.

A single, normal foot-substitution can disrupt the fabric of such verse in a surprising way. Consider the sixth line in this passage from Williams's "To Mark Anthony in Heaven" (1920):

    ˘ /   ˘ /   ˘ /
    I hope | it was | because

    ˘   /   ˘ /   ˘ /
    you knew | her inch | by inch

      ˘   /   ˘ / / ˘
    from slant | ing feet up | ward

˘ ˘ / ˘ ˘ /
to the roots | of her hair
˘ / ˘ / ˘ /
and down | again | and that
x / / /
you | saw her
˘ / ˘ / ˘ / ˘
above | the bat | tle's fur | y—

Like the poem itself, the passage is mostly iambic and mostly trimeter, and suddenly: "you saw her." The appearance is of great freedom, but the anacrusis (omitted initial syllable) and spondee are no less normal, really, than the anapests of "to the roots of her hair," and no less metrical.

Less noticeably, the volatility may be observed in "Pastoral," in the whole foot that vanishes in turning my fake pentameter, "When I | was young | er it | was plain | to me," into Williams's two lines. The foot "-er it" *disappears* into e-s ending and anapest. The same thing happens with "-es of" in "admir | ing the hous | es of | the ver | y poor." These feet (and their promoted stresses) are exactly the despised tick-*tick* of the metronome; but getting rid of them, though it may be mistaken for the freedom of free verse, doesn't make the lines less metrical. For the record, a scansion:

˘ / ˘ / ˘
When I | was young | er
˘ ˘ / ˘ /
it was plain | to me
˘ ˘ / / ˘ ˘ ˘ /
I must | make some | thing of | myself
x / ˘ /
Old | er now
˘ / / /
I walk | back streets
˘ / ˘ ˘ / ˘
admir | ing the hous | es
˘ ˘ / ˘ /
of the ver | y poor:
/ / ˘ / ˘ /
roof out | of line | with sides

⌣ ∕ ∕ ⌣
the yards clut | tered

⌣ ∕ ∕ ⌣ ∕ ∕ ⌣
with old chick | en wire, ash | es,

∕ ⌣ ⌣ ∕ ∕
furni | ture gone wrong;

⌣ ∕ ⌣ ⌣ ∕ ∕ ⌣
the fen | ces and | outhou | ses

x ∕ ⌣ ∕ ⌣ ∕
built | of bar | rel-staves

⌣ ∕ ⌣ ∕ ⌣ ∕
and parts | of box | es, all,

⌣ ∕ ⌣ ∕ ⌣ (∕)
if I | am for | tunate,

x ∕ ⌣ ∕ ⌣ ∕
smeared | a blu | ish green

⌣ ∕ ⌣ ⌣ ∕ ⌣
that prop | erly weath | ered

∕ ⌣ ⌣ ∕
pleases | me best

⌣ ∕ ∕ ⌣
of all col | ors.

∕ ∕
No one

⌣ ⌣ ∕ ∕
will be | lieve this

⌣ ∕ ∕ ⌣ ⌣ ⌣ ∕ ⌣
of vast im | port to | the na | tion.

Twelve lines are dimeter, seven trimeter, and one each monometer and te-trameter. There are 27 iambs—a strong plurality—and, notably, seven bac-chics (four in the description of the yards in lines 9–11 and three in the proud irony of the final lines).

Although short lines seem quick or unexpected, such phrasal verse is plainly metrical. So is a second kind of verse in short lines, which uses radical enjamb-ment (between adjective and noun, between preposition and article, and so on), like that Pound pioneered in "The Return" (1912):

See, they return; ah, see the tentative
Movements, and the slow feet,
The trouble in the pace and the uncertain
Wavering!

For the record, a scansion:

>   ∕   ∕   ◡ ∕   ◡   ∕   ◡   ∕   ◡ (∕)
> See, they | return; | ah, see | the ten | tative
>   ∕   ◡   ◡   ◡   ∕   ∕
> Movements, | and the | slow feet,
>   ◡ ∕   ◡ (∕) ◡   ∕   ◡   ◡   ◡ ∕   ◡
> The trou | ble in | the pace | and the | uncer | tain
> x   ∕   ◡ (∕)
> Wav | ering!

Williams's first use of the device of radical enjambment appears in "Hic Jacet" (1913) in the Byronic rhyme, "prosper-loss, for / Kind heaven fills their little paunches." By the following year, it begins to appear casually in his phrasal poems, like "Metric Figure": "as the sea / sliding above / submerged whiteness." Radical enjambment is a feature of the very first poems Marianne Moore began publishing in 1915. My impression is that she relished syllabics in part for their apparent justification of such arbitrary line-breaks as those in "To a Steam Roller":

Were not "impersonal judgment in aesthetic
matters, a metaphysical impossibility," you
might fairly achieve
it. As for butterflies ...

A scansion:

>   ◡   ∕   ◡   ∕   ◡◡   ∕   ◡ (∕) ◡ ∕ ◡
> Were not | "imper | sonal judg | ment in | aesthe | tic
>   ∕ ◡   ◡ ∕   ◡ ∕   ◡◡ ◡ ∕   ◡∕ ◡◡ ∕
> matters, | a met | aphys | ical | impos | sibil | ity," you
>   ◡   ∕   ◡ ◡ ∕
> might fair | ly achieve

(´) ‿   ‿ ╱   ‿ ╱
it. As | for but | terflies ...

Cummings, too, impressed by "The Return," began to experiment boldly in 1916, as with line-breaks and spacings of "the little lame balloonman whistles far and wee." And in that year the popular poems of Don Marquis, supposedly written by a cockroach named Archy, began to show up in *The New York Sun*. Having the soul of a "vers libre bard" who had died, Archy composes by diving headfirst onto the keys of a typewriter, one at a time. "mehitabel was once cleopatra" begins:

> boss i am disappointed in
> some of your readers they
> are always asking how does
> archy work the shift so as to get a
> new line or how does archy do
> this or do that they
> are always interested in technical
> details when the main question is
> whether the stuff is
> literature or not
> i wish you would leave
> that book of george moores on
> the floor
> mehitabel the cat and i want to
> read it ...

What begins as satire of the artsy-literary quickly turns out to be its most lovable and perhaps most successful embodiment. The Archy poems have been continuously in print since.

Sorting the variety of enjambment will be a useful study. Sometimes it is expressive, as in "uncertain / Wavering" or "to get a / new line." Sometimes the torque is very strong, as in "might fairly achieve / it" or in Robert Creeley's "the darkness sur- / rounds us" in "I Know a Man." Often, however, the enjambment seems merely routine or generic, as it also often is in traditional verse to fill out the meter:

Is come indeed, when I should see behind me
The inevitable prosecution of
Disgrace and horror, that, on my command ...
(*Anthony and Cleopatra* 4.14.64–66)

Let us not burden our remembrances with
A heaviness that's gone. (*The Tempest* 5.1.199–200)

In the second bit, the promoted stress is presumably on "-ces," Shakespeare intending "with" as an e-s ending to avoid the untidy anapest. But such radical enjambment may also be expressive, as it seems in the melting stress at the end of the middle line here:

Our revels now are ended. These our actors,
As I foretold you, were all spirits, and
Are melted into air, into thin air ... (*The Tempest* 4.1.148–150)

In *Twentieth Century Pleasures* (69-70), Robert Hass no doubt reads the purpose of Williams's radical enjambments correctly:

So Frost was wrong to say that free verse was like playing tennis without a net. The net was the resisting of the iamb. A lot of William Carlos Williams's individual perceptions are a form of iambic music, but he has arranged them so that the eye breaks the iambic habit. The phrase—"a dust of snow in the wheeltracks"—becomes

a dust of
snow in
the wheeltracks

and people must have felt: "yes, that is what it is like; not one-TWO, one-TWO. A dust of / snow in / the wheeltracks. That is how perception is. It is that light and quick." The effect depends largely on traditional expectation.

The reader had to be able to hear what he was not hearing.

Alan Williamson has also noted (149–51) Williams's covert and therefore surprising engagement with traditional meter. Scanning as "an all-but-perfect pentameter" the opening line of a well-known passage in Paterson, "Without invention nothing is well spaced," Williamson finds "Williams dismantling and rebuilding the pentameter line in a seemingly endless struggle." He concludes by suspecting that "Williams invokes the ghost of that line oftener, in subtler ways, than most of his disciples realize."

Williams himself seems to have been aware, at least on occasion, of the metrical doubleness of his short lines. In a 1950 interview, John W. Gerber asks what makes "This Is Just to Say" a poem. Williams answers, "In the first place, it's metrically absolutely regular.... So, dogmatically speaking, it has to be a poem because it goes that way, don't you see!" (qtd. in Perloff 90).

In a curious lapse, Marjorie Perloff decides that Williams doesn't mean meter, he means stanza shape. Williams, she says,

> mistakes sight for sound: on the page the three little quatrains look alike; they have roughly the same physical shape. It is typography rather than any kind of phonemic recurrence that provides directions for the speaking voice. (90–91)

Williams is joshing the interviewer, I have no doubt. But he means what he says:

Forgive | me they | were deli | cious so sweet | and so cold.

Since such poems use enjambment to disjoin or disguise metrical cadences, scansion may sometimes usefully read feet across *line-breaks* in order to notice those cadences. The dovetail feet are obvious and, in any case, only replace anacrusis or extra-syllable endings. I will show the dovetail scansion beside the lines:

THIS | IS JUST | TO SAY

I have eat | en

the plums |

that were | in

the | icebox |

and which |

you were prob | ably

sav | ing

for break | fast

Forgive | me	∪ ╱ | ∪
they | were deli | cious	╱ | ∪ ∪ ╱ | ∪
so sweet |	∪ ╱ |
and so cold	∪ ∪ ╱

The rhythm is open and quick, easy-going: nine anapests, five iambs, and one each pyrrhic and spondee, along with the anacrusis in the title. Stanzas group into five, four, and five feet, the first two stanzas (along with the title) making the first of the poem's two sentences. Omission of punctuation (other than that implied by capitalizing "Forgive") suggests the informality of a jotted personal note.

Kirby-Smith notes accurately of Cummings (250), "In some poems typography is a thin disguise for traditional metrics," but he fails to see a similar doubleness of rhythmic and visual in Williams's "The Attic Which Is Desire," of which he remarks (247–48):

> [A]lmost everything about this poem is visual.... But, to restate an earlier argument, he could never have remained so resolutely free of iambic rhythms had he not possessed them so thoroughly [in his early devotion to Keats] as to be able always to avoid them.

But of course Williams doesn't avoid iambs in the poem. Rather, like Cummings, he disguises them. The poem may be read aloud as easily as seen on the page; and if we read as Williams mostly did, taking no account of line breaks, the iambs are unmistakable.

THE AT | TIC WHICH IS | DESIRE	∪ ╱ | ∪ ∪ ╱ | ∪ ╱ |
the un | used tent |	∪ ╱ | ╱ ╱ |
of	∪
bare beams |	╱ ╱ |
beyond | which	∪ ╱ | ∪
direct | ly wait |	∪ ╱ | ∪ ╱
the night	∪ ╱ |
and day— |	∪ ╱ |
Here	╱

from | the street | ˘ | ˘ / |
by   ˘

```
*   *   *
*   S   *
*   O   *                    / |
*   D   *
*   A   *                    ˘
*   *   *
```

ringed | with   / | ˘
run | ing lights | / | ˘ / |

the dark | ened   ˘ / | ˘
pane | / |

exac | tly   ˘ / | ˘
down | the cen | ter | / | ˘ / | ˘

is | / |
transfixed   ˘ /

The count: one trochee, one spondee, one bacchic, two anapests, and 19 iambs. After line 9, *all* the feet are iambs.

The hypothesis I am setting out is consistent with Williams's prosodic views and, perhaps, completes them, clarifying even his often confusing comments about the variable foot. Williams was decisive: "to my mind, there is no such thing as free verse. It's a contradiction in terms. The verse is measured. No measure can be free" (Wagner-Martin 38).

Alone among poets and prosodists of his time, Williams intuited the chaos of our understanding of meter: "We don't, any more, know how to measure the lines and therefore have convinced ourselves that they can't be measured" (*Selected Letters* 331). And: "Without measure we are lost. But we have lost even the ability to count.... there is no one among us who is consciously aware of what he is doing" (*Selected Essays* 340).

The problem, he argued, lay in our conception of the foot: "The rigid impositions imposed on us by the regularly measured foot (which Whitman felt but did not properly know what to do with) are to be understood only when we conceive of it as a fault in the foot itself' (*Selected Letters* 334). The foot had to be altered to reflect the language. "It is," he says, "a technical point but a point of vast importance" (321). The variable foot, then, may be merely the continuum-foot of English verse which, at last correctly described, may be variously iamb / trochee / spondee / anapest / Bacchic / pyrrhic. Williams couldn't know that, like him, poets since Gascoigne and Shakespeare have been working at cross-purposes with an incomplete or mistaken prosody.

As we grow accustomed to thinking of all verse as metrical, we will realize that regularities are *achieved*, made to coalesce from the metrical field of the language, rather than a perfect given from which any divergence (substitution or variation) is a loss or falling off. There will, naturally, be various sorts and degrees of regularity, including even the very strictest in the old-fashioned sense.

The notion of metrical form as preexisting and somehow, therefore, either splendid or sterile, is a misleading stereotype. In "The Shape of Poetry" (278-306), Paul Lake interrogates Pound's distinction that "some poems may have form as a tree has form, some as water poured into a vase," as well as the prosodic implications of A.R. Ammons's "Corson Inlet." Using analogies in fractal geometry and chaos science, Lake argues persuasively that

> Once we look at how poems actually take shape, it becomes clear that Ammons and Pound are wrong: The rules of formal poetry generate not static objects like vases, but the same kind of bottom-up, self-organizing processes seen in complex natural systems such as flocking birds, drifting sand dunes, and living trees.

II. On Justice on Stevens, with Asides

The politics of it aside, English verse is quite simple:
"Things are more like they are now than they ever were before."
—Dwight D. Eisenhower

Donald Justice manages almost entirely without the clumsiness of scanning-marks in his landmark essay, on "The Free Verse Line in Stevens" (176–204). Implicit in the essay are carefully arranged distinctions both between free verse and accentual meter, and then between free verse and accentual-syllabic meter. His argument that, ultimately, Stevens's unrhymed pentameters modulate into free verse is persuasive—so much so that, when Thom Gunn notes (in a 1995 *Paris Review* interview with Clive Wilmer) that "Stevens invented one amazingly subtle kind" of free verse, he is undoubtedly referring to Justice's essay.

My recollection of Justice as an indefatigable and accurate scanner sent me back to the essay looking for bacchic feet. Though he calls bacchics merely "an unusual version of the trisyllabic foot" (199), there they were, a useful dozen or so from early and late in Stevens's oeuvre, including (in my scansions)

˘ ⁄ ⁄ ˘ ˘ ⁄ ˘ ⁄ ˘ (⁄) ˘ ⁄
A white pig | eon it is, | that flut | ters to | the ground ...

˘ ⁄ ⁄ ˘ (⁄) ˘ ⁄ ˘ ⁄ ˘ ⁄
A thing fi | nal in | itself | and, there | fore, good ...

⁄ ⁄ ˘ ⁄ ˘ ⁄ ⁄ ˘ ⁄ ˘ ⁄
All men | endure. | The great cap | tain is | the choice ...

⁄ ⁄ ˘ ⁄ ˘ ⁄ ⁄ ˘ ⁄ ˘
Wreathed round | and round | the round wreath | of au | tumn ...

"In Stevens' practice," Justice notes (200), the foot "is a step in the direction of turning the line loose, making it free."

Rereading the essay, however, I am troubled by Justice's casualness in dealing with the larger issues. To say this is not to single out Justice, since the failing is general among metrists, few of whom even try to be precise. As soon as we posit the existence of free verse, the line between what is free and what is metrical becomes a crux; and differing assumptions make even discussion difficult. Like pedants in Swift's Lagado, we unpack our bundles of examples and so converse for an hour or so without communication. A large part of the verse of the twentieth century remains off the prosodical maps.

Justice begins by distinguishing "the two types of free-verse line Stevens favored—one short, one long" (176). The essay falls into two parts. Let's take them in order. The short-line verse "is shaped syntactically":

> [T]hat is, it stops at the end of a phrase or clause and does not break across the phrase or contrary to it. J. V. Cunningham has called it, condescendingly, a kind of "parsing" meter, visually diagrammed by the line divisions. The point of the line divisions, however, seems to be not merely to follow the grammarian's parsing but to suggest a principle of order a little aside from grammar, implying a conscious and deliberate ordering of the phrases into units having a recognizable rhythmical as well as syntactical identity. The sense of line becomes in itself a shaping force, a partial guide to the composition of the phrases and to their linkage.

As example, he offers "Disillusionment of Ten O'Clock."

> The houses are haunted
> By white night-gowns.
> None are green,
> Or purple with green rings,
> Or green with yellow rings,
> Or yellow with blue rings.
> None of them are strange,
> With socks of lace
> And beaded ceintures.
> People are not going
> To dream of baboons and periwinkles.
> Only, here and there, an old sailor,
> Drunk and asleep in his boots,
> Catches tigers
> In red weather.

Justice notes that, given the parsing rule, "lines 8 and 9 could with equal reason be printed as one line" or lines 10 and 11 "be divided, with somewhat more reason, after *dream* instead of after *going*," thus: "People are not going to dream / Of baboons and periwinkles."

So, though the parsing rule "does have a certain use, it is neither exact nor sufficient." The further principle of order, "a little aside from grammar," is that the poem's lines are pretty obviously organized upon some sort of accentual basis, though the basis is just as obviously a somewhat flexible one. It is not that each line *must* contain two accents but that each line *may* and probably will do so.... What matters is to recognize that the basic line contains a certain number of accents from which departures will occur; and this fact seems plain enough to be regarded as a clear organizing principle. It might not be pretty, but a mathematician would find it easy enough to devise a formula such as "2 accents plus or minus 1 (or more)" to describe this line in action. (179)

Since legitimate departures would include a line with twenty accents or with only one, or apparently with none, it is hard to see how the rule might exclude any line at all or serve either poet or reader as an "organizing principle."

This may not be quite the non sequitur it seems since we can *count* each line by its accents, and when we find a *pattern*, such verse is no longer free but has become accentual meter. Justice's example, though he quotes only lines 14–20, is "The American Sublime":

And the sublime comes down
To the spirit itself,
The spirit and space,
The empty spirit
In vacant space.
What wine does one drink?
What bread does one eat?

He comments: "Each of its lines has two accents, unvaryingly; a few might be read differently—this is always true—but no other reading is necessary" (182). As I have argued elsewhere (*Meter in English*, 16, 322–324), the problem of the so-called accentual meter is precisely that—it *is* "always true" that lines "might be read differently." Telling clearly and unambiguously what are stresses is difficult. To me, "And the sublime comes down" here and the line "One grows used to the weather" have three stresses naturally, not simply as a matter of performance; and the line "Shall a man go barefoot" has, plausibly, four stresses. So Justice's distinction between free verse and accentual meter seems unreliable. By comparison, the great advantage of accentual-syllabic meter is that it essentially resolves this difficulty: "comes down," whether iamb or spondee, counts as *one* foot, so nothing much depends on hearing the stressing differently. Here, however, our perception of the poem as being either metrical or free is at stake—and is unresolvable, except by a critical wave of the hand, as in Justice's "no other reading is necessary," which dismisses all interpretations but his own.

Similar arbitrariness undermines his argument that, despite varying line lengths, the "strict stanza patterns" of "The Death of a Soldier" keep the poem from being free verse and allow "the accentual meters to be heard and understood" (183):

Life contracts and death is expected,
As in a season of autumn.
The soldier falls.

He does not become a three-days personage,
Imposing his separation,
Calling for pomp.

Death is absolute and without memorial,
As in a season of autumn,
When the wind stops,

When the wind stops and, over the heavens,
The clouds go, nevertheless,
In their direction.

"The first line of each stanza may be read with four accents, the second with three, and the third with two. All of this can be done quite naturally," writes Justice—but not, I must interject, with either reliability or consistency. "As" in lines 2 and 8 and "In" in line 12 must be counted as stresses, though not "When" in lines 9 and 10. The secondary accent in "separation" in "Imposing his separation" must be counted, but *not* the secondary accents in "absolute" and "nevertheless." Nor the one in "personage," even without which line 4 has *five* stresses rather than the requisite four:

$$\text{/ \quad / \quad\quad / \quad / \quad / \quad (/)}$$
He does not become a three-days personage

Justice simply counts "-days" as unstressed, swallowing the natural emphasis.

What seems obvious is that measuring by accents is imprecise, whether it is free verse or accentual meter we are trying to count. Nor can measuring by accents provide much information. Justice himself shrugs, saying of "Disillusionment of Ten O'Clock" at one point (179, his italics) that "One line has three accents for certain, and several others appear to have two *or* three," while "two lines probably stretch out to four accents and one perhaps to as many as five." We may compare such indecision with a metrical scansion of the poem:

The hou | ses are haunt | ed

By white | night-gowns.

None | are green,

Or pur | ple with | green rings,

Or green | with yel | low rings,

Or yel | low with | blue rings.

None | of them | are strange,

With socks | of lace

People | are not go | ing

To dream | of baboons | and per | iwink | les.

On | ly, here | and there, | an old sail | or,

Drunk and | asleep | in his boots,

Catch | es tig | ers

In red weath | er.

Lines vary from monometer to tetrameter. There are 21 iambs among 38 total feet. This scansion plainly makes the poem's rhythm more available for discussion than does Justice's imprecise measurement by accents. (Metrical scansion of "The Death of a Soldier," which I leave to the reader, is similarly revealing.)

Justice almost makes a similar point about the iambs of the second section of "Peter Quince at the Clavier," which, rhymes aside, "might serve as a model for the line of 'Disillusionment of Ten O'Clock" (185). I quote the first eight lines:

In the green water, clear and warm,
Susanna lay.
She searched
The touch of springs,
And found
Concealed imaginings.
She sighed.
For so much melody.

"It is true that the meters are iambic, with scarcely an exception," Justice remarks, "but the overall design remains 'free.'" "Overall design" apparently refers to variation in line-length, though quotation marks around "free" suggest some reservation or ambiguity about this definition of the term. The expansion and contraction of line-length are more rapid than in "Disillusionment of Ten O'Clock," but the pattern of variation isn't dissimilar in kind from the dimeters, then trimeters, then dimeters, then tetrameters of that poem, with its patterned diminution in the last four lines: tetrameter, trimeter, dimeter, monometer.

Before the present moment, the argument that all verse is metrical—measurable by the same system—has never seemed credible. No one, including Eliot himself, took seriously his statements in "Reflections on *Vers Libre*" that lines of free verse "are usually explicable in terms of prosody. Any line can be divided into feet and accents," and that there is no reason "why there should not be lines (as there are) divisible only into feet of different types." Eliot's reason for putting aside this account is that such "scansion tells us very little," because the purpose of scansion is to detect "repetition of effect," that is, "pattern."

It is clear, however, that other methods of counting lines of free verse (or of accentual verse, if it exists at all) tell us less, much less, and do so very unreliably.

When we take account of the bacchic foot (as I argue above, in "Recovering the Genetic Code of English Verse"), we arrive at the possibility of a fresh understanding of meter. Our notions of meter have hitherto been largely *prescriptive*, adducing rules. Poets have sometimes ventured outside the rules, and occasionally, over time, the rules have bent—for instance, in freely allowing in syllabic substitution, although opposition to this concession continues even now. (In their essays in *Meter in English*, for instance, Timothy Steele and Dana Gioia insist that anapestic substitution can shift verse out of accentual-syllabic meter.) A similarly puritanical rule requiring uniformity of line-length except in special cases has surfaced repeatedly ever since *Tottel's Miscellany* in 1557 corrected Wyatt's tetrameter, "It was no dream. I lay broad waking," to a pentameter. (Kirby-Smith, for instance, argues that Herbert's "The Collar" and Milton's "Lycidas" are free verse, not accentual-syllabic meter.) Permissible latitude in both foot-types and line-lengths remains sharply contested.

I have no quibble at all about the value of metrical regularity. Meter is pattern, but pattern is always, necessarily, in some measure free—in the relatively differing syllables that fulfill it, and of course in the substitutions and other conventions (such as extra-syllable endings) that modify or extend it. The question is, at what point do these accumulating little freedoms produce a change in *kind* (for this is the assumption) from metrical verse to free verse? At what point does one non-iambic foot, or one varied line length, become one too many? To ask the question in this form is to suggest that it is unanswerable. Patterns even a good deal less than strict are also patterns, and we lose nothing in being aware of the whole spectrum from paradigmatic regularity to even the outermost irregularity. Indeed, we will gain much in the precision of rhythmic analysis.

In short, meter may now be construed as *descriptive*, that is, as a system of measurement which does not furnish rules or imply aesthetic or ethical judgment. It is from this perspective that I have approached Justice's essay.

When Justice turns to Stevens's long-line free verse, he argues that the poet, during "the forty years from 1915 to 1955" (191), loosened the unrhymed iambic pentameter until, "toward the end, Stevens evidently felt quite comfortable writing a long line that has become in essence 'free,' yet without ever quite losing touch with its source in the old heroic line, which more and more bends to his will without losing its shape." At the beginning of the essay Justice had seemed quite firm: "the two types of free-verse line Stevens favored—one short, one long." But now he hedges: "in essence 'free,'" "a relative freedom" (194), or "this nearly 'free' long line" (195). He elaborates:

The gradual evolution of the line can be seen as one more example of the classic pattern of the poet's development, in which the young poet first masters a type of traditional verse and then, maturing, treats its laws with more and more familiarity and confidence, leading to a *degree of freedom*. In Shakespeare's blank verse a similar progress or, depending on one's point of view, decline may be traced.... Likewise with Stevens, the fresh, untroubled blank verse of "Sunday Morning" gives way gradually to the looser blank verse of "Notes toward a Supreme Fiction" and, a little later, "Esthetique du Mal," only to end in the much loosened and stretched pentameters of "To an Old Philosopher in Rome," "St. Armorer's Church from the Outside," and "The World as Meditation." To include "Prologues to What Is Possible" would be to push the case about as far as it could be taken. (192, my italics)

Since the verse in Shakespeare's late plays isn't free verse in any modern sense, the parallel hardly advances Justice's claim as to Stevens. Nor does the verse of "The World as Meditation" or "Prologues to What Is Possible" seem accurately described as pentameters, as we will see. Nor, indeed, is it clarifying that Justice regards the late Stevens's line as "still 'foot-verse,'"

which is to say that the syllables gathered about each verse accent, though varying to some degree, are distributed in a limited number of recurring and identifiable groupings. This was not true of the loose accentuals of "Disillusionment of Ten O'Clock." For the purpose of definition it may be enough to say that Stevens' long line based on the iambic pentameter can be described as "free" when two conditions are met. One: when within a basically pentameter passage a few hexameters or tetrameters, rarely any line longer or shorter than these, are mingled randomly, yet without leading to metrical incoherence. Two: when as many non-iambic feet as iambic appear, as well as occasional lines or feet not easy to classify or interpret. (193–194)

An important point to make is that "Disillusionment of Ten O'Clock" is *also* foot-verse, as we have seen, although less regular than the foot-verse iambics of the section of "Peter Quince at the Clavier." We may in effect graph all of these poems using the two variables of line-lengths and foot-types. Albeit unnamed, the bacchic foot must count as one of Justice's "limited number of recurring and identifiable groupings." The bacchic lets us make metrical sense even of the line that, in Justice's argument, "represents the final stage in the loosening of Stevens' long line, and it comes very late" (202):

˘ ′ ˘ ˘ ′ ˘ ˘ ′ ′ ˘ ′ ˘ ′ ′

One thinks | where the hous | es of | New Eng | land catch | the first sun

Although irregular, the line strikes me as easily explicable as hexameter—which is the norm of its poem, "A Discovery of Thought." The poem shows several other clear bacchics, as in line 4:

′ ˘ ˘ ′ ˘ ′ ˘ ′ ′ ˘ ′ ˘ ′

One is | a child | again. | The gold beards | of wat | erfalls

Stevens's use of bacchics is consistent from as early as "Le Monocle de Mon Oncle" in 1918.

The pyrrhic foot also occurs often in Stevens, both early and late—as, for example, in "Le Monocle de Mon Oncle":

˘ ′ ˘ ˘ ′ ˘ ˘ ˘ ˘ ′ ˘(′) ˘ ′

But note | the uncon | scion | able treach | ery | of fate

In "To an Old Philosopher in Rome":

˘ ′ ˘ ′ ˘ ˘ ′ ˘ ˘ ˘ ′ ˘ ′ ˘

Become | the fig | ures of heav | en, the | majes | tic move | ment

Here, followed by a bacchic, in "Valley Candle":

˘ ′ ˘ ′ ˘ ′ ˘ ˘ ˘ ′ ′ ˘

My can | dle burned | alone | in an | immense val | ley.

Returning to the argument that, ultimately, Stevens transmutes his pentameters into free verse, we may look at the four late poems Justice mentions, "To an Old Philosopher in Rome," "Prologues to What Is Possible," "The World as Meditation," and "St. Armorer's Church from the Outside." When we apply his definition (which I have quoted), it turns out not to be confirming. The condition that "as many non-iambic feet as iambic appear" is met *in none* of the four poems. My tabulations of the various feet:

	∪ /	/ ∪	∪ ∪ /	/ /	∪ / /	∪ ∪	x /	non-iambic
Philosopher	257	89	17	16	6	16	1	= 145
Prologues	166	61	11	8	6	14	2	= 102
World	85	32	6	4	5	9	0	= 56
St. Armorer's	135	52	11	2	6	12	0	= 83

The poems register, then, in order: 64% iambic, 62% iambic, 60% iambic, 62% iambic. For what it's worth, a count of "Disillusionment of Ten O'Clock" (21 iambs, 17 non-iambs) shows the poem as 55% iambic.

If we count the four poems by line-lengths, these are the results:

	5-feet	6-feet	7-feet	8-feet	9-feet
Philosopher	75	6			
Prologues		1	23	10	2
World	7	13	4		
St. Armorer's	43	1			

In two poems, a pentameter norm is a little stretched. In the other two, it seems entirely speculative to claim that the line has "become in essence 'free,' yet without ever quite losing touch with its source in the old heroic line, which more and more bends to [Stevens's] will without losing its shape" (191). One might as easily argue that, say, the tetrameters of "Two Illustrations That the World Is What You Make of It" are essentially free, being contractions of the blank verse line.

Justice's essay, in short, brilliantly spotlights Stevens's metrical variety, but does not demonstrate or clarify the intended distinctions between meter and free verse. All of us have hitherto worked to as little effect: the problem is insoluble.

With the recovery of the bacchic foot, however, we now may be able to understand meter in English as a purely descriptive system of measurement that applies to *all* verse. That is the hypothesis that must be tested.

The Notion of Modern Accentual Meter

Modern accentual meter does not exist, so this essay is the history—in my view—of a delusion.

The notion refers to measuring verse lines by counting speech stresses only, without regard to the number or placement of unstressed syllables (if any) among the stresses and, therefore, without regard to the pacing or rhythm of the stresses. Since the succession of stresses *is* the metrical pattern, there can be no promotion or, for that matter, demotion in this meter, although ambiguity as to what counts as a stress—among the myriad levels of stress in speech or performance—will almost inevitably make any scansion arbitrary. Whether such a meter is sufficiently audible and distinctive to work in modern English seems doubtful. Neither the passages offered as examples of accentual meter nor the rather fitful arguments as to its theory are reassuring.

The earliest contemporary reference I find to accentual meter is in Helen Gardner's 1950 *Art of T.S. Eliot* (15–35), so I take her to be the critical fountainhead of the accentual revival. (Notably, she doesn't mention Coleridge or "Christabel.") "The creation of this metre is perhaps Mr. Eliot's greatest poetic achievement," she wrote. This "new metre," in which "he was taking up and remaking for his own purposes, or perhaps we might say finding his way back to, the medieval tradition of accentual verse," comes into existence in the plays and most notably in *Four Quartets*, wherein "the number of syllables is of no importance, nor is the disposition of stressed and unstressed syllables."

Only stresses are counted. And the count need not be regular—any passage will necessarily have an arithmetical norm from which, to avoid monotony, it may vary and to which it may return. Both a three-stress and a six-stress line fit in a four-stress passage (Gardner shows caesuras):

     /   /   / /
Midwinter spring | is its own season
    / /   /
Sempiternal | though sodden towards sundown,
     /   /   /   /
Suspended in time | between pole and tropic.
        / /   /   /   /
When the short day is brightest, | with frost and fire,

    / / /   /   /   /
The brief sun flames the ice, | on pond and ditches,

   /   /   /   /
In windless cold | that is the heart's heat,

   /   /   /
Reflecting in a watery mirror

   /   /   /   /
A glare that is blindness | in the early afternoon.

Similarly, an eight-stress line fits in a five-stress passage, a two-stress line in a six-stress passage, and so on. Any verse at all can be counted in this way, though whether such counting amounts to a "metre" is a good question.

  Moreover, Gardner is quite arbitrary as to what she counts. Secondary stresses sometimes count ("constellation" has two stresses) but sometimes not ("afternoon" above has one). She counts "as" in "in their *dancing* / *As* in their *living* | in the living *seasons*," but not "When" in the fourth line above—nor "run-" in "*Whis*per of running *streams*, | and *win*ter *light*ning." She counts a stress for "into" in one line, but not in another. In a six-stress passage, "neither" doesn't count in three lines, but does in two others:

      / /   /   /   /   /
At the still point of the turning world. | Neither flesh nor fleshless;

       /   /   / / /   /
Neither from nor towards; | at the still point, there the dance is,

      /   /   /   /   /   /
But neither arrest nor movement. | And do not call it fixity,

      /   /   /   /   /   /
Where past and future are gathered. | Neither movement from nor towards,

      /   /   /   /   / / /
Neither ascent nor decline. | Except for the point, the still point,

        /   /   /   /
There would be no dance, | and there is only the dance.

Although the passage has been chosen to exemplify six-beat accentual meter, lines vary from four to seven stresses. Gardner's arbitrariness as to what are stresses matters, since the count *determines* the lines' measurement. Note that, in English, performance or context will often let us disagree about speech stresses—as, here, in the sixth line I would incline to count "no" as also stressed. Although such variability of interpretation throws off the measuring of lines by accentual meter, it does not affect measuring by accentual-syllabic meter—which (through spondees and pyrrhics, or promotions) allows pentameters, for instance, to vary from as few as two or three speech stresses to as many as seven or eight, without changing the line-counts. This is part of the genius of English meter.

It will turn out that Gardner's scansions are conservative compared to what is ahead. In 1951, in "Poetry and Drama" (*On Poetry and Poets* 88), Eliot himself confided that, for *The Family Reunion* and the plays that followed, he had worked out "a rhythm close to contemporary speech,"

> in which the stresses could be made to come wherever we should naturally put them. a line of varying length and varying number of syllables, with a caesura and three stresses. The caesura and the stresses may come at different places, almost anywhere in the line; the stresses may be close together or well separated by light syllables; the only rule being that there must be one stress on one side of the caesura and two on the other.

John Frederick Nims ("Our Many Meters" 186) has scanned for us two lines in this accentual meter:

> /   /   /
> Why should we stand here like guilty conspirators, | waiting for some revelation ...
> /   /
> In a horrid amity of misfortune? | why should we be implicated, brought in and
> /
> brought together ...

It is worth observing that the meter of such lines, whatever it is, bears no resemblance whatever to the Old English meter that is its presumed source.

Although this meter is patent nonsense, Northrop Frye gave it a slanting imprimatur, noting—a modest correction—that "Mr. Eliot speaks of the rhythm of *The Cocktail Party* as a three-beat line, but I usually hear four beats, and so apparently do most of the actors" (*Sound and Poetry*, xx). Incorporating that piece into his *Anatomy of Criticism* (1957), Frye revises the comment:

> In the verse rhythm of *The Cocktail Party*, which perhaps most clearly foreshadows the development of a new rhythmical center of gravity between verse and prose in modern speech, we go back to a rhythm very close to the

old four-accent line. Perhaps what is taking shape here is a long six-or-seven beat accentual line finally made practicable for spoken dialogue by being split in two. (270)

This second version seems muddier, somewhat more grandiose; two *perhaps's* in two sentences suggest Frye was getting cold feet.

Neither Eliot nor Frye scans lines from *The Cocktail Party* or, for that matter, from any of the other of his plays. So adjudicating their differing views as to the meter's being three- or four- (or six- or seven-) beat would be interpretative guesswork. I find virtually no lines conforming to Eliot's prescription and few enough that I'd credit as either three- or four-beat. The majority—like the lines Nims scans above—are far from being either. "The only man I ever met who could hear the cry of bats" (Act I, Scene 1), for example, strikes me as plainly having seven stresses (six iambs, one anapest).

It is also telling that Frye is promoting the relation of music to poetry. As he remarks in *Sound and Poetry* (xvii), "To read poetry which is musical in our sense we need a principle of accentual scansion, a regular recurrence of beats with a variable number of syllables between the beats. This corresponds to the general rhythm of music in the Western tradition, where there is a regular stress accent with a variable number of notes in each measure." Here is part of the same argument in *Anatomy of Criticism* (251):

A four-stress line seems to be inherent in the structure of the English language. It is the prevailing rhythm of the earlier poetry, though it changes its scheme from alliteration to rhyme in Middle English; it is the common rhythm of popular poetry in all periods, of ballads and of most nursery rhymes. In the ballad, the eight-six-eight-six quatrain is a continuous four-beat line, with a "rest" at the end of every other line. This principle of the rest, or a beat coming at a point of actual silence, was already established in Old English. The iambic pentameter provides a field of syncopation in which stress and metre can to some extent neutralize one another. If we read many iambic pentameters "naturally," giving the important words the heavy accent that they do have in spoken English, the old four-stress line stands out in clear relief against its metrical background. Thus:

$$\text{/} \quad \text{/} \quad \quad \text{/} \quad \quad \text{/}$$

To be, or not to be: that is the question.

／　　　　　／　　　　　　／　　　　　／
Whether 'tis nobler in the mind to suffer

　　　／　　　　　／　　　　　　／　　　　　／
The slings and arrows of outrageous fortune,

　　　／　　　　　／　　　　　／　　　　　／
Or take up arms against a sea of troubles ...

Apparently, except for the larger metrical background of the play (iambic pentameter), the lines of Hamlet's soliloquy could be scanned as being in accentual meter.

In "The Concept of Meter" (1959), W. K. Wimsatt and Monroe C. Beardsley—stung by the "musical view" represented by Frye—defended the primacy of the "relative stress," the richness and potential for "tension" or "interplay," of traditional accentual-syllabic meter. In contrast, they point out, "the stress pattern of [accentual] meter is so nearly the same as the stress pattern of the syntax and logic that there is nothing for the meter to interplay with" (165). This is the reason, they suggest, "why the greatest English poetry (Chaucer, Shakespeare, Milton, Pope, Wordsworth) has after all been written in the more artful syllable-stress meter—not in the older, simpler, more directly natural strong-stress meter."

Wimsatt and Beardsley easily get the better of this argument, but—in my view—at a fateful cost: they endorse the notion of a modern accentual meter.

They do so parenthetically and rather off-handedly, as if we already know clearly what the term means. Thus, they refer to the "older (and newer) English strong-stress meter" and a page or two later to "the very old (and recently revived) meter of strong stress with indeterminate or relatively indeterminate number of syllables between the stresses," listing "*Beowulf, Piers Plowman, Everyman*, Spenser's *February Eclogue*, Coleridge's *Christabel*, the poetry of G. M. Hopkins (who talks about 'sprung rhythm' and 'outrides'), the poetry of T.S. Eliot, and many another in our day" (155). Given this miscellany, it is hard to work out their position. Does the inclusion of "Christabel" mean that they accept Coleridge's mistaken description of his meter, or do they count verse mixing iambs and anapests as being in accentual meter? Who are the "many another"? What does the careful hedging of "or relatively indeterminate" mean?

In a finale probably too clever by half, Wimsatt and Beardsley turn the tables on Frye. Given relative stress and the fact that iambic pentameters will often have "one somewhat lighter stress," Frye's claim that the lines of Hamlet's soliloquy resemble stress-meter "is not very remarkable" (166). "But," they go on, "if a poem written on the whole in a meter of four strong stresses, with indeterminate number of syllables, at some point tightens up, counts syllables, and tilts minor accents into an iambic pentameter, this is something else." The rest of Wimsatt and Beardsley's essay is worth examining in full (166–67):

> A wise and shifty modern poet, always in search of rhythmical invention, writes a stanza containing in the middle such a line as:

> Her hair over her arms and her arms full of flowers,

and at the end:

> Sometimes these cogitations still amaze
> The troubled midnight and the noon's repose.

This is playing in and out of the metrical inheritance. Part V of *The Waste Land* begins:

> After the torchlight red on sweaty faces
> After the frosty silence in the gardens
> After the agony in stony places ...

Coming after four parts of a poem largely in strong-stress meter, these lines, with their marked swinging parallel of construction, will most likely be read at a fast walk as strong stress meter, four stresses to the first, three each to the second and the third. But each is also a perfectly accurate pentameter line, each complicated in the same two traditional ways, the inverted beginning and the hypermetric ending. ("Whether 'tis nobler in the mind to suffer ...")

It is probably not until about the time of Mr. Eliot and his friends that the free and subtle moving in and out and coalescing of strong-stress and syllable-stress meters in the same poem, the same stanza, begins to appear with any frequency. This is something remarkable in the history of metrics. But the understanding of it depends precisely upon the recognition of the few homely and sound, traditional and objective, principles of prosody upon which we have been insisting throughout this essay. Without recognition of the two distinct principles of strong-stress and of syllable-stress meter, it seems doubtful if anything at all precise or technical can be said about Mr. Eliot's peculiar rhythms and tensions.

The underlying point again is the superiority of the accentual-syllabic heritage, which "Mr. Eliot and his friends" confess by tightening up poems and—shiftily—returning to the iambic pentameter.

The implication of rescue by pentameters ("at the end," "after four parts of a poem largely written in strong-stress meter") misrepresents both poems. I am not clear that either poem has been demonstrated to be "written on the whole in a meter of four strong stresses, with indeterminate number of syllables." *The Waste Land* seems too complicated a case for easy generalization; and Gardner held that the new beginning—Eliot's introduction of accentual meter—came only "after *The Waste Land*." In her view, Eliot was still working changes on the English heroic line: "we might say that on the whole up to *The Waste Land* Mr. Eliot's verse could be 'scanned' with as much or as little propriety as most English post-Spenserian verse can be" (16). As to "La Figlia che Piange," it is worth testing Wimsatt and Beardsley's claim that the poem is in accentual meter:

    / ‿ ‿ / ‿ / ‿ (/) ‿ /
    Stand on | the high | est pave | ment of | the stair—
    / ‿ ‿ / ‿ /
    Lean on | a gar | den urn—
    / / ‿ / / ‿ ‿ /
    Weave, weave | the sun | light in | your hair—
x / ‿ / ‿ ‿ / ‿ ‿ / ‿ /
    Clasp | your flow | ers to you | with a pained | surprise—
    / ‿ ‿ ‿ / ‿ /
    Fling them | to the ground | and turn
    ‿ ‿ / ‿(/) ‿ / ‿ ‿ ‿ /
    With a fug | itive | resent | ment in | your eyes:

    ‿ / / ‿ / / ‿ ‿ /
    But weave, weave | the sun | light in | your hair.
    ‿ / ‿ ‿ / ‿ /
    So I | would have had | him leave,
    ‿ / ‿ ‿ / ‿ / ‿ /
    So I | would have had | her stand | and grieve,

˘ ╱   ˘   ˘   ╱
So he | would have left
˘   ˘   ╱   ╱   ˘ ╱ ˘ ╱   ˘   ╱
As the | soul leaves | the bod | y torn | and bruised,
˘   ˘   ╱   ˘╱   ˘   ╱   ˘(╱)   ˘   ╱
As the mind | deserts | the bod | y it | has used.
x ╱   ˘   ╱
I | should find
˘   ╱   ˘╱   ˘ ˘   ˘   ╱   ˘   ╱
Some way | incom | para | bly light | and deft,
˘   ╱   ˘   ╱   ˘   ╱   ˘   ╱
Some way | we both | should un | derstand,
╱ ˘   ˘   ╱   ˘ ˘ ˘ ╱   ˘   ╱   ˘ ˘ ╱
Simple | and faith | less as | a smile | and shake | of the hand.
˘   ╱   ˘╱   ˘   (╱)   ˘ ╱   ˘   ╱   ˘
She turned | away, | but with | the au | tumn weath | er
˘   ╱   ˘ ˘ ˘╱ ˘╱   ˘   ╱   ˘ ╱
Compelled | my imag | ina | tion man | y days,
x ╱   ˘ ╱   ˘   ╱   ˘   ╱
Man | y days | and man | y hours:
˘   ╱ ╱   ˘   ˘   ╱   ˘   ˘   ╱   ╱   ˘   ╱   ˘
Her hair o | ver her arms | and her | arms full | of flow | ers.
˘ ˘ ╱   ˘   ╱   ˘   ╱   ˘   ╱   ˘ ╱   ˘
And I won | der how | they should | have been | togeth | er!
╱   ˘   ˘   ╱   ˘ ╱   ˘ (╱) ˘ ╱
I should | have lost | a ges | ture and | a pose.
╱   ╱   ˘   ╱   ˘╱   ˘   ╱   ˘╱
Sometimes | these cog | ita | tions still | amaze
˘   ╱   ˘   ╱   ╱   ˘   ˘   ╱   ˘ ╱
The trou | bled mid | night and | the noon's | repose.

The poem scans readily as accentual syllabic—indeed, a good deal more readily than it would in "a meter of four strong stresses." It shows a moderate variety of line-length that conforms to Eliot's practice at the time (and to the model of "Dover Beach"): Among its 24 lines appear 13 pentameters and 6 tetrameters.

Like Frye and like Eliot himself, Wimsatt and Beardsley demonstrate absolutely nothing about what they call the "distinct principle" of this "newer" and "recently revived" strong-stress meter, including its identity with or difference from the Old English original. But the notion is passed along, with enhanced authority.

Their essay appeared in the December 1959 issue of *PMLA*. Its last two paragraphs are quoted (beginning at "A wise and shifty modern poet ...") in the third edition of Robert Penn Warren and Cleanth Brooks's *Understanding Poetry* (1960), the Preface to which is dated January 24, 1960. The new accentual meter rates no mention at all in the long chapter "Metrics" (119–80), but appears in a brief addendum to "old native meter" in the "Notes on Versification" at book's end (568–70), where Gardner's *Art of T S. Eliot* is also quoted.

Brooks and Warren appear puzzled themselves, noting that "In some of the modern developments of the old native meter, there may be more or fewer than four beats to the line." They mention, as "reflect[ing] more or less strongly" that meter, Hopkins's "The Windhover" and poems by Auden and Empson as well as Eliot. "Some of the poems just mentioned are rather easily scanned in terms of the conventional metrical pattern," they add—though they don't say whether such poems should be scanned so now or may be taken as written in *two* meters at once. Brooks and Warren focus on a poem by Robert Graves, of which they say: "On the whole, it would seem best to abandon the conventions of normal English verse and to scan "Rocky Acres" in terms of a pattern of four strong beats, with feet of a varying number of weak syllables." However, they offer their students no advice at all on finding *the* four beats in lines like:

With harsh craggy mountain, moor ample and bare

or

The rocks jut, the streams flow singing on either hand.

And so the deed is done! Modern accentual meter entered the textbooks—a notion little tested and certainly not convincingly or precisely demonstrated, but with considerable authority behind it (Gardner, Eliot himself, Frye, Wimsatt and Beardsley, Brooks and Warren). In 1964, Harvey Gross (*Sound and Form* 25) can affirm without doubt that "Modern poets have revived strong-stress meter." In 1965, Paul Fussell (*Poetic Meter and Poetic Form* 11) can include accentual as one of the four meters in English.

Now, two generations past the third edition of Warren and Brooks's *Understanding Poetry* (1960) and long since the time when PhDs in English were relieved of the duty of learning Anglo-Saxon, this folly of a modern accentual meter is the received wisdom; although I doubt anyone hearing or reading the following lines could identify the first two as being metrically equal and equivalent four-beat lines and the third as being one beat *shorter*, a three-beat line:

Dull roots with spring rain ...
I think I understand your Lordship better than anybody ...
How can you sit in this blaze of light for all the world to look at?

What is oddest in this brief history is the assumption that a meter, after some 500 years of disuse, can be revived and instantly heard, as if no cultural factors impinged other than the nature of the (also very changed) language itself. Also assumed is that the Old English four-stress pattern can be successfully varied to three-stress or six-stress patterns, and so on, as well as to patterns mixing lines of different numbers of stresses, and that this revived meter can function without one or several of its normal elements, which include stress-heightening alliteration, distinct medial caesuras, and the formulaic syllabic patterning of half-lines. Signaling half-lines in oral performance by striking the strings of a harp is another element usually missing in modern accentual verse.

A Messy Complication

In 1965, when Fussell listed accentual as one of the four meters in English, he applied a quite different and utterly confusing interpretation of the term—without saying he was doing so or discussing the sleight-of-hand. He conflated mere trisyllabic *substitution* with accentual *meter*.

We have noted Brooks and Warren's puzzlement about "some of the modern developments of the old native meter," in which "there may be more or fewer than four beats to the line," and about examples of the revived meter which "are rather easily scanned in terms of the conventional metrical pattern," that is, with iambs and anapests (568–69). But their third edition was going to the printer, so they hastily quoted and relied in Gardner and on the two paragraphs by Wimsatt and Beardsley. But Wimsatt and Beardsley have also shown a similar but opposite reservation when they hedge as to accentual meter's "indeterminate *or relatively indeterminate* number of syllables between the stresses" (155, my emphasis).

The problem is that definitions of accentual meter offer no limiting or guiding condition, so that even lines like

              ／   ／   ／   ／
And miles to go before I sleep

fit the description fully and accurately. Consider Fussell's definition: "While in syllabic meter only the syllables are counted, in accentual meter only the accents are. Syllables may vary in number per line" (9)—or may not, of course.

Fussell codifies this muddle in *Poetic Meter and Poetic Form* by offering as examples of accentual meter only two poems, Yeats's "Why Should Not Old Men Be Mad?" and Auden's "September 1, 1939," both readily scannable in accentual-syllabic meter with trisyllabic substitution, a convention that Fussell—quite inconsistently—also accepts (34, 58, 69). He quietly hi-jacks the term accentual meter without even a discussion of the sort of verse Gardner, Eliot, Frye, Wimsatt and Beardsley, Brooks and Warren, and indeed Harvey Gross had posited and assumed they were considering.

In his chapter "The Historical Dimension" Fussell notes that "the great phenomenon in nineteenth century English versification is the rejection of strict accentual-syllabism in favor of accentualism. This is to say that the use of trisyllabic substitution in duple metrical contexts becomes the technical hallmark of the age" (71). Fussell seems to have noticed none of the anapests in Shakespeare or in Milton, say. Oddly, among the many useful scansions in *Poetic Meter and Poetic Form*, he *never* offers an accentual scansion, that is, one in which "only the accents" are counted. Even when he scans snippets of the Yeats and Auden poems (97, 58), his primary examples of accentual meter, he invokes metrical feet—improperly, it would seem, since accentual meter presumably disallows the convention of feet.

Fussell's second example, Auden's "September 1, 1939" (of which he quotes one stanza), is cited by Dana Gioia in *Meter in English* ("Meter-Making" 85–86) and discussed in some detail ("Completing" 315–16), so I will not repeat the discussion here. Instead, we may focus on Fussell's first example, "Why Should Not Old Men Be Mad?" of which he quotes (but does not scan) the opening eight lines, noting that "we find four stresses per line, although the number of syllables varies from seven to nine" (9). His claim that the poem is in accentual meter is a willful misdesignation, since it is, as Brooks and Warren would say, "rather easily scanned in terms of the conventional metrical pattern." Let's consider the poem:

x / ⏑ / / / ⏑ /
Why | should not | old men | be mad?

x / ⏑ / ⏑ / ⏑ /
Some | have known | a like | ly lad

⏑ / ⏑ / / / ⏑ /
That had | a sound | fly-fish | er's wrist

/ ⏑ ⏑ / ⏑ / ⏑ (/)
Turn to | a drunk | en jour | nalist;

⏑ / ⏑ / / / ⏑ /
A girl | that knew | all Dan | te once   5

/ ⏑ / / ⏑ ⏑ ⏑ /
Live to | bear chil | dren to | a dunce;

⏑ / ⏑ ⏑ / ⏑ / ⏑ /
A Hel | en of so | cial wel | fare dream,

/ ⏑ ⏑ / ⏑ (/) ⏑ /
Climb on | a wag | onette | to scream.

⏑ / ⏑ ⏑ / ⏑ ⏑ / ⏑ /
Some think | it a mat | ter of course | that chance

⏑ / / / ⏑ / ⏑ /
Should starve | good men | and bad | advance,   10

⏑ / ⏑ / ⏑ / ⏑ /
That if | their neigh | bours fig | ured plain,

⏑ / ⏑ / ⏑ / ⏑ /
As though | upon | a light | ed screen,

⏑ / ⏑ / ⏑ / ⏑ /
No sin | gle sto | ry would | they find

⏑ ⏑ ⏑ / ⏑ / ⏑ /
Of an | unbro | ken hap | py mind,

⏑ / ⏑ / ⏑ ⏑ ⏑ /
A fin | ish wor | thy of | the start.   15

/ / / / ⏑ ⏑ ⏑ /
Young men | know noth | ing of | this sort,

⏑ / ⏑ / / / ⏑ /
Observ | ant old | men know | it well;

⏑ / ⏑ / ⏑ / / /
And when | they know | what old | books tell,

⏑ / ⏑ / ⏑ / ⏑ /
And that | no bet | ter can | be had,

<pre>
    /   /   ᵕ /   /   /   ᵕ /
Know why | an old | man should | be mad.   20
</pre>

Despite omitted initial syllables in lines 1 and 2, the poem's iambic tetrameter takes hold quickly and firmly. Trochaic inversions, spondees, are rare. Three anapests (among the poem's *eighty* feet) hardly disturb the pattern.

I have scanned pyrrhics in lines 6, 14, 15, and 16, rather than equally possible promotions, in order to test Fussell's accentual claim, "four stresses per line." But, in fact, lines 1, 3, 5, 10, 16, 17, and 18 show *five* stresses and line 20 *six* stresses. Lines 14 and 15 show only *three* stresses. So Fussell's notion of measuring the poem as four-stress is inaccurate for ten—half!—of its twenty lines.

The pretext for Fussell's misdesignation is presumably the minimal variation in the number of unstressed syllables in lines mixing iambs and anapests. But an unvarying one or two syllables between metrical stresses is quite different from the wide and irregular variation predicated for accentual meter—from zero to, who knows, five or more unstressed syllables between stresses. And the familiar convention of trisyllabic substitution seems utterly preferable to the frequent, basic inaccuracies and ambiguities (for which no explanation is ever offered) of Fussell's sort of accentual misdesignation. Such misdesignation, sponsored by the premier metrical handbook of the past thirty-some years, is now received wisdom.

A recent example. William Harmon (123) cites Yeats's "Easter 1916" as in three-beat accentual meter, though he scans none of it. But consider my scansion showing speech stresses:

<pre>
      /   / /   /
Hearts with one purpose alone
           /   /   /
Through summer and winter seem
        /   /
Enchanted to a stone
        /   /   /
To trouble the living stream.
</pre>

Lines with *four* or with *two* stresses don't fit the alleged three-stress accentual pattern at all. But the passage scans smoothly, and informatively, as accentual-syllabic trimeter:

> /   ꞈ   /   /   ꞈ   ꞈ/

Hearts with | one pur | pose alone

>   ꞈ   /   ꞈ   ꞈ   /   ꞈ   /

Through sum | mer and win | ter seem

>   ꞈ   /   ꞈ   ꞈ   ꞈ   /

Enchant | ed to | a stone

>   ꞈ   /   ꞈ   ꞈ   /   ꞈ   /

To trou | ble the liv | ing stream.

Clearly, for "Easter 1916," Harmon's "counting by accents only, not by rhythmic feet" works poorly, providing at best a fuzzy description of the verse. Yeats himself would have been surprised by the ascription of accentual meter to the poem, since he could only have believed he was writing in accentual-syllabic meter with anapestic substitution—like Blake, like Shelley.

In Derek Attridge's *Poetic Rhythm: An Introduction* (1995), we may note a further variant on this interpretation of accentual meter. Attridge proposes to replace foot-scansion by a new system of beats and offbeats. Of the two meters he finds in English, stress (accentual) meter and syllable-stress (accentual-syllabic) meter, only the first allows what we would call trisyllabic substitution—and "stress meter, with very few exceptions, always falls into a four-beat rhythm" (63). Despite being trimeter, "Easter 1916"—surprisingly—is not an exception. Attridge can manage this, because his new system scans what he calls "unrealised" or "virtual" beats and offbeats—beats and offbeats representing syllables that, as he puts it, are "not actually present in the words of the verse" (58). "By contrast," he explains, "beats which are present" in the words "are called *actual beats*."

Harmon had to ignore lines with two or four speech-stresses in order to claim "Easter 1916" as three-beat accentual. Attridge sees the difficulty in his own claim that the poem is four-beat accentual (*Rhythms* 326–29):

> The foundation of [Yeats's] forms is a metrical pattern of three realized beats followed by an unrealized beat, although it must be said that the rhythmic freedom of the verse subdues this structure to the point where the unrealized beat is only a dim presence; as there are no realized fourth beats at all, there is no strong expectation of one ....

Despite all, nonetheless, Attridge gets where he is heading. "Yet," he says, "when it becomes appropriate for the underlying [four-beat] rhythm to emerge strongly into the open, as in the final lines of the poem ... it does so very readily." And he scans:

> I write it out in a verse—
> o B o B o   B   [o B]
>
> MacDonagh and MacBride
> o B o B o B   [o B]
>
> And Connolly and Pearse
> o B o B o   B   [o B]
>
> Now and in time to be,
> B   o B o B   [o B]
>
> Wherever green is worn
> o B o   B   o B   [o B]

"Now and in time to be" is four-beat accentual meter, emerged strongly into the open? Harmon and Attridge agree that Yeats's poem is in accentual meter, though we may take our choice whether the verse is three-beat or four-beat.

I said that accentual meter is a delusion. It is in fact a nest of delusions.

Aside from a belief in a sudden revival about 1950, there is another and more credible history of how medieval accentual meter enters twentieth-century poetry in English. It appears in Jakob Schipper's *History of English Versification* (1910). The short of it is that, as early as the eleventh century, the Old English alliterative line began gradually to change under the influence of both Medieval Latin and Norman-French poetry, due to "the constantly growing intercourse between the British Isles and the continent" (Schipper 64–67). Final rhyme tends to replace alliteration, and "the unaccented syllables are interposed between the accented ones with greater regularity" (80), as may be observed in Layamon's *Brut* and in *King Horn* in the thirteenth century. Later, as a consequence of an initial unaccented syllable not permitted in the Old English line (which had a descending rhythm), alliterative verse "becomes in Middle English ascending, and is brought into line with the rhythm of the contemporary even-beat metres" (91). As Schipper says (97), the alliterative line began "to accommodate its free rhythm of four accents bit by bit to that of the even-beat metres, especially to the closely related four-foot iambic line, and thus to transform itself into a more or less regular iambic-anapestic metre." This evolution is evident in *Piers Plowman* and *Sir Gawain and the Green Knight* in the fourteenth century, in ballads or lyrics like "I Have Labored Sore" and "Western Wind" in the fifteenth, and in the lines George Gascoigne cites in 1575 as written in "other kindes of Meeters" we have used in times past:

   ᴗ ╱   ᴗ ᴗ ╱   ᴗ   ╱   ᴗ ᴗ╱
No wight | in this world | that wealth | can attain
   ᴗ╱   ᴗ ᴗ╱   ᴗ ╱ ᴗ ᴗ ╱
Unless | he believe | that all | is but vain ...

or in lines of what was probably meant, in 1599, to seem an archaic song:

     ᴗ ╱   ᴗ ᴗ ╱   ᴗ   ╱   ╱   ╱
Do noth | ing but eat, | and make | good cheer ...
    ᴗ ╱ ᴗ ᴗ ╱ ᴗ ᴗ ╱   ᴗ ╱
Be mer | ry, be mer | ry, my wife | has all ... (*2 Henry IV* 5.3.18, 35)

It was this natural iambic-anapestic mixing, developed from Anglo-Saxon ac-
centual meter, which was proscribed about 1557, in an effort at literary propriety,
by the strict disyllabic compromise between classical foot-meter and romance
syllabic meter. Shakespeare and others cheated, particularly on the stage, as in

    ᴗ ᴗ ╱   ᴗ   ╱   ᴗ ╱   ᴗ ╱   ᴗ ╱
I beseech | your Gra | ces both | to par | don me, (*Richard III* 1.1.84)

or with the device of apostrophes which I doubt were always observed in per-
formance, as in

     ᴗ   ╱   ᴗ╱   ᴗ   ╱   ᴗ ╱   ᴗ ╱
And board | ed her | i' th'wan | ton way | of youth (*All's Well That Ends Well* 5.3.210)

This iambic-anapestic mixing reemerged in the poems of Blake, Burns, and
others at the end of the eighteenth century, as in Coleridge's

    ᴗ ᴗ ╱   ╱   ╱   ᴗ ╱ ᴗᴗ ╱
By thy long | grey beard | and glit | tering eye ...

And, in the two hundred years since that line was written, it has been used
naturally and elegantly by poets as varied as Shelley, Tennyson, Hopkins, Frost,
Stevens, and Bishop.

    Trisyllabic substitution in the disyllabic line is our legacy from Old English
verse, but it is *not* accentual meter.

Very Like a Meter

Do you see yonder cloud, that's almost in shape like a camel?
—Hamlet, speaking to Polonius (*Hamlet* 3.2.850)

The rhythms of English are made by successions of syllables that carry differing levels of stress. Both the number of syllables and the placement among them of the differing stresses determine any particular rhythm—what Robert Hass sums up as "the pacing of the stresses" ("Prosody" 148). Meter is a system of measurement that lets us abstract or approximate, and so compare and discuss, the actual rhythms of verse lines. When a metrical pattern is fairly regular, meter also works before the fact by creating an expectation which we enjoy hearing fulfilled or, sometimes, take as fulfilled even when it isn't (the convention we call "promotion"). In that sense at least, meter and speech are interactive, with meter providing a formality that affects the way in which we respond to the fluidity of speech.

Historically, in English, there were taken to be four basic metrical patterns, each given its name by the foot that mainly composed it: iambic (‿ ⁄), trochaic (⁄ ‿), anapestic (‿ ‿ ⁄), dactylic (⁄ ‿ ‿). Five iambs fitting together, for instance, Lego-like, measure an iambic pentameter line; and so on. To keep a pattern from becoming monotonous, occasionally one of the other feet may replace a basic foot without really changing the pattern (the convention we call "substitution"). At least two other feet, pyrrhic (‿ ‿) and spondee (⁄ ⁄), which can't form a pattern, may also replace a basic foot. Substitutions supply a significant part of lines' rhythmic variety, allowing more of the fluidity of speech and creating expressive gestures in the rhythm. Substitution works, because we do not experience the pattern as broken by the variants. The system of feet is like having six slightly different "inches" that can be used interchangeably.

This traditional English meter coalesced from (and describes) the successful practice of poets. Essentially not prescriptive, it nonetheless guides later poets and evolves as they write new poems successfully. From our present perspective, for instance, it does not seem very useful to distinguish between the four metrical patterns which, given substitution, have always in some measure—and increasingly—overlapped. Since 1557 (the publication of Tottel's *Miscellany*) iambic has been the principal and now seems the one essential pattern. With the experience of many more poems, we may discard the dactyl as an English foot without loss, replacing it among the six English feet with the bacchic (‿ ⁄ ⁄), which has long had a hidden presence in our verse. Robert Pinsky

(66) also finds the dactyl "unnecessary."

The twentieth century has been a time of great flux and experimentation in poetry. New kinds of verse seemed to be written *outside* the traditional system. Since they were invariably written in reference to that system, however, they will likely come to seem a further evolution within it. That is, "free" verse will turn out also to be metrical, measurable, within the same system.

Meantime, syllabic meter and accentual meter have been put forward as measuring (and justifying) some of the new, theoretically nonmetrical verse. As their names suggest, these "meters" are merely spun-off elements of traditional accentual-syllabic meter. One counts *only* syllables, with no regard to the number or arrangement of stresses: te-te-te-te-te-te-te-te-te-te, and so on. The other counts only stresses, with no regard to the number or arrangement of unstressed syllables: thump-thump-thump-thump-thump-thump, and so on.

Neither approximates or measures actual rhythms or anything else of importance or interest about verse lines; and since the determination of stress inevitably turns arbitrary or subjective, the second cannot even count stresses reliably and, in fact, measures nothing at all.

Traditional meter has long since developed simple ways of absorbing the problems involved in counting the syllables and accents of English. Let's look at the problems and these solutions—and at the inadequacy of syllabics and accentuals to account even for passages offered as exemplary of these "meters."

Syllables. These can be counted. Ambiguities are few: words like "fire" or "flower" may be either one or two syllables in speech, even for the same speaker—an oddity that Shakespeare apparently plays on in Sonnet 124:

$$\text{/} \quad \cup \quad \cup \quad \text{/} \quad \cup \quad \text{/} \quad \cup \quad \text{/} \quad \cup \quad \text{/} \quad \cup$$

Weeds a | mong weeds, | or flowers | with flow | ers gath | er'd

But this seems a minor difficulty, and poets as dissimilar as Marianne Moore and Philip Levine have found counting syllables a useful resistance in writing verse. But that is a quite different thing from syllabics as a meter, since it turns out that exact syllable-count doesn't matter much in English because we can't really *hear* it. Our attention keeps being distracted by hearing and counting stresses. English prosody was confused about counting syllables once before, roughly between 1500 and 1800—from whenever changes in the language made Chaucer's meter unintelligible until the appearance of poems like Blake's "The Sick Rose," Southey's "The Cross Roads," and Coleridge's "The Rime of the Ancient Mariner."

The first half of the sixteenth century was a time of great metrical uncertainty and experimentation. Wyatt (1503–1542), for instance, could write

They fle from me that sometyme did me seke

and, in the next line, the metrically almost unintelligible

With naked fote stalking in my chambre.

As John Thompson points out (2), "Wyatt seems to have been the first poet to use [the iambic line] in modern English to any extent, his way of using it is hard to define, and no explanation of his practice has ever been generally accepted." Probably, in the second line here, he was just counting ten syllables on the model of Romance syllabism which had come to England with the Normans in 1066 and was powerfully renewed, for Wyatt, by the example of the Petrarchan sonnet. Only in Tottel's *Miscellany* did iambic emerge "clearly as the guiding metrical pattern" (Thompson 3). Tottel's editor (or editors) took pains not only to regularize Wyatt's pattern of stresses but also to correct his syllable counts where these were irregular. Thus, Wyatt's "This maketh me at home to hounte *and to hawke*" was repaired to read "... to hunt *and hauke*," banishing the anapest.

The new iambic consensus represented in Tottel's *Miscellany* was more an iron law than a guiding principle. It imposed on literary verse a restriction to disyllabic feet and a strict equivalence of syllables from line to line. This consensus accomplished much. It reconciled two tempting (and competing) metrical systems which English poets and readers knew—classical foot-meter and Romance syllabism. It firmly established iambic, based on stress rather than on quantity, as the natural pattern for the system of English verse. And the flowering that followed quickly proved the value of the pruning.

But this clarification came at a cost. It pushed aside for 250 years what Jakob Schipper (97) called "the more or less regular iambic-anapestic metre" into which the Old English alliterative line had transformed itself well before Wyatt. We know this "iambic-anapestic" verse in "Western Wind" (circa 1500)—"And I *in my bed* again"—and of course in Frost's "The Road Not Taken."

The poet George Gascoigne wrote faithfully within the restricting iambic-syllabic compromise, but he saw the loss. In 1575, in "Certain Notes of Instruction Concerning the Making of Verse or Ryme in English" recalling "our father Chaucer," he noted:

[W]ho so ever do peruse and well consider his workes, he shall finde that although his lines are not alwayes of one selfe same number of Syllables, yet beyng redde by one that hath understanding, the longest verse and that which hath most Syllables in it, will fall (to the eare) correspondent unto that whiche hath fewest sillables in it: and like wise that whiche hath in it fewest syllables, shalbe founde yet to consist of woordes that have suche naturall sounde, as may seeme equall in length to a verse which hath many [more] sillables of lighter accentes. And surely I can lament that wee are fallen into such a playne and simple manner of wryting, that there is none other foote used but one.... (467–68)

George Puttenham also accepted the iambic-syllabic compromise in *The Arte of English Poesie* (1589), arguing capably against classical feet in English other than the "*Iambique* and sometime the *Trochaike* which ye shall discerne by their accents, and now and then a *dactill* keeping precisely our symphony of rime without any other mincing measures" (140–41). By "now and then a *dactill*" I suspect he means a trochaic inversion to start a line, because exact syllabic precision was now required. How exact, we may judge by Puttenham's almost comic efforts to justify the extra-syllable (or feminine) ending without disturbing the syllable count. This exception is allowable, he says (85), "for that the sharpe accent falles upon the *penultima* or last save one sillible of the verse, which doth so drowne the last, as he seemeth to passe away in maner unpronounced, and so make the verse seem even." He returns to the question (143), adding that the extra-syllable ending "is in a maner drowned and supprest by the flat accent, and shrinks away as it were inaudible and by that meane the odde verse comes almost to be an even in every man's hearing." George Saintsbury (1: 298) describes the strict syllabic consensus as "this strange self-tyranny," noting that "For more than two hundred years it mastered the schools, if not exactly the courts, of the Muses with us; it can be seen almost within the last generation; I am not sure that it has not partisans even now."

And so the seventeenth and eighteenth centuries became the Age of Apostrophes, despite Shakespeare's later anapestic cheating on the stage. A further infusion of heady French influence followed the Restoration in 1660. Dryden remodeled *Anthony and Cleopatra* in *All for Love* (1678). In *The Art of English Poetry* (1702), of which nine editions appeared over sixty years, Edward Bysshe was firm: "The Structure of our Verses, whether Blank or in Rhyme, consists in a certain Number of Syllables; not in Feet compos'd of long and short Syllables, as the verses of the Greeks and Romans" (1). Bysshe neglects to say that accents fall on the even syllables, but he is explicit that, "in a Verse of 10 Syllables," "the Seat of the accent ... must be either on the 2d, 4th, or 6th," thus producing "the Pause," that is, "a Rest or Stop that is made in pronouncing the Verse, and that divides it, as it were, into two parts; each of which is call'd an Hemistich, or Half-Verse" (3–4).

If this sounds a little like a description of French verse, that is because it is. As A. Dwight Culler notes in the introduction to the Augustan Reprint Society facsimile of Bysshe's 1708 edition (from which I have been quoting), Bysshe "took almost his entire prosodical system" from the French section of the *Quatre Traitez de Poësies, Latine, Françoise, Italienne, et Espagnole* (1663) of Claude Lancelot. "Critically," Culler comments, "[Bysshe's 'Rules'] are nothing; but historically, they dominated the popular prosodic thought of the eighteenth century" (iv–v). A vestige of that old authority may be glimpsed even now in the entry for syllabic verse in Babette Deutsch's *Poetry Handbook* (81). She offers as examples, before going on to Marianne Moore, passages of "strictly ten-syllable lines" by Milton and Pope.

Syllabics does not work as a meter in English because we cannot hear the count of syllables. In *The Sounds of Poetry* (128), Robert Pinsky observes of these lines of Moore's "The Fish"—

Of the crow-blue mussel-shells, one keeps ...
The barnacles which encrust the side ...

—that "while my fingers tell me that there are nine syllables in each ..., my ear cannot." In *The Best American Poetry 1990* (275), Richard Wilbur notes that he wrote "the second part of "A Wall in the Woods: Cummington" in syllabics "in hopes of embodying the fluent skittering of the chipmunk." Here are the third and fourth stanzas:

There is no tracing
The leaps and scurries with which
He braids his long castle, ra-
Cing, by gap, ledge, niche

And Cyclopean
Passages, to reappear
Sentry-like on a rampart
Thirty feet from here.

The rhythms, he reports, however, "are apparently strong enough to have disguised, for some good readers, the 5-7-7-5 syllabic pattern." Despite what may be a clue in "ra-/Cing," the section seems from its first line ("He will hear no guff") firmly metrical, mixing 78 iambs or other disyllabic feet with 14 anapests and one bacchic ("his long cas-" in the third line quoted above). The stanzaic pattern of dimeters framing two trimeters is maintained in all but three lines that count one extra foot, like

$$x \ / \quad \cup \ / \quad \cup \ /$$
Thir | ty feet | from here.

Do note the wonderfully burrowing rhymes of Cyc- and *like* in that stanza.

The short of it is, syllabics are as fragile as the quantities of Campion's "Rose Cheek'd Laura," because accents dominate and won't be ignored.

Although proponents of syllabic meter usually advertise it as strict, maintaining "a fixed syllable count," the poems they offer as exemplary often do not keep the count—with nary a word of explanation. For instance, Alfred Corn (118) cites Moore's "The Steeple Jack," quoting stanza 1:

Dürer would have seen a reason for living
in a town like this, with eight stranded whales
to look at; with the sweet sea air coming into your house
on a fine day, from water etched
with waves as formal as the scales
on a fish.

He notes the syllable count of the lines as 11, 10, 14, 8, 8, and 3, which he describes as applying "uniformly throughout the remainder of the poem." But that is not true. Only the fourteen- and one of the eight-syllable lines keep the count. Two *eleven*-syllable lines turn out to have ten and twelve syllables:

cattails, flags, blueberries and spiderwort ...
is not right for the banyan, frangipani, or ...

A *ten*-syllable line has eleven:

place has a school-house, a post-office in a ...

An *eight*-syllable line has nine:

waifs, children, animals, prisoners ...

A *three*-syllable line has four:

at the back door ...

Perhaps Corn has just counted carelessly. More likely, since the problem shows up in virtually every account by proponents of syllabic meter, they haven't really counted at all. Actual, exact syllable count isn't the point. What counts is the idea. It should be possible, on occasion, for a divergence from the fixed syllable-count to be a significant variation, as substitution in metrical poems may effect a meaningful lilt in rhythm. But with syllabics, since we can't hear small changes in the count, the effect must be intellectual, not rhythmical, as with Moore's *ten*-syllable line in a nine-syllable position in "The Mind Is an Enchanting Thing": "it's conscientious inconsistency." In any case, a reader would be hard put to know, or to recall, the equivalent syllable-counts of lines a stanza apart. Moore herself, when she revised, often didn't bother to restore the syllabic equivalence.

It should also be possible for a poem that doesn't keep the count to be seen as defective or to be judged as no longer in syllabic meter. But proponents steadfastly refuse to describe or even to consider the limits of syllabic divergence. A twenty-nine line poem with a divergence of twenty-seven syllables from the pattern can still be passionately defended as exemplary of syllabic meter (Wallace, "Completing" 319). For proponents to say they didn't notice, or that it doesn't matter, confesses the emptiness of syllabic meter.

Accents. Because what counts as a stress may be problematical or arbitrary, accentual meter—counting lines by stresses only—does not work in modern English. Among the myriad levels of stress in speech, context often determines what we hear as stressed. In itself, for instance, the word "among" carries stress on its second syllable; but both syllables are relatively unstressed in the line of Sonnet 124:

$$\text{/ } \cup \quad \cup \text{ / } \quad \cup \text{ / } \quad \cup \text{ / } \quad \cup \text{ / } \quad \cup$$
Weeds a | mong weeds, | or flowers | with flow | ers gath | er'd

Just as anapests and bacchics let traditional meter deal with variability in the count of syllables, so spondees, bacchics (again), and promotion give it ways to absorb the ambiguities of stress. The genius of this homegrown accentual-syllabic meter is that the number of syllables in equivalent lines, or the number of stresses, or both, may vary; and we can nonetheless identify the equivalence and discuss precisely the differences of such lines.

We may remind ourselves how elastically our meter works with stresses. Consider Ben Jonson's "Song" from *Cynthia's Revels:*

> Slow, slow, fresh fount, keepe time with my salt teares;
> Yet slower, yet, ô faintly gentle springs:
> List to the heavy part the musique beares,
> > Woe weepes out her divisions, when shee sings.
> > Droupe hearbs, and flowers,
> > Fall griefe in showers;
> > Our beauties are not ours:
> > > O, I could still
> (Like melting snow upon some craggie hill,)
> > > drop, drop, drop, drop,
> Since natures pride is, now, a wither'd Daffodill.

Lines 1, 2, 3, and 9 are pentameters, the first with nine stresses:

$$/ \quad / \quad / \quad / \quad / \quad / \quad \cup \quad / \quad / \quad /$$

Slow, slow, | fresh fount, | keepe time | with my | salt teares

The others have only five stresses, though each line varies their arrangement a little; and in line 9 the clearly weakest stress, virtually a promotion, centers the line (and hill?) with its melting:

$$\cup \quad / \quad \cup \quad / \quad \cup \, (/) \quad \cup \quad / \quad \cup \quad /$$

(Like melt | ing snow | upon | some crag | gie hill,)

Spondees ("Droupe hearbs," "Fall griefe") give the dimeters of lines 5 and 6 three stresses, which is the number in the (similarly indented) trimeter of line 7. A comparable linking appears in the flush-left lines, the last of which, also slowed by the emphatic commas, is a somewhat surprising hexameter—its six feet and six stresses registering the poem's heavy rhythm in a somewhat different way.

Traditional meter counts these lines easily and scansion provides a useful way to discuss both their equivalences and their differences. We have no difficulty tracking the iambic stress-positions that measure line 1, or recognizing as dimeters lines 5, 6, 8, 10. It wouldn't change the equivalences, though it might refocus discussion, if someone reported hearing as stressed "Yet" in line 2, "Our" or "not" in line 7, or "some" in line 9—or didn't hear stresses on "my" in line 1, "when" in line 4, or "-on" in line 9. In short, traditional scansion absorbs a good deal of variability in our perception of stress.

Accentual meter can absorb none. In that system of counting, lines 9 and 10 are equivalent *if* we agree that "upon" receives no stress; otherwise not. And our agreement would tell us nothing about the rhythm of the two "equal" lines: "(Like melting snow upon some craggie hill,)" and "drop, drop, drop, drop."

At one point, Corn shows a healthy skepticism (21–22, his italics): "the main problem with using stress alone as a basis for meter is that there is too much room for disagreement about which syllables actually *receive* stress." Nonetheless, he buys the system; and lest readers not have audio recordings to check the stressing, he advises

poets using accentual meter to mark the stronger stresses and not to leave us in doubt as to where they fall. (Granted, such visual markers are a distraction as we read a poem; but perhaps they could be indicated in a footnote.)

Along with "Christabel," he mentions as "important examples" of accentual meter Auden's "Epithalamium," albeit without discussing or scanning any of either poem, though he then scans a bit of Auden's "His Excellency."

"Christabel" is ever a historical landmark for proponents of modern accentual meter, despite the fact that the poem is definitively *not* in accentual meter. Coleridge's sloppy account may give a false impression when he claims its meter as "being founded on a new principle; namely, that of counting in each line only the accents, not the syllables." But the latter are in fact also counted and, as he adds, "may vary from seven to twelve"—which is the number one would expect for accentual-syllabic tetrameter that can range from all iambic (with perhaps an omitted initial syllable) to all anapestic. The unstressed syllables fall quite regularly, either one or two, between the stresses:

```
x   /    ᴜ /    ᴜ /    ᴜ /
Hath | a tooth | less mas | tiff bitch ... (line 7)
  ᴜ   ᴜ  /   ᴜ (/)  /   ᴜᴜ  /   ᴜ (/) /
Save the grass | and green herbs | underneath | the old tree ... (line 542)
```

(Note the bacchic feet in line 542, no doubt felt as anapests in 1816.) Though it doesn't change the metrical identity of the poem, line 277 has thirteen syllables: "And didst bring her home | with thee | in love | and char | ity." As Deutsch remarks (80), "Coleridge's arithmetic was not as good as his ear for rhythm."

Nor is a "new principle" involved. In the song that opens *Marriage à la Mode* (1673), Dryden combined iambic and anapestic lines in parallel quatrains of a single stanza:

> Why should a foolish marriage vow,
> > Which long ago was made,
> Oblige us to each other now,
> > When passion is decayed?
> We loved, and we loved, as long as we could,
> > Till our love was loved out in us both;
> But our marriage is dead, when the pleasure is fled:
> > 'Twas pleasure first made it an oath.

(Note the bacchics in lines 6 and 8: "was loved out" and "-ure first made.") Much earlier, in the February eclogue of *The Shepheardes Calender* (1579), Spenser experiments with tetrameters loosely mixing iambs and anapests. A few lines:

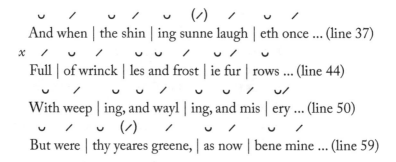

And when | the shin | ing sunne laugh | eth once ... (line 37)

Full | of wrinck | les and frost | ie fur | rows ... (line 44)

With weep | ing, and wayl | ing, and mis | ery ... (line 50)

But were | thy yeares greene, | as now | bene mine ... (line 59)

(Note the bacchics in lines 37 and 59.) Spenser is using the "iambic-anapestic metre" into which, as Schipper pointed out, the old native, alliterative, accentual meter had been transformed long since. This mixed measure, set aside by the compromise of 1557, was perceived as "common and popular" and so was thereafter "seldom admitted above stairs" (Saintsbury 2: 420) Yet Saintsbury notes passionately (1: 174),

> In all folk-song and ballad-writing it perseveres, while the persistent and
> ferocious persecution of it, and the critical disapproval of it, for two hundred

years and more, cannot drown it or burn it or bury it. Earth and water and fire may combine against it, but it abides victoriously in the air, the element of poetry, and descends again at the right time.

It was there, in song and ballad, that Dryden and for less trivial purposes Blake, Southey, and Coleridge found it.

So the historical antecedents cited by proponents of modern accentual meter are spurious. To assess how well the meter works, let's look at Corn's other examples.

Auden's "Epithalamion" is a ceremonial poem in eight sixteen-line stanzas, meticulously rhymed. (Auden misses with one rhyme pair in stanza 4: *more-saw*, but matches it exactly in the poem's only other miss, in stanza 7: *law-war.*) As to meter, Corn doesn't even say what the poem's stress-norm is, but we may usefully try the first four lines of the last stanza:

> ⁄   ⁄   ⁄
> Vowing to redeem the State,
>   ⁄   ⁄   ⁄   ⁄
> Now let every girl and boy
>   ⁄   ⁄
> To the heaven of the Great
>   ⁄   ⁄   ⁄
> All their prayers and praises lift ...

Plainly, the lines are not counted by speech stresses, as *two, three, and four* of these show up. Moreover, if we consider promotions on "to" in the first line and on "To" and "of" in the third, the lines all scan as iambic tetrameter with the initial syllable omitted—like much of Milton's "L'Allegro." And that, with a scattering of anapests, *is* the meter of the poem, except for the dimeters (like "Wish us joy") in which each stanza ends. The poem's ceremonial rigidity seems both remarkable and deliberate. "Epithalamion" in no way bears out Corn's assertion that its form is accentual meter.

Corn also finds what he is looking for, even though it isn't there, in Auden's "His Excellency." He scans six of the poem's thirty-one lines this way:

And the ROUGH FUture
Of an inTRANsiGEANT
And the beTRAYing SMILE,
BeTRAYing, but a SMILE:

That that is NOT, is NOT;
ForGET, forGET.

"Nearly everyone," he says,

> will agree that the syllables notated here in upper case all receive stress, and we see that there are two of these per line. Meanwhile, the syllable count is as few as four and as many as six, with stresses falling in several different places: therefore this is accentual verse.

Actually, everyone should doubt that stress on "GEANT" since, unlike (say) "intoxicate," the word "intransigeant" doesn't carry a secondary stress and, moreover, the line sounds awful. Aware of some difficulty, Corn explains—irrelevantly as well as inaccurately—that "accentual-*syllabic* meter (as opposed to purely accentual meter) would certainly place stress" on that syllable. But the difficulty is that he has miscopied the line: "Of an intransigeant *nature* / And the betraying smile."

And he mistakes the poem's meter, which is clearly a mixture of accentual-syllabic dimeters and trimeters. A line like

$$\breve{\ }\ \diagup\ \ \diagup\ \ \diagup\ \ \breve{\ }\ \diagup$$
Let him | not cease | to praise,

won't reduce to two-beat accentual. And there is plenty of "room for disagreement" about "but" and "that" in the third and fourth lines he quotes. Once one uses the proper template, other lines fall into place:

$$\diagup\ \ \breve{\ }\ \ \breve{\ }\ \ \diagup$$
All that | was thought
$$\breve{\ }\ \diagup\ \ \breve{\ }\ \diagup\ \ \diagup\ \diagup$$
As like | as not | is not;
$$\breve{\ }\ \ \diagup\ \ \breve{\ }\ \ \breve{\ }\ \ \breve{\ }\ \diagup$$
When noth | ing was | enough
$$\breve{\ }\ \diagup\ \ \breve{\ }\ \diagup$$
But love, | but love,
$$\breve{\ }\ \ \breve{\ }\ \ \diagup\ \ \diagup\ \ \breve{\ }$$
And the | rough fu | ture
$$\breve{\ }\ \breve{\ }\ \ \breve{\ }\diagup\ \ \breve{\ }\ \breve{\ }\ \diagup\ \ \breve{\ }$$
Of an | intran | sigeant na | ture,

$(\diagup)$ ⌣   ⌣

And the | betray | ing smile,

⌣ ╱   ⌣ ╱   ⌣ ╱
Betray | ing, but | a smile:

⌣ ╱   ⌣ ╱   ╱ ╱
That that | is not, | is not;

⌣ ╱   ⌣ ╱
Forget, | forget.

Even the poem's ironic rhymes, off-rhymes, and identities begin to appear.

Though very like a meter, neither accentuals nor syllabics will function as one in English.

The Metrical Laws of Ted Hughes

The Poet Laureate of England devotes most of the long, recent essay "Myths, Metres, Rhythms" to a reinterpretation of all English verse based on two "laws."[13] His starting point is the last line of an early poem, "The Horses" (1957), to which a reviewer objected at the time and the meter of which Hughes believes his reinterpretation will explain and justify. Since Hughes's scansion of the line "Hearing the horizons endure" is more than interesting, I will come to it (as Hughes does) in due course. First, for the rest of English verse, which he redivides between "orthodox metre" and "unorthodox metre."

"Orthodox metre" includes free verse as well as strict iambic pentameter (and so on). In this meter,

> each line moves from beginning to end under a single metrical law, using each syllable's 'natural quantity' (the emphasis and time-value given to it in natural, conversational speech) in such a way that the metrical law is self-evident and cannot be mistaken. (320–21)

He does allow one variation—what we usually call a promotion (that is, counting a stress in a position where natural quantity isn't doing the job)—as in a line of the passage Hughes cites from Addison's "Letter from Italy, to the Rt. Honourable Charles Lord Halifax, 1701":

---

[13] Appointed in 1984, Ted Hughes remained England's Poet Laureate until his death in 1998. *-Eds.*

```
        x  /  x  /  x   x   x  /   x    /
```
Conspire to trouble your repose with rhyme

The line, Hughes says, "can be read without this deformity only if the voice imposes, forcibly, *a musical interpretation* on the possibilities" (322, his italics).

There are a number of similar variations in traditional meter which Hughes (perhaps pointedly) ignores: the common trochaic inversion (or the common omission of the unstressed initial syllable) in the first foot of iambic lines, and the common substitution of (say) anapests or spondees for paradigmatic iambs. Although "imposing, forcibly," like "deformity," seems to overstate the difficulty of these minor conventional adjustments, they all would require "a musical interpretation." And since just such musical interpretations or impositions turn out to be the characteristic feature of "unorthodox metre," one wonders whether "orthodox metre" isn't limited to free verse and *completely* regular metrical verse.

I suspect that Hughes's definition is faulty. If the "single metrical law, using each syllable's 'natural quantity'" also implies a strict alternation of unstressed and stressed syllables, most free verse won't fit the category. If it doesn't imply that (as Hughes's use of the term "the law of 'natural quantities'" in discussing unorthodox meter certainly doesn't), then free verse is the only verse following that "single law" of quantities and so—very oddly—is the only verse that fits the category of "orthodox metre."

Coming to "unorthodox metre," Hughes describes it this way: "It lives within a tension between two laws: the law of 'natural quantities' and the law of the 'hidden' pattern of stresses." The line doesn't move "under a single simple law of 'natural quantities.'" "Instead, it explores its way through a field of flexing contrapuntal tensions between two simultaneous but opposed laws—that is to say, between a law of 'natural quantities' set in opposition to the law of a fixed, basic metric pattern" (336). His first instance of unorthodox meter is Coleridge's "Christabel," from which he cites a "crucial" line in which he finds only three stresses rather than the required four:

```
            /        /        /
```
Which is lord of thy utterance, Christabel

The voice, therefore, "is whipped forcibly into the dance step by the law of the beat" and must pronounce "Chrîstábĕl." If this seems very like the promotion required to fix the "deformity" in Addison's line, it is—the difference apparently being that now Hughes admires the slight variation and its effect.

I have questions about his interpretation of the meter of "Christabel," but they will be clearer after we consider his second example of unorthodox meter.

Having noted that Coleridge's "new principle" of counting only stresses "turns out to be the very same thing as Hopkins's 'sprung rhythm'" (329), Hughes goes onto line 6 of "The Windhover." "Read in the usual way, under a simple, single, metrical law, following natural quantities" (337), Hughes predicts (correctly) that an orthodox reader would come up with

As a skate's heel sweeps smooth on a bow-bend: the hurl and gliding

(The law of quantities here, note, seems not to imply alternating unstress and stress.) Hughes miscounts, calling this a "seven stress interpretation" (337), but perhaps he means only that a reader might scan the line as having seven feet, following natural quantities and the normal conventions of foot-meter, as I do:

As a | skate's heel | sweeps smooth | on a | bow-bend: | the hurl | and glid | ing

An unusual line—ending in two iambs, but having two of the familiar pyrrhic/spondee combinations (which we know in Shakespeare's Sonnets) as well as a third spondee and an extra-syllable ending. If we manage with the two iambs of

When to | the ses | sions of | sweet si | lent thought

we can certainly credit Hopkins's line, finding part of its special rhythmic or musical effect in the shift from expected pentameter to heptameter—it approximates the old "fourteener."

Hughes will have none of that, though, insisting—oddly—that "as far as accents go, the whole sonnet is orthodox," as in its pentametric first line: "I caught this morning morning's minion, king-" (339). So he requires demotions (I insert the x's):

As a skate's | heel sweeps smooth | on a bow- | bend: the hurl | and gliding

The artificiality of repressing the values of spoken English, and so of turning

Hopkins's line to four anapests and an iamb, seems to me a mixed blessing—particularly since the process is exactly the one used to produce the doggerel of Clement Moore' s "'Twas the Night Before Christmas," making a tetrameter (with false anapests) of

˘   /   ˘ ˘ /   ˘ ˘ /   ˘˘ /

The moon | on the breast | of the new- | fallen snow

which in a more serious context might register as a pentameter:

˘   /   ˘ ˘ /   ˘ ˘ / / / ˘ /

The moon | on the breast | of the | new-fal | len snow

Hughes, however, waxes ecstatic over turning the line into doggerel:

> [T]o a modern ear the line now springs into life in a new way. It becomes a marvelously suggestive, intricate, clear sequence of actions that mimes, very precisely, a particular sequence in the bird's flight. That "skate's heel" phrase, formerly heavy with the G force of the skater's momentum kneeling into the long bend, is now light, electrified, aloft. It reproduces the forceful, slicing parabola of the small falcon's body, tensed and compacted by the pressure of the wind against it, wings half-closed, half-open, and braced. This physically intimate sense of a taut, hurtling missile steered at unnatural speed by a crouching pilot, on a veering balletic arc, against and through and over a hard, invisible resistance, is jammed into the reader's effort of suppressing and forcibly overriding the bumping turbulence of heavy beats that the words of the whole line, by natural quantity and stubborn, refractory shape, try to assert against the internal assertion of only five accents. This same, slightly off-balance, brilliantly constantly-corrected balance produces those flickering, stabbing touches of the wings, trimming the ailerons, that carry the bird across and up off the page like a hallucination.
>
> Once the reader is faced with performing this flight, there is no way to get out of it. The natural quantities of the words used and the five stress law of the hidden pattern are braced against each other in a wind-tunnel of counterpointed tensions so extreme that the voice is snatched beyond kinaesthetic co-operation into something more like anaerobic emergency. The reader has to get air-borne—has to levitate into song....
>
> This leaping of the gulf, from speech into song, breaks a sound-barrier....

And so on for two paragraphs (340–341).

Hughes's allegiance to what he calls "the new, modern wave of the accentual tradition" (343) involves a good deal of disingenuousness (to credit him at least with knowing what he is doing). The second law, defined initially as "the law of the 'hidden' *pattern* of stresses" and "the law of a fixed, basic metric *pattern*" (my italics), became instantly "the law of the beat" (336); then, it became "the five stress law of the hidden pattern" (340); soon, it becomes "the hidden law of the five stress line," "the five stress basic pattern" (341), merely "the required five beats" (346), and so on. Beats, in the unvaryingly correct number, *are* the pattern. The placement of unstressed syllables, if any, and thus any real pattern in the pacing of the stresses, are theoretically irrelevant. Hence, Hughes's iron refusal to consider the option of treating Hopkins's line as having seven feet, although poets have often used lines of varying length in plainly metrical poems—Herbert in "The Collar," Arnold in "Dover Beach," Frost in "After Apple-Picking"—not to mention the hexameters and tetrameters with which Shakespeare occasionally paces the pentameters of *King Lear* (about which, more shortly).

In fact, without acknowledging it, Hughes uses pattern—the anapestic pacing I pointed out—to fix on syllables to stress and demote in Hopkins's line. Picking five of the eight natural stresses is hardly a foregone question, and yet the choice isn't discussed. An unorthodox reader might well opt, say, for stressing the clause's subject and verb, which Hughes demotes:

$$x \quad x \quad x \quad / \quad / \quad \quad x \quad \quad x \ x \ / \quad x \quad \quad x \quad / \quad x \quad x \ x$$
As a skate's heel sweeps smooth on a bow-bend: the hurl and gliding

Or—and why not?—

$$x \ x \quad / \quad \quad / \quad / \quad \quad x \quad \quad x \ x \ / \quad x \quad \quad x \quad / \quad x \quad x \ x$$
As a skate's heel sweeps smooth on a bow-bend: the hurl and gliding

in which smoothing down "smooth" and, after the stress on "hurl," leveling the stress-bump on "glid-" would wonderfully mime the line's actions.

It seems clear, similarly, that Hughes's electing to find his fourth stress on the word "Christabel" responds to that line's pattern as foot-meter and to the rhyme—rather than, say, on the thematically more meaningful "thy":

$$/ \quad \quad / \ / \quad \quad \quad \quad /$$
Which is lord of thy utterance, Christabel

It is also hard to suppose that Hughes, hearing the word "Christabel" as having naturally only one stressed syllable, would nonetheless leave "-bel" unstressed in this line with its four other natural stresses:

> /　　/　　/　　　/
> Hush, beating heart of Christabel

But promoting "-bel" and demoting one of the natural stresses would seem merely arbitrary—indeed, holding to a real metrical pattern.

It is worth looking again at Hughes's claim that in "Christabel" the rhythm of natural speech "is locked into that four stress pattern" (333) by which the voice "is whipped forcibly into the dance step by the law of the beat" (336)—adding stresses when they fail to appear as natural quantities, demoting stresses when too many appear. Since I hold that the poem is entirely foot-meter with anapestic substitution—as Schipper saw in describing it as "iambic-anapestic metre" and as Saintsbury saw in dismissing Coleridge's "new principle" contemptuously—I will scan the examples, showing the syllables' natural quantities.

Although foot-meter easily responds to the following trimeters, Hughes may not be entirely comfortable in scanning four stresses in

> ᵕ　　/　　ᵕ ᵕ　ᵕ　/
> How drow | sily | it crew ...
> ᵕ　ᵕ /　ᵕ ᵕ　ᵕ　/
> To the la | dy by | her side ...

Nor is it easy to guess which two natural stresses Hughes or his "liberated," unorthodox reader will demote in each of these lines:

> /　ᵕ　　/　　/　　/ /　ᵕ　/
> Sixteen | short howls, | not o | ver loud ...
> ᵕ　ᵕ　　/　　　/　　　/　　ᵕ /　　/　　/
> Of the huge, | broad-breast | ed, old | oak tree ...

He will easily find his four stresses in this dimeter:

> /　　/　　　　/　　/
> Tu—whit!—— | Tu—whoo!

But how about the same owls in

$$\cup \quad / \quad \cup \quad / \quad \cup \quad / \quad \cup \quad /$$
From cliff | and tower, | tu—whoo! | tu—whoo!
$$/ \quad / \quad / \quad / \quad \cup \quad / \quad \cup \quad /$$
Tu—whoo! | tu—whoo! | from wood | and fell ...

without diminishing the mimetic effect or making the lines unsayable without stresses on "cliff," "tower," "wood," and "fell."

To fast-forward, Hughes tortures a tetrameter from *King Lear*, which I would scan:

$$/ \quad / \quad \cup \quad / \quad / \quad / \quad \cup \quad /$$
Hear, Na | ture, hear! | Dear God | dess, hear!

Because the line occurs in a pentameter context, however, Hughes insists on reading it as having *five* beats. So he needs to demote only "Dear," which does little harm, although there is some loss as to meaning and in muting the internal rhyme. His main mischief is in attributing two wildly absurd scansions to an orthodox reader following only the law of natural quantities. Such a reader, Hughes says, "might well find" (346):

$$/ \quad x \; x \quad / \quad x \quad / \; x \quad /$$
Hear, Nature, hear! Dear Goddess, hear ...

$$x \quad / \; x \quad / \quad x \quad / \; x \quad /$$
Hear, Nature, hear! Dear Goddess, hear!

Like choosing a passage by Addison to represent orthodox meter, these misrepresentations of the normal speech stresses on "goddess" and "nature" must be counted as willful.

Similarly, Hughes brings Wyatt into the unorthodox fold by requiring five stresses for lines easily read as tetrameters (355):

$$\cup \quad / \quad \cup \quad / \quad \cup \quad \cup \quad / \quad \cup \quad / \quad \cup$$
That nowe | are wyld | and do not | remem | bre ...
$$\cup \quad / \quad / \quad / \quad \cup \quad / \quad / \quad / \quad \cup$$
It was | no dreme: | I lay | brode wak | ing ...

Stranger than tetrameters in a pentameter context, surely, is his accentual
scansion of the first, for which he borrows Hopkins's notion of "in some man-
ner distributing" a single stress over several syllables (362):

That nowe are wyld and do not remembre

"Musical interpretation," he says (363),

> has to brace the required three heavy stresses "in sane manner" against [the
> natural quantities], and once again forcibly slow the whole phrase down. It
> does this by letting that "wyld"—which is the peak in the power graph of
> the whole line—requisition the "and" as a carrier of its own stress.

This, he adds, "'fetches out' the musical beauty and truth of feeling."

We come now to the final couplet of Hughes's "The Horses," a poem in
which "the 'governing principle' is a line of five accents" (364). (He appears not
to like the term "law" applied to him.) Others, he reports, "always scanned" the
penultimate line:

Between the streams ( ) and the red clouds, hearing curlews

Demoting the natural stress on "clouds," however, isn't enough for Hughes. "In
my own head I had never heard the line as anything but" (365):

Between the streams ( ) and the red clouds, hearing curlews

We are thus empowered by the novel device of scanning as stressed even a
pause without punctuation and dividing a prepositional phrase.

He then offers two scansions of the poem's last line. "The shape of the
phrase," he says, "oscillates somewhere between interpretations that look
slightly different—but only as two parts of a harmony. For another reader I
would scan it ..."

     /   / / /   /
Hearing the horizons endure

in which "hor-" is the only truly unstressed syllable. "But," he continues,

> to my ear, spellbound as it is by the unorthodox tradition, the most natural thing is to hear it slightly more plastically shaped, almost (but not quite) as:

     / x   x   x / /   / /
Hearing the horizons endure

> ... the final four stresses heap up one from behind the other, all prolonged and all at different levels, until the last one, "-ure," is held into the blue distance, like the recession of horizons behind horizons in the Pennine moorland being described.

It might be diverting to discover how Hughes finds the required five stresses in earlier lines of the poem, in, for instance,

Making no sound

and especially in the line

I turned

I would be disappointed if in the end he hid behind that "*in general* the 'governing principle' is a line of five accents" (my italics), opting out of a law he applies liberally to everyone else, including Wyatt, Shakespeare, Coleridge, and Hopkins.

III. Dragons in the Verse Patch

> If Shakespeare had never existed we would not miss his works, for there would be nothing missing.
>
> —Richard Poirier, *The Renewal of Literature*

In *The Work of Poetry* (1997), John Hollander offers a startling judgment: that our present is a time of pervasive prosodic uncertainty and confusion, like that spanning the end of the fifteenth century and the beginning of the sixteenth. For poets of his generation, whose first books appeared not long after 1950 (146),

> verse was still part of our verbal culture. We all knew a good deal about verse, and whether we wrote free verse or not, it all came from choices made in light, not in darkness. By this I mean that an ear for various modes of English verse could allow one to tune in on one's own rhythmic wavelength. Not so subsequent generations. Now we are in a time rather like the hundred years before Surrey—when Chaucer's pentameter line had been forgotten, and tone-deaf attempts to write it produced with tin ears. The computer on which I have been writing these remarks establishes, under the heading "style," a typeface it calls "the default." In generations subsequent to ours, all but some of the youngest poets of today write in a default mode, they are bound to free verse because they can hear nothing else, rather than coming to it—and to a mode of it all their own—by knowledgeable choice. This is one of the reasons why poetry has gotten so toneless.

For this sorry state Hollander blames primary school teachers who no longer require kids to memorize and recite verse (174). He blames "professionalized academics in departments of literature" who have let poetry "rapidly [become] marginal" among their concerns (150), a charge Hollander ironically (or confessionally) tropes in a sentence about his students' recalling "many of the texts themselves, of Stevenson's *Child's Garden of Verses*" (129). (Not poems, *texts*.) So instruction in the technicalities of verse has largely shifted from courses in literature to courses in creative writing, whose teachers he blames for running workshops as "free-form group therapy sessions" (150).

But Hollander overlooks the obvious: the prosodic uncertainty and confusion at the end of the twentieth century is a result of prosodic confusion and uncertainty. On the free verse side he sees the problem (*Work* 173):

> One trouble with the teaching of verse writing today is that there is no useful conventional terminology for the description, taxonomy, and analysis of different modes of free verse.

On the metrical side, it has been a half-century roiled by frequent and enormous novelty. The fragile consensus that existed in 1950 has been shredded by linguists like Trager and Smith, Halle and Keyser, Derek Attridge, and—recently—Richard D. Cureton (*Rhythmic Phrasing in English Verse* [1991]). Poet-metrists like Timothy Steele and Alfred Corn have adopted four levels of stress for scanning, unsettling, or upending the traditional binary system. Two new meters, syllabics and accentuals, have gained wide currency, though both are unproved and of dubious value. Lifted from *The New Princeton Encyclopedia of Poetry and Poetics* by one of its editors, T.V.F. Brogan, *The New Princeton Handbook of Poetic Terms* has no entry for meter at all. Scansion has become slapdash, arbitrary, or willfully impressionistic.

Meter is a convention (or system of conventions) that, in order to work, depends on both agreement and ready compliance. Alternative scansions are sometimes unavoidable, but the LCD (lowest common denominator) rule always applies—that is, we should opt for the scansion that is simplest and closest to the metrical norm. When influential critics deliberately trash the conventions, Hollander doesn't have far to look for a significant cause of the present prosodical mess. Let's consider instances of misscansions by Paul Fussell, Harvey Gross and Robert McDowell, Annie Finch, Helen Vendler, and Hollander himself (along with a cameo appearance by Northrop Frye). Supposing that these critics would rather be accused of mischief than of ignorance, I have chosen my title to give them due regard.

(1) In *Poetic Meter and Poetic Form* (34–35), wishing to demonstrate how "An unanticipated reversal in the rhythm … implies a sudden movement, often of discovery or illumination," Fussell records the opening of Robert Frost's "Come In" this way:

```
˘ ˘ /      ˘ ˘ /      ˘ ˘ /
As I came | to the edge | of the woods,
  /     ˘ ˘         /
Thrush music | | —hark!
```

After the anapests of line 1, Fussell notes, "Frost reverses completely to a dactylic movement, and then presents a caesura and a monosyllable as the equivalent of a complete foot."

This account of line 2 is inaccurate in several ways. The word *music* cannot be scanned as two unstressed syllables; it has an unambiguous speech stress. Except in doggerel, where metrical pattern overrides natural inflection to produce an artificial rhythm, demotion is not a convention of English meter. (Students are well advised to *begin* a scansion by marking the stresses they hear in speech, as these will provide an armature for assessing the rest of each line.) Moreover, we do not construe feet to conform to *phrasing*. As Fussell acknowledges, when he scans a line by Pope on the very next page, a foot may contain a caesural pause. So there is no dactyl. There isn't even a "dactylic movement." We must scan spondee | iamb:

```
      /    /  ˘  /
Thrush mus | ic—hark!
```

For more than thirty years now, Fussell's deliberate errors have been standard instruction for tens and tens and tens of thousands of students, contributing to the prosodic confusion Hollander identifies.

(2) Hard cases make bad law. W.H. Auden's "Musée des Beaux Arts" has been characterized variously as free verse, as metrical, and as beginning metrically before it "ambles into prose." Although my immediate purpose is to present a misscansion of the poem's last two lines by Harvey Gross and Robert McDowell (241–42), I should put my scansion in the record:

```
˘ /    / ˘   ˘ /    ˘ /   ˘ /
About | suffer | ing they | were nev | er wrong,
 ˘  /    / ˘    ˘ /    ˘ /   ˘ /
The Old | Masters: | how well | they un | derstood
˘ /   ˘   ˘/   ˘  /    ˘/    /
Its hu | man posi | tion, how | it takes place
```

˘   /   ˘   /   ˘ /   ˘   ˘ /   ˘ ˘   ˘ /   ˘ ˘

While some | one else | is eat | ing or op | ening | a win | dow or |

/   /   ˘   /   ˘ ˘ /

just walk | ing dul | ly along;

/   ˘   ˘ /   ˘ ˘ /   ˘˘   ˘ /   ˘ ˘   ˘ /   ˘

How, when | the ag | ed are rev | erent | ly, pas | sionate | ly wait | ing

(/) ˘   ˘/   ˘ ˘   /   ˘   /   ˘   ˘ /

For the | mirac | ulous birth, | there al | ways must be

/   ˘   ˘   ˘   /   /   ˘ ˘   /   ˘ ˘   /   ˘   /   ˘

Children | who did | not spec | ially want | it to hap | pen, skat | ing

˘ ˘ /   ˘ ˘   /   ˘ ˘   /

On a pond | at the edge | of the wood:

˘   /   ˘ ˘ /

They nev | er forgot

˘ /   ˘   ˘   /   ˘ /   ˘ (/)   ˘   /   ˘ /

That e | ven the dread | ful mar | tyrdom | must run | its course

/ ˘   / ˘   ˘ /   ˘   /   ˘ /   ˘ /

Any | how in | a corn | er, some | untid | y spot

˘   ˘ /   / /   ˘   ˘   /   ˘ /   ˘ ˘ /   ˘ ˘   /

Where the dogs | go on | with their dog | gy life | and the tor | turer's horse

/ ˘   ˘ /   ˘ (/)   ˘ /   ˘ ˘ /

Scratches | its in | nocent | behind | on a tree.

˘   /   ˘ /   ˘ ˘   ˘ /   ˘   ˘ /   ˘ ˘   /   ˘/

In Breu | ghel's *I* | *carus*, | for in | stance: how ev | erything turns | away

/ /   ˘ ˘   /   ˘ ˘ ˘/   ˘   ˘   /   ˘   /

Quite lei | surely from | the disas | ter; the plough | man may

˘   /   ˘   /   ˘ ˘ /   ˘ /

Have heard | the splash, | the forsak | en cry,

˘ ˘ /   ˘ ˘ /   ˘ ˘ /   ˘ /   ˘ ˘   /   /

But for him | it was not | an impor | tant fail | ure; the | sun shone

˘˘ /   ˘ ˘   ˘   /   / /   ˘/   ˘ /   ˘ ˘   /

As it had | to on | the white | legs dis | appear | ing in | to the green

/ ˘   ˘ ˘   ˘/   ˘ /   ˘˘   /   ˘ /   ˘ /

Water; | and the | expen | sive del | icate ship | that must | have seen

/   ˘   ˘/   ˘ ˘   / /   ˘ /   ˘ ˘ /

Something | amaz | ing, a | boy fall | ing out | of the sky,

˘   /   ˘   ˘ /   ˘ ˘   /   /   ˘/

Had some | where to get | to and | sailed calm | ly on.

Nothing can be gained by lingering over the merely terminological distinction between meter and free verse. The poem is very irregular, with lines ranging from two to ten feet, although a fairly clear norm centers on six pentameters and six hexameters. Rhymes occur twice in adjacent lines (14 and 15, 18 and 19), but are separated by as many as five and six lines (2 and 8, 6 and 13). Line 3 is unrhymed. The poem is also plainly metrical, if we mean measurable in the traditional accentual-syllabic way. I count 55 iambs and 32 anapests, with a scattering of other disyllabic feet. The advantage of information in this metrical description seems unmistakable.

Gross and McDowell scan lines 1–2 as I do, but line 3 this way (they show only stresses, so I take the liberty of inserting breves):

$$\breve{}\; / \quad \breve{}\; \breve{}\; / \quad \breve{} \quad \breve{}\; \breve{}\; / \quad /$$

Its hu | man posi | tion; | how it takes place

They comment: "The unsettling trochee in the second foot of the first two lines and the anomalous third line pull the rhythm away from blank verse" (241). I agree about the divergence from blank verse, but don't find line 3 "anomalous." It is a tetrameter, with (I think properly) an iambic stress on "how" and a bacchic foot in the fourth position. Since the bacchic has only recently been claimed as one of the limited number of standard feet in English meter, Gross and McDowell's difficulty is understandable. They continue: "Succeeding lines amble into prose," and they quote (unscanned) lines 5–8. This seems an inaccurate claim even by their lights, since they credit Whitman's "non-metrical prosody" and explicitly call "mistaken" Eliot's characterization of Whitman as "a great prose writer" (Eliot, "Introduction" 10). Auden's lines are prosy, yes; "prose," no; and, as my scansion shows, amenable to description in metrical terms.

Coming to lines 20–21, Gross and McDowell comment, "The final lines fall in approximate dactyls, suggesting, perhaps, Icarus's spiraling descent":

$$/ \; \breve{} \; \breve{} \quad / \; \breve{} \; \breve{} \quad / \; \breve{} \; \breve{} \quad / \; \breve{} \; \breve{} \quad /$$

Something a | mazing, a | boy falling | out of the | sky,

$$\breve{} \quad / \; \breve{} \; \breve{} \quad / \; \breve{} \; \breve{} \quad / \quad \breve{} \; \breve{} \quad /$$

Had | somewhere to | get to and | sailed calmly | on.

Gross and McDowell go to considerable trouble to achieve this result, and their "approximate" suggests they know they are fudging. As dactylic, both lines end in double catalexis (though the missing unstressed syllables aren't indicated); and presumably initial hypercatalexis is invoked to produce the extra unstressed syllable that, standing outside the foot-scansion, begins line 21. Moreover, entirely improper demotions of speech stresses on "fall-" and on "calm-" are required. That the poem ends as it began, with a quite scannable pentameter, gets lost in the needless shuffle.

(3) The success of lessons like those taught by Fussell and Gross may be found in Annie Finch's *The Ghost of Meter*. Misscanned dactyls are her favorite foot throughout, and though without mentioning Gross, she cites Auden's final line as "the most regular dactylic line in the poem," which she sees as characterized otherwise by "dactylic absence" and, thus, as alluding to the dactylic hexameters of the classical epics (14–15). Here is how Finch interprets a line of Whitman's "Inscription" to *Leaves of Grass*, calling the line "almost perfectly dactylic, with an initial hypermetrical syllable" (39)—scanned as I interpret her intention:

ᵕ / ᵕ ᵕ / ᵕ ᵕ / ᵕ ᵕ / ᵕ ᵕ

Yet | utter the | word Demo | cratic, the | word En-Masse.

Finch persists, although she notes, "The line could also—and perhaps even more properly—be scanned as iambs and anapests."

Or consider a line in "The Waste Land," which Finch describes as introducing "the first consistent dactylic rhythm in the entire poem" (110):

/ ᵕ ᵕ / ᵕ ᵕ / ᵕ ᵕ / ᵕ

Who is the | third who walks | always be | side you?

If we accord "walks" its natural speech and metrical stress, however, there are no dactyls in the line, and no "consistent dactylic rhythm":

/ ᵕ ᵕ / ᵕ / / ᵕ ᵕ / ᵕ

Who is | the third | who walks | always | beside | you?

(4) Hollander himself is a victim or perpetrator of the present prosodical confusion. Although he doesn't go as far as Fussell, Gross, and Finch, who happily mute speech stresses to get the wanted effect, Hollander himself seems drawn to vivid scansion for the last line of this stanza of Stevenson's "Windy Nights":

Whenever the moon and stars are set,
Whenever the wind is high,
All night long in the wind and the wet,
A man goes riding by.
Late in the night when the fires are out,
Why does he gallop and gallop about?

The poem is simply metered, iambic with some anapestic substitution, and the last line may be scanned neutrally with a normal trochaic inversion:

$$\text{/} \quad \cup \quad \cup \text{/} \quad \cup \quad \cup \quad \text{/} \quad \cup \quad \cup \text{/}$$

Why does | he gal | lop and gal | lop about?

But Hollander, commenting on "the three pounding dactyls of the couplet that reinforced the opening d'*dah* da rhythm of 'when*e*ver'" (*Work* 131), seems to prefer

$$\text{/} \quad \cup \quad \cup \quad \text{/} \quad \cup \quad \cup \quad \text{/} \quad \cup \quad \cup \quad \text{/}$$

Why does he | gallop and | gallop a | bout?

I am completely mystified as to how the rhythm of "whenever" is reinforced by "pounding dactyls," and indeed as to why "pounding" anapests wouldn't do as well, since scanning anapests would conform more closely to the metrical pattern of the poem.

This is a sort of scansion which, as recently as 1975 (*Vision and Resonance* 4), tempted Hollander's disapproval:

For example, a student, responding first to the fairly schematic movement of a standard set piece like Andrew Marvell's "Coy Mistress" poem, may exclaim appreciatively over the speeding up of the rhythmic pace of "But at my back I always hear / Time's winged chariot hurrying near" with its dactylic rush, and observe the continuation of the falling rhythm in "And yonder all before us lie / Deserts of vast eternity." Our demythologizing, here using a mode of exorcism no more arcane than historical grammar, would have to dampen his appreciative ardor with the observation that the last of these lines—the original form, "desárts," accented on the second syllable—was still for Marvell quite regularly iambic.

I quote extensively because the questions raised are interesting and because, except for the mistaken ascription of "dactylic," my sympathies go with the student, who I hope held his or her own and is now teaching creative writing somewhere.

I don't know how Marvell pronounced "Desarts," nor how Hollander knows how Marvell pronounced it. But I'd guess that Pope, using the obsolete form in "To roam the howling desart of the Main" (*Odyssey*, IV, 748), put the accent on the first syllable. So conceivably, reading a trochaic inversion for both "Desarts" and "But at," as the student should have done instead of lighting on dactyls, isn't demon possession. Since the student's amended text, which Hollander quotes here and presumably assigned, doesn't show the Ur-text, I will do so, scanning as well. I take it from *The Poems of Andrew Marvell*, edited by Hugh MacDonald (1952):

> / ⌣ ⌣ / ⌣/ ⌣ /
> But at | my back | I al | waies hear
> / / ⌣ / ⌣⌣ / ⌣⌣ /
> Times wing | ed Char | riot hur | rying near:
> ⌣ / ⌣ / ⌣ / ⌣ /
> And yon | der all | before | us lye
> / ⌣ ⌣ / ⌣/ ⌣(/)
> Desarts | of vast | Eter | nity.

In the first and last lines, trochaic inversions, and in the second line anapests—all rather than dactyls. For the inversions, no explanation is needed since Marvell uses them frequently, as in "Vaster | than Em | pires, and | more slow" (line 12).

Between the "Western Wind" poet and Blake, trisyllabic substitution was pretty much ruled out of English verse, though poets (including Shakespeare and Donne) sometimes cheated, as I hope Marvell is doing here. The Ur-text faithfully shows apostrophes for syllables not to be pronounced, as in "And now, like am'rous birds of prey," in "Like wat'ry Lines and Plummets fall," in "th' industrious Bee," in "the Glories of th' Almighty Sun," in "pow'r," "flow'r," or past verbs like "preserv'd," "prepar'd," "reckon'd." But notably *not* in "Charriot," "hurrying," or—just below—"echoing," all three syllable words. The first can be managed naturally enough as two syllables, but "hur-ying near" or "ech-wing Song" strike me as silly as well as missing the little expressive rhythms the student also found appropriate. Perhaps Marvell did so as well, quietly slipping into the old iambic-anapestic derived from the Anglo-Saxon line.

The student may have been led into mis-ascribing dactyls by the problem of alternative scansions, which the mirror-image iambic and trochaic, anapestic and dactylic "meters" of the tradition caused, producing much needless muddle about plainly iambic poems like Milton's "L'Allegro" or Blake's "The Tyger." (Or perhaps he or she hadn't been listening when Professor Hollander passed along the advice that a difficult line will often resolve easily, once the speech stresses have been marked, by working *backwards* from the line's last stress.)

We may study a quite different sort of alternative scansion in Hollander's account—which I quote entire (*Work* 216)—of George Meredith's "Love in the Valley":

Then there is the beautiful Theocritean idyll, "Love in the Valley," with its surging trochaic lines (but very free with extra unstressed syllables) alternating with a *dum* da da da *dum* da da da *dum* da da da *dum*—and yet so wonderfully varied in the different syntactic and rhetorical patterns disposed among them. Thus the opening stanza

> Under yonder beech-tree single on the greensward
>   Couched with her arms behind her golden head,
> Knees and tresses folded to slip and ripple idly,
>   Lies my young love sleeping in the shade.
> Had I the heart to slide an arm beneath her,
>   Press her parting lips as her waist I gather slow,
> Waking in amazement she could but not embrace me:[14]
>   Then would she hold me and never let me go?

and, later on,

> This may I know: her dressing and undressing
>   Such a change of light shows as when the skies in sport
> Shift from cloud to moonlight; or edging into thunder
>   Slips a ray of sun; or sweeping into port
> White sails furl; or on the ocean borders
>   White sails lean along the waves leaping green.

---

[14] In a later analysis of this line, Wallace will note Hollander's "miscopied word-order," correcting "but not" to "not but." -*Eds.*

> Visions of her shower before me, but from eyesight
> Guarded she would be like the sun were she seen.

The inexorable, purely accentual four-beat rhythms, the pastoral delight in the air of continuing erotic promise, the profusion of pictorial moments, all combine in a poem that is simply gorgeous.

Hollander seems to ascribe three different meters to the poem. Trochaic lines, he tells us, alternate with a sing-along pattern that might be described as first-paeonic (∕ ᴗ ᴗ ᴗ) tetrameters; and somewhere there are "inexorable, purely accentual four-beat rhythms." The exposition seems utterly jumbled. Although lines 1 and 3 are plausibly trochaic hexameters (with an extra syllable, and so a dactyl, in "folded to"), lines 2 and 4 aren't anything like "*dum* da da da *dum*" at all. Line 2 would be most simply scanned as iambic pentameter with trochaic inversion:

$$\text{∕ \quad ᴗ \quad ᴗ \quad ∕ \quad ᴗ ∕ \quad ᴗ \quad ∕ \quad ᴗ \quad ∕}$$
Couched with | her arms | behind | her gold | en head

Line 4 is essentially symmetrical—iambic or trochaic pentameter, depending on where we prefer to register the missing syllable:

$$\text{x ∕ \quad ᴗ ∕ \quad ∕ \quad ∕ \quad ᴗ (∕) \quad ᴗ \quad ∕}$$
Lies | my young | love sleep | ing in | the shade ...
$$\text{∕ ᴗ \quad ∕ \quad ∕ \quad ∕ ᴗ (∕) ᴗ \quad ∕ \quad x}$$
Lies my | young love | sleeping | in the | shade

Line 5 is iambic pentameter with e-s ending:

$$\text{ᴗ ∕ \quad ᴗ \quad ∕ \quad ᴗ \quad ∕ \quad ᴗ \quad ∕ \quad ᴗ \quad ∕ \quad ᴗ}$$
Had I | the heart | to slide | an arm | beneath | her

None of the poem's 208 lines fits the "*dum* da da da *dum*," paradigm. Though not alternating, line 7 has the needed thirteen syllables and isn't far off if a reader can know to avoid the accentual-syllabic promotion of "in" and—improperly—to demote the probable speech stress on "she." Correcting Hollander's miscopied word-order, we would have:

／ ᵕ (ᵕ) ᵕ ／   ᵕ (ᵕ)   ᵕ   ／ ᵕ ᵕ ／ ᵕ

*Wak*ing in a*maze*ment she could *not* but em*brace* me.

But disconnecting the accentual-syllabic expectation, once it is started, in order to interpret a few lines differently, seems a fragile mechanism. And we probably do best to regard "*dum* da da da *dum*" as merely, well, performative impressionism. Reading a poem as being in two meters simultaneously is needless confusion.

The same difficulty (now of three meters simultaneously) attends Hollander's attribution of "purely accentual four-beat rhythms"—if in fact this isn't what he means by "*dum* da da da *dum*," despite this rhythm's apparent regulation of three unstressed syllables between the stresses. In any case, all but three or four of the sixteen lines he quotes have five or more pretty clear stresses. There is nothing "inexorable" about the four main or metrical stresses among the seven stresses in, say, "White sails lean along the waves leaping green" or (correcting Hollander's miscopied "into") in "Shift from cloud to moonlight; or edging over thunder ..." Frye had noted (*Anatomy of Criticism* 254–55) that Meredith's poem "is most easily scanned as a four-stress line very similar in its rhythmical make up to Lydgate's," but *the* four metrical stresses seem neither clearer nor more convincing in Frye's musical scansion:[15]

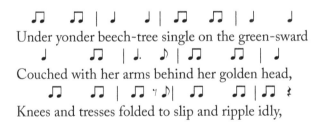

Under yonder beech-tree single on the green-sward

Couched with her arms behind her golden head,

Knees and tresses folded to slip and ripple idly,

There is no reason why "gold-" doesn't carry a stress instead of "-hind" in line 2; and the rests in line 3 are obviously manipulative, the first in order to accommodate "-ed to slip" which would be an anapest in normal scansion. Moreover, Frye's interpretation depends entirely on the arbitrary assumption that we *must* scan four bars to the line, an assumption for which I see no justification whatever.

---

[15] For context, we turn to Northrop Frye: "After the death of Chaucer and the change from middle to modern English, we find ourselves in the strange metrical world of [John] Lydgate" (252), one characterized by "a line with four main stresses and a variable number of syllables between the stresses" (253). -*Eds.*

Perhaps Hollander's muddle of the third alternative scansion reflects only his inability to avoid and his unwillingness to correct Frye's assertion.

(5) Helen Vendler believes students need very little instruction in meter. Of the 656 pages of *Poems, Poets, Poetry* (1997), she devotes maybe fifteen to rhythm, meter, and free verse altogether—six pages in the main text, nine in an appendix. The account is sketchy. Caesura gets two sentences and one example, but enjambment is never mentioned or discussed. She notes that "Feet of comparable length can freely substitute for each other," but says nothing at all about substituting feet *not* of comparable length, so an anapest in an iambic line may seem inexplicable. And so on. She makes one notable innovation, referring to line *width* rather than length, though she doesn't explain why this static and merely spatial term might be superior to the familiar one that also suggests (appropriately) both direction and duration. Free verse she defines as "verse in which the lines are of different widths, and which does not rhyme in any regular way." ("The Collar," "Dover Beach," and "After Apple-Picking" become free verse?) She veers in an instant from mere junk to sublime junk (607, her italics):

> The unit of free verse seems to be the breath: there is a breath limit to the long line of free verse (reached by Whitman and Ginsberg, to give two notable examples). The theoretical appeal of free verse is that it admits an element of chance; it offers a model not of a teleological or providential universe but of an *aleatory* one, where the casual, rather than the fated, holds sway.

The mere inadequacy of *Poems, Poets, Poetry* prepares one not at all for Vendler's utterly perverse scansion of Sonnet 126 in *The Art of Shakespeare's Sonnets* (533–38). It is hard to imagine an alternative scansion more alternative. Having chosen trochees and amphibrachs as primary, Vendler scans with these feet almost as generously as she can, and—the other main eccentricity—allows as many monosyllabic feet as she needs to fill out the pentameters. As guide, here is a tabulation of the result:

trochees	12
amphibrachs	12
iambs	12
monosyllabics	11
pyrrhics	8

spondees 5
total: 60

What seems to be a hypermetrical unstressed syllable ("Dost") begins line 2. I assume that a printer's error shows "goest onwards" in line 6 as ∪ / / rather than as ∪ / ∪, and so both accept her count of twelve amphibrachs and reproduce her scansion exactly:

∪ / ∪ / ∪ / / ∪ / /
O thou // my love / ly boy // who in / thy power

∪ / / / ∪ / ∪ / ∪ /
Dost / hold Time's / fickle / glass // *his sickle* / hour

∪ / ∪ / ∪ / ∪ / ∪ /
Who hast / *by waning* / grown // and therein / show'st

∪ / ∪ / ∪ ∪ ∪ / / /
Thy lovers / with'ring // as thy / sweet self / grow'st

∪ / ∪ / ∪ / ∪ ∪ ∪ /
If Nature // sovereign / mistress / over / wrack

∪ / ∪ / / / ∪ / ∪ /
As thou / *goest onwards* / still will / pluck thee / back

∪ / ∪ ∪ / / ∪ ∪ ∪ /
She keeps thee / to this / purpose // that her / skill

∪ / ∪ / ∪ / ∪ / ∪ /
May Time / disgrace // *and wretched* / minutes / kill

∪ ∪ ∪ / ∪ / / / ∪ / ∪
Yet fear her // O thou / minion / of her / pleasure

∪ ∪ ∪ / ∪ / / / ∪ / ∪
She may / detain // but not / still keep / *her treasure*

∪ / ∪ ∪ ∪ / / ∪ ∪ /
Her audit // though de / layed // answered / must be

∪ / ∪ / ∪ ∪ ∪ / ∪ /
And her / *quietus* // is to / render / thee.

Vendler provides justifications for electing trochees and amphibrachs. As to amphibrachs:

> Because two lines have already begun with an amphibrach followed by a caesura—

$$\breve{}\ \diagup\ \breve{} \qquad\qquad \breve{}\ \diagup\ \breve{}$$
If nature // and *Yet fear her //*

—the ring of *Her audit* comes as a fatal confirmation of both the futility of natural tenacity and the ominous warning. There are (by my count) nine other amphibrachic feet besides these three, and their presence serves to highlight the amphibrachic conclusive word *quíetus*.

This begs the question. It has not been argued, nor even stated, that these snippets involve amphibrachs, so in no sense can it be said that two lines have "already begun" with amphibrachs. The claim seems to negate the convention that metrical feet are construed across phrase-boundaries, even at punctuated caesuras. As to trochees:

Because of the number of significant disyllabic words accented on the first syllable, such as *answer* and *audit*, the poem falls into a trochaic and amphibrachic rather than an iambic pattern. (I say this because given the two possible scansions of, say, line 5—

> *Iambic:*　If Na- / ture sove- / reign mis- / tress o- / ver wrack
> *Trochaic:*　If / Nature / sovereign / mistress / over / wrack

—I prefer the one which keeps words intact.) On this principle—and noticing how many of the first syllables of these lines are negligible in relation to the import of the second and following syllables—I would scan the lines as follows, italicizing the amphibrachs.

The natural preponderance in the language of disyllabic words stressed on the first syllable hardly seems, at this date, a reason for replacing traditional iambic scansion. Vendler's "I prefer" turns instantly into "this principle," although it negates the convention that metrical feet cross word-boundaries (and are not word-determined). She applies the new principle only erratically, however, dividing between two feet the words "lovely" in line 1 and "delayed" in line 11. The consideration of foot to wordshape[16] is presumably irrelevant, in any case, since only one of Vendler's twelve amphibrachs, *quietus*, comes in amphi

---

[16] A term from linguistics (and applied most commonly in sign language), *wordshape* charts the binary relationship between "syllabicity" and "morphemicity" in establishing units of language. -*Eds.*

brachic, a fact that makes it less than probable that the eleven non-wordshape amphibrachs will "highlight" *quietus* for readers who haven't happened upon her odd scansion of the poem.

The simplest way of assessing Vendler's scansion is just to rearrange the verticals marking off feet. The poem's rhythm is of course identical, since feet are merely notional, a system of measurement.

```
 ◡   /    ◡   /   ◡  /    /  ◡   /   /
O thou | my love | ly boy, | who in | thy power
    ◡   /   /    /    ◡  /   ◡   /   ◡  /
Dost hold | Time's fick | le glass, | his sick | le hour;
   ◡  /   ◡   /   ◡   /    ◡   /   ◡   /
Who hast | by wan | ing grown, | and there | in show'st
  ◡  /   ◡   /   ◡  ◡   ◡   /   /  /
Thy lov | ers with | 'ring, as | thy sweet | self grow'st;
  ◡ /   ◡   /    ◡   /    ◡  ◡   ◡  /
If Na | ture (sov | ereign mis | tress o | ver wrack),
  ◡   /   ◡   /   ◡   /   ◡   /   ◡   /
As thou | goest on | wards still | will pluck | thee back,
   ◡   /    ◡  ◡   /  /   ◡   ◡   ◡  /
She keeps | thee to | this pur | pose, that | her skill
   ◡   /   ◡  /    ◡   /    ◡   /   ◡   /
May Time | disgrace, | and wretch | ed min | utes kill.
  ◡   /   ◡  ◡   ◡  /   /  ◡  ◡   /   ◡
Yet fear | her, O | thou min | ion of | her pleas | ure,
  ◡   ◡    ◡ /   ◡  /   /  /   ◡   /   ◡
She may | detain, | but not | still keep | her treas | ure
  ◡  /   ◡   ◡     ◡ /    /  ◡    ◡  /
Her au | dit (though | delayed) | answered | must be,
  ◡   /    ◡/  ◡  ◡   ◡ /    ◡  /
And her | quie | tus is | to ren | der thee.
```

This is a passable scansion, although it seems too generous with pyrrhics. A tabulation:

iambs	44
pyrrhics	9

| spondees | 5 |
| trochees | 2 |

The word "over" (line 5) carries a stress in speech and "goest" (line 6) is the main verb of its clause (imagine the stresses in saying as neutrally as possible, "as you go onwards"). Even if routine promotions like "of" in line 9 are resisted, several other words in metrical-stress positions (and perhaps "thee" in line 7) seem charged with enough meaning in context to deserve stresses. In line 4, for instance, "as" is the fulcrum of paradoxical simultaneity between "lovers withering" and "self grows't." In line 10, "may" seems to imply an ominous sense of what is merely permitted.

Nonetheless, this scansion is far preferable to Vendler's identical but eccentric trochaic/amphibrachic scansion because it remains clearly based on a rhythmic pattern regular enough to hear. Expectation and variation can operate. It records (and lets us discuss) the poem's use of meter, indeed, of the very meter Shakespeare presumed he was using.

Vendler's eccentric scansion first blurs or overrides the perception of that traditional meter *and* then attempts to replace it by an arbitrary and merely intellectualized imposition of *any* fancied feet whatever. There would equally be no answer to an assertion of, say, a mollossus in line 4:

$$\smile \, / \, \smile \qquad / \qquad \smile \quad \smile \, \smile \qquad / \quad / \quad /$$
Thy lovers | with'ring | as thy | *sweet self grows't*

Students, and critics with perhaps less restraint than Vendler, will have a field day.

Oddly, having gone to the trouble of misscanning the poem, Vendler makes little use of all those trochees, amphibrachs, and monosyllabics, other than to note that "The effect of the prosody is to suggest that easy conversational intonation in which Shakespeare excels all other poets"—though, elsewhere, she comments on a plea's "evenness of iambic rationality" (564) or finds "the poet's inner 'rebellion'" being felt in two lines' initial trochees (460). But one can well imagine the vivid scansions inspired by the authority of Vendler's methodology.

The metrical uncertainty and confusion Hollander has observed seems quite out of control at century's end.

Of Anapests, Apostrophes, and Shakespeare's Deaf Hen

Anapests approximate an essential little rhythm of the language. Their exclusion from literary verse after Tottel's *Miscellany* in 1557 brought on what George Saintsbury calls "the ugly apostrophe, which invaded English books in the seventeenth century, and persevered into the eighteenth" (1: 172). Perfectly melodious words had to be crippled in order to fit the disyllabic meter. To avoid anapests poets said and readers heard—or they pretended to say and hear—"th'oaks," "th' utmost," "th'uncouth," "vi'lets," "dang'rous," "mell'wing," and of course something like "heav'n" for "heaven"; although, as John Thompson points out (78), "the use of *heaven* as one syllable is purely conventional since the phoneme *n* is syllabic." So perhaps "he'n" is how it went.

Were words like "thoaks" and "tembrace" really pronounced so in verse? "I do not believe they ever were," Saintsbury said. And poets certainly cheated in blank verse for the stage, especially Shakespeare in the later plays. Consider Lear's

/ / ꞈ / ꞈ / ꞈꞈ/ ꞈ /
Smite flat | the thick | rotun | dity o' | the world

Heard so, the anapest would be difficult to get rid of. If we try the less appealing

ꞈ (/) ꞈ ꞈ /
Smite flat | the thick | rotun | dity | o' the world

we might get "o' th' world," but that sounds like "oath" and loses the wonderfully enunciated "o'," which is surely the point of this apostrophe.

Traditionalist and rebel, Milton had read his Shakespeare and did not scruple to make free with anapests early and late, in sonnet or epic, as Saintsbury documents (2: 207–72). A sampling from *Paradise Lost*:

ꞈ ꞈ /
Creat | ed hug | est that swim | the o | cean stream ... (1.202)

ꞈ ꞈ/
Of ri | ot ascends | above | their loft | iest towers ... (1.499)
ꞈꞈ

ꞈ ꞈ/
If true, | here on | ly, and | of deli | cious taste ... (4.251)

<pre>
              ᵕ   ᵕ   ╱   ᵕ ᵕ   ╱
And rap | ture so oft | beheld? | Those heav | enly shapes ... (9.1082)
</pre>

Of the last, Saintsbury remarks: "Does anybody really believe that Milton would have run the risk of the substitution of 'And rapture *soft* beheld'?" Saintsbury holds that Milton was a conscious and even experimental prosodist; so Milton's freedom might well have loosened the restraint of 1557 on anapests well before Blake, had not the Restoration also restored the authority of French theory.

My purpose here is to point out a collateral damage: the unawareness of bacchic feet. Bacchics (ᵕ ╱╱) approximate a little rhythm as natural in the language and in English verse as the anapest, if less frequent. Even when anapests were allowed in the artifice of song, they provided an easy hiding place for bacchics, as in Dryden's song in *Marriage à la Mode*:

<pre>
      ᵕ   ╱   ᵕ   ╱   ╱   ᵕ ╱   ╱   ᵕ ᵕ ╱
He found | the fierce pleas | ure too hast | y to stay ...
</pre>

The musical pace that may want to slur "fierce" and "too" into unstressed syllables, in order to thump on the beat, can hardly be appropriate in more serious contexts. Consider Wyatt's line in "The First Satire":

<pre>
      ᵕ   ╱   ᵕ   ╱   ╱   ᵕ ╱   ᵕ   ╱
To make | the crow sing | ing as | the swane ...
</pre>

which was altered in Tottel's *Miscellany* thus:

<pre>
      ᵕ   ╱   ᵕ   ╱   ᵕ ╱   ᵕ ╱   ᵕ   ╱
To make | the crow | in sing | yng, as | the swanne ...
</pre>

Consider Othello's

<pre>
      ᵕ   ╱   ᵕ   ╱ ᵕ ╱   ᵕ ╱ ╱   ᵕ ╱
I kissed | thee ere | I killed | thee: no way | but this ... (5.2.358)
</pre>

or Lear's

<pre>
      ᵕ   ╱   ᵕ (╱)   ᵕ   ╱   ╱ ᵕ╱   ᵕ ╱
You sul | phurous | and thought-ex | ecut | ing fires ... (3.2.4)
</pre>

In Sonnet 29, if we put aside "he'n" and just pronounce the words as spoken English, we have

> ˘ / ˘ / / ˘ / ˘ / ˘ /
> And trou | ble deaf heav | en with | my boot | less cries ...

In *Paradise Regained* (1.140):

> / / ˘ / ˘ / / ˘ / / /
> O'er-shad | ow her; | this man born | and now | up-grown ...

In *Samson Agonistes* (127, 938):

> / / ˘ / ˘ / ˘ / / ˘ ˘ /
> No strength | of man, | or fierc | est wild beast | could withstand ...

> / ˘ ˘ / ˘ / ˘ / ˘ / /
> If in | my flower | of youth | and strength | when all men ...

The six lines of Shakespeare and Milton are unambiguously iambic pentameters, in which the bacchics appear as simple substitutions. Notably, only Dryden's line might be described as being in anapestic "meter," like "'Twas the Night Before Christmas" or Browning's "How They Brought the Good News from Ghent to Aix." In such poems, bacchics may be relatively frequent but slurred-over in performance in order to impose a rhythm, as perhaps in Browning's "James Lee's Wife":

> ˘ / ˘ ˘ / ˘ / / ˘ ˘ /
> The swal | low has set | her six young | on the rail ...

As Charles O. Hartman argues ("Some Responses" 113), however, the bacchic is a natural substitution "in anapestic verse, just as the spondee and trochee are in iambic verse." It isn't Hartman's intention to allow bacchics in "iambic verse," but I see no alternative to scanning them wherever they appear. As with spondees, there may be occasional ambiguity, due to interpretation, in ascribing bacchics, although such uncertainty will usefully focus discussion on the rhythm of a particular line or passage.

A similar ambiguity in scanning occasionally links trisyllabic feet and line length. We know that poets may deliberately vary line length, as Shakespeare does with tetrameters and hexameters in *King Lear*, or as Wyatt does in the tetrameter "It was no dreme: I lay brode waking" among the pentameters of "They Flee from Me Who Sometime Did Me Seek." So Wyatt's nine-sylla-ble line about "the crow singing as the swane," quoted above, may be cred-ited as a tetrameter among pentameters. One might scan an anomalous monosyllabic foot—

$$x \quad /$$
To make | the crow | sing | ing as | the swane ...

but that changes nothing, providing a mere rationalization of a pentameter, which seems little better than the weak emendation in Tottel. Both alterna-tives are pointless. The line, as written, sounds fine. So we may scan a tetrame-ter with a bacchic foot in the second position.

There may be instances harder to decide. Saintsbury, although he passion-ately advocates anapests and freely accepts hexameters in Milton's blank verse, describes this line of *Paradise Lost* (8.299) as having "one of Milton's curious ditrochaic (or paeonic) openings." He intends this scansion:

$$/ \;\; \cup \quad / \;\; \cup \quad \cup \;\; / \quad \cup \;\; / \quad \cup \;\; /$$
To the | Garden | of bliss, | thy seat | prepar'd

But nothing, not even metrical stress position, supports the promotion of "To." A simpler scansion would be:

$$\cup \;\; \cup \;\; / \quad \cup \;\; \cup \;\; / \quad \cup \;\; / \quad \cup \;\; /$$
To the Gar | den of bliss, | thy seat | prepar'd

This scansion may or may not be more correct than Saintsbury's, though I think I prefer it as being simpler. The line is easy and natural, and there is no need to deploy arcane terms. My point is just to note the possible metrical ambiguity in such cases.

Let's look carefully at two poems in which bacchic feet may be use-fully scanned, Blake's "The Wild Flower's Song" and Sharon Olds's "Quake Theory." The Blake:

> ˘ ˘ ´ ˘ ˘ ´ ˘
> As I wan | der'd the for | est,
> ˘ ´ ´ ˘ ´
> The green leaves | among,
> ˘ ´ ˘ ´ ´ ˘
> I heard | a Wild Flow | er
> ´ ˘ ˘ ´
> Singing | a song.
> ˘ ´ ˘ ˘ ´
> I slept | in the earth
> ˘ ˘ ´ ˘ ´
> In the si | lent night.
> ˘ ´ ˘ ˘ ´
> I mur | mur'd in fears
> ˘ ˘ ´ ˘ ´
> And I felt | delight.
>
> ˘ ˘ ´ ˘ ˘ ´
> "In the morn | ing I went,
> ˘ ´ ˘ ˘ ´
> As ros | y as morn,
> ˘ ´ ˘ ´ ´
> To seek | for new joy:
> ˘ ˘ ´ ˘ ´
> But I met | with scorn."

Bacchics in lines 2, 3, and 11 are unmistakable, linking "The green leaves," "a Wild Flow | er," and "for new joy" among the dimeters that otherwise mingle ten iambs, ten anapests, and a trochaic inversion. Especially notable is Blake's modulation in the last three feet—"for new joy: But I met with scorn"—from bacchic to anapest to the relative (and rejecting?) abruptness of iamb. Blake's small satire on the rejection of the natural seems relevant to my argument.

As we might expect, the little rhythm in English represented by the bacchic foot emerges significantly in the twentieth century, in the ready disguise of so-called free verse. Consider Olds's "Quake Theory," in which the foot provides an expressive rhythmic motif:

˘ / / ˘ / / ˘/ ˘ / ˘
When two plates | of earth scrape | along | each oth | er
˘ ˘ / ˘ ˘ / ˘
like a moth | er and daught | er
˘ ˘ / ˘ /
it is called | a fault.

˘ ˘ / ˘ / / ˘ / ˘ / ˘
There are faults | that slip smooth | ly past | each oth | er
˘ / ˘ / ˘ / ˘ / /
an inch | a year, | with just | a faint rasp
˘ ˘ / / ˘ ˘ / / ˘ ˘ /
like a | man run | ning his | hand o | ver his chin,
˘ / ˘ / ˘
that man | between | us,
˘ ˘ ˘ / ˘ / / ˘˘ / ˘ / ˘ /
and there | are faults | that get stuck | at a bend | for twen | ty years.
˘ / / ˘ / ˘ ˘ / ˘ ˘/ ˘ / /
The ridge bulg | es up | like a fath | er's sarcas | tic forehead
˘ ˘ / / / ˘˘ / ˘ / ˘ / ˘
and the whole | thing freez | es in place, | the man | between | us.

˘ ˘ / ˘ ˘ / ˘ / ˘ / ˘
When this hap | pens, there will | be heav | y dam | age
˘ ˘/ ˘˘/ ˘˘ ˘ / ˘ / ˘(/)
to indus | trial ar | eas | and leis | ure res | idence
˘ ˘ / /
when the | deep plates
/ ˘ ˘ / /
final | ly jerk past
˘ / ˘˘ / ˘ ˘ ˘ / ˘
the ter | rible pres | sure of | their con | tact.

˘ / /
The earth cracks
˘ / ˘˘ / ˘ / / ˘/ ˘ / ˘
and in | nocent peo | ple slip gen | tly in | like swim | mers.

Ten bacchics, among sixty-three total feet (including twenty-six iambs and six-teen anapests), are probably unusual, but it seems sure that bacchics will show up often in more recent "free" verse, once we begin to scan it.

Behind the Trochaic Mirror

Alternative scansions have muddled English prosody almost from the beginning.

It was a reasonable assumption in 1589 that, like Greek and Latin verse, English verse should have several meters. So George Puttenham recognized "*Iambique* and sometimes the *Trochaike*" (140–41). In due course anapestic and dactylic meters were added.

The problem with these mirror-image pairs—especially iambic and trocha-ic—is that both meters often appear in a single poem. Moreover, a series of conventions sprang up that could justify a line in either meter as being also in the other. Consider the last two lines of Jonson's "Epitaph on Elizabeth, L. H.," which is usually considered a poem in trochaic meter:

$$\acute{}\;\cup\quad\acute{}\;\cup\quad\acute{}\;\cup\quad\acute{}\;x$$
Fitter, | where it | died, to | tell

$$\acute{}\;\cup\quad\acute{}\;\cup\quad\acute{}\;\cup\quad\acute{}\;x$$
Than | that it | lived at | all. Fare | well.

The superscript *x* marks the legitimate omission of the unaccented syllables of each final "trochaic" foot. This convention goes by the term "final catalexis." The initial syllable of the last line ("Than") is considered metrically *extra*—that is, is not counted—so the line scans as four trochees (with final catalexis in the last of course). This convention of an added, not-counted syllable goes by the term "initial hypercatalexis" or "anacrusis." So, trochaic "meter."

But, notice, both lines may *also* be in iambic meter:

$$x\;\acute{}\quad\cup\;\acute{}\quad\cup\;\acute{}\quad\cup\;\acute{}$$
Fit | ter where | it died, | to tell

$$\cup\;\acute{}\quad\cup\;\acute{}\quad\cup\;\acute{}\quad\cup\;\acute{}$$
Than that | it lived | at all. | Farewell.

The last line requires no fixing, and the other needs only the convention of "initial catalexis"—the legitimate omission of the unaccented syllable of the first foot—to count as being in iambic meter.

R.M. Alden made this point in 1909 (227–28). The distinction between iambic and trochaic meters, he said,

> is, after all, a superficial one, depending not on the nature of the rhythm concerned but on where we begin to count. Such verse as "Spied a blossom passing fair" has the same rhythm whether we think of it as iambic verse with the first syllable missing, or trochaic verse with the last syllable missing. Such a verse as "We met an host and quelled it" has the same rhythm whether we think of it as iambic verse with an extra syllable at the end, or as trochaic verse with an extra syllable at the beginning.

T.S. Omond had made the point in 1903 (61–62):

> These are really subdivisions of the same metre. Our poets, as has been already noted, pass backwards and forwards from one form to the other at their pleasure. Critics have professed to find different effects in the two types; but in view of this interchangeability such professions must be received with distrust.

Alden adds (230, his italics): "It may be worthwhile in the same connection to point out that it is also true that there is no *necessary* difference of rhythm between the iambic and anapestic measures, as is shown by the ease with which some poems glide from one into the other without any obvious change of rhythmical character"—and he cites the verse "called by Schipper 'iambic-anapestic,' in which one cannot be certain which is the prevailing type."

It will therefore be a great clarification at last, as I argued in *Meter in English* ("Meter" 28–30; "Completing" 298–303, 330–338), to conclude that there is one meter in English, its base being iambic. We may drop trochaic, anapestic, and dactylic "meters" from the textbooks, as I did in *Writing Poems* (1982; 4th ed. 1996). No one will miss them or wish for them back.

A side benefit is that we may also drop the dactyl as an English foot since, it turns out, there will never be an occasion requiring its use in scansion. Its place among the six English feet may be taken by the bacchic (∪ ⁄ ⁄), a foot essential in any case.

A further side benefit is that we may shed the less-than-useful as applied to meter or rhythm. These terms work as pale reflections of iambic and trochaic. (Iambic is "duple rising meter"; trochaic, "duple falling meter," and so on.) But of course *both* iambic and trochaic regularly go up *and* down, rise *and* fall, so these terms were never very informative, though they are still offered to describe—impressionistically—the rhythm of lines' ending on a stressed or on an unstressed syllable. Alfred Corn, for instance, quotes only the second of these three lines from Sonnet 29:

> Haply I think on thee, and then my state
> (Like to the lark at break of day arising
> From sullen earth) sings hymns at heaven's gate ...

The line, Corn notes (46),

> concludes with the foot "arising," an iamb plus an extra weakly stressed syllable. Lines using this variation are said to conclude with "falling rhythm," or a "dying fall," which is usually soothing, lulling, graceful ....

The rhythm of Shakespeare's line comes far more from syntax and powerful enjambment than from that extra syllable, and is of course better described by *any* image at all than by "falling." No doubt Corn will want to reconsider his example.

There are still critics who find "different effects" in iambic and trochaic. David Weiss in "Rapping Scops," for instance, fancying Marvell and Blake as modern rappers, holds that "a hip-hop CD of English verse might just make the charts" (167). The reason? "Metrical patterns produce an aura, call it mood or rhythmic thought; from each pattern emanates a broad, predominant spirit" (168). In "The Tyger," for example,

> Blake is making us feel the spirit of the trochaic. It asserts itself in this poem whenever the divine is manifest—the divine, that is, in the form of the overwhelming, the fierce, the destructive.

Blake's "Lamb," however, "comes in iambic form.... It is a kinder, gentler rhythm" (169). Weiss sums up:

> [I]t makes good sense for the lamb to be iambic. Partly, this is because trochaic and iambic are rhythmic opposites (*Motherfucker* versus *My dearest child*), and Blake's tyger and lamb are spiritual flipsides of each other.

Nevertheless, it turns out that, for Weiss, "the trochaic does have a tender side, too, which peeks out, for example, in lullabies." And, in "London," the iambic also shows up in "a new role ... an ugly one—the dystopic as normative":

> In every cry of every man
> In every Infant's cry of fear
> In every voice, in every ban
> The mind-forged manacles I hear.

"The iambic tetrameter of the first three lines of this stanza," Weiss writes, "is all about sameness and uniformity, mechanical and unvarying—a rhythmic figure for oppressiveness." He continues:

> Still, it has momentum; it's forceful and hammering. There's undeniable power here. But it's bad power, coercive. It makes you want to scream. Blake, too, wants to shriek, and he does it in the next stanza through the trochaic. This is another face of the trochaic: indignation, flaring into outrage. (170–71)

Weiss's enthusiasm is probably inimitable, so we need say no more about this mere impressionism. But two of his procedures in scanning seem untrustworthy enough to deserve comment. One is attributing a meter to each line of a poem, separately; and the other is, apparently, to determine *each* line's meter by its first foot. Both procedures may be observed in his account of stanza 1 of "The Tyger" (168). He quotes lines 1–2, comments, then quotes lines 3–4:

> Tyger, Tyger, burning bright
> In the forests of the night.

> The scop is tight with tetrameter, but he's turned the meter upside down. It's coming out trochaic, not iambic. Even the anapestic second line picks up the trochaic feel. It's like a chant, but he's a subtle sort of druid, and the first stanza is, in fact, a virtual catalogue of meters, now trochaic again, now iambic:

> What immortal hand or eye
> Could frame thy fearful symmetry?

If I follow this, Weiss says that the meter of lines 1 and 3 is trochaic (although both are in fact just symmetrical and might be scanned equally as iambic, with omitted initial syllable, or as trochaic, with omitted final syllable). The meter of line 4 is iambic. But the meter of line 2 is *anapestic*? Presumably Weiss intends

> ⏑ ⏑ ╱
> In the for | ests of | the night …

though he notes that the line also "picks up the trochaic feel" (due, I'd guess, to the wordshape of "forests").

The same dubious procedure seems to be at work when Weiss describes the following line of Hopkins's "Pied Beauty" as "strictly a trochaic one" (173). His foot-division would presumably be:

> *x*
> Glory | be to | God for | dappled | things—

"What follows, 'for dappled things,' feels iambic" to Weiss, however. Such "metrically androgynous" lines, he decides, are "not iambic *or* trochaic—but both at the same time" (his italics).

Defining a line's meter by its first foot seems risky, especially for lines beginning with pyrrhics, spondees, or trochaic inversions—instances of which either don't show up or receive no comment in Weiss's essay, as when he quotes this line of Sonnet 129 (mistaking it as Sonnet 116):

> Savage, | extreme, | rude, cru | el, not | to trust …

Presumably he would call the line's meter trochaic, as he would this line (also Shakespeare's):

> Hover | through fog | and filth | of air …

which he quotes (170) but does not scan.

Having two different and competing ways of describing the same thing has often produced confusion in our prosody, as it does in Weiss's essay. Simplicity and clarity, then, will be the great advantages of recognizing that there is only one meter in English. Poets may still opt for disyllabic regularity, or trisyllabic regularity; but meter will have become a single system of *measuring* all verse, however irregular.

This is a new, liberating, and essential mindset.

Albeit in a way that Weiss didn't intend, he is correct. Meter in English is "not iambic *or* trochaic—but both at the same time."

Alternatives to Foot-Meter

From Otto Jespersen's "Notes on Metre" (1900) to Derek Attridge's *Poetic Rhythm: An Introduction* (1995), attempts to replace foot-scansion with a new system invariably posit a strict alternation of unstressed and stressed syllables, unwittingly carrying forward Tottel's notorious disyllabic restriction of 1557. Such systems founder on the fact of trisyllabic substitution. Quite natural to English verse, exactly linking "Western Wind" (circa 1500) and "The Road Not Taken" or "Le Monocle de Mon Oncle," trisyllabic substitution has plainly withstood the test of time.

Attridge tries to get around the problem by holding that there are *two* basic meters in English, "stress [accentual] meter" and "syllable-stress [accentual-syllabic] meter." The first allows what we call trisyllabic substitution; the second, which Attridge identifies closely with the pentameter line, doesn't. He presents the latter as strict (138):

> In syllable-stress verse the poet has to choose, as the basis of the meter, between separating the beats of the line by one syllable or separating them by two syllables; that is, between duple meter and triple meter. There is no possibility of moving between these options in the same line, as there is in stress verse ....

Historically, Attridge's two basic meters were never in fact separate meters. Nobody knows where the regular alternation of unstressed and stressed syllables came from, but it occurs in both popular and literary verse. The occasional appearance of an extra unstressed syllable—trisyllabic substitution—is equally early and traditional, as George Gascoigne's comments about "our father Chaucer" (467-68) show. In his First Satire, Wyatt uses trisyllabic substitution even in pentameters:

$$\smile \quad \smile \quad /$$

And call | crafft coun | sell, for prof | fet styll | to paint

—and Spenser experiments with it in his May Eclogue (86, 266):

$$\cup \ \cup \ /$$
Eke cher | ish his child, | if in | his wayes | he stood ...
$$\cup \quad \cup \quad /$$
I am | a poore Sheepe, | albe | my col | oure donne ...

Nor is the phenomenon unfamiliar in pentameters by Shakespeare, Milton, Wordsworth, Browning, Yeats, Frost, Stevens, and others. For instance, as Attridge knows, in Wordsworth's *The Prelude* (5.57.79):

$$\cup \ \cup \ /$$
That once | in the still | ness of | a sum | mer's noon ...
$$\cup \ \cup \ /$$
A stone, | and in | the op | posite hand, | a shell ...

Or in the blank verse of Browning's *The Ring and the Book* (11.1379):

$$\cup \quad \cup \ / \quad \cup \cup \ / \qquad \cup \quad \cup \ /$$
From the ter | rible pa | tience of God? | "All which | just means ..."

So Attridge's confining of trisyllabic substitution to stress meter seems odd, since "stress meter, with very few exceptions, always falls into a four-beat rhythm" (63). When he finally does cite one instance of trisyllabic substitution in a pentameter—

$$\cup \ \cup \ /$$
What youth | ful moth | er, a shape | upon | her lap
Honey of generation has betrayed

—he does so in a two-paragraph section called "Free double offbeats" (125–26), where the distinction between his two basic meters falls apart.

In the second paragraph, in the sentence before he quotes Yeats's lines, he remarks that "the adding of a single unstressed syllable to a line of syllable-stress verse does not unduly disturb the duple meter." So there *is* a "possibility of moving between these options in the same line." And in the first paragraph of the section, he had noted:

Syllable-stress meter can be used with varying degrees of strictness. Not only may a particular line be regular or irregular, depending on the variations it employs, but a particular poem, poet, or age will often have a characteristic kind and degree of strictness.... Of course, to loosen up syllable-stress verse beyond a certain point turns it into something else: either stress verse (if it is four-beat, and conforms to the conditions for strict stress verse) or a kind of free verse.

Attridge doesn't explain what that "certain point" is, so his parting caveat seems pointless.

Neither "Among School Children" nor *The Ring and the Book* is four-beat or conforms to the conditions for strict stress verse," so they may be in syllable-stress meter or—depending on that uncertain point—in free verse. Despite conforming, ballad stanzas without anapests and Marlowe's "Come live with me and be my love" are in syllable-stress, not stress, meter. And, as Attridge himself allows (138), "triple syllable-stress meter is scarcely distinguishable from triple stress meter, since in both forms the triple meter establishes a powerful rhythm that tends to fall into the four-beat formation and to override the normal pronunciation of words."

The late admission that "syllable-stress meter can be used with varying degrees of strictness," suggests that Attridge's system has itself become more important than the verse it presumably exists only to describe. Central as disyllabic regularity may be to it, and as conceptually tempting, English verse somehow always escapes that artifice a little.

IV. Mr. Pinksy Sets a Problem

Meter in Merwin's Free Verse

> Strawberry wives lay two or three great strawberries at the mouth of their pot, and all the rest are little ones.
> —Sir Francis Bacon, *A Collection of Apophthegms* (1625)

It is almost a commonplace to note that poets whose free verse we most admire were trained in meter. Early in the century, Pound, Williams, Stevens of course; later, Theodore Roethke, Robert Lowell, Elizabeth Bishop, James Wright, Louis Simpson, W.S. Merwin. For Merwin the significant transition occurred in his fifth collection, *The Moving Target* (1963); and the full evolution into free verse was accomplished in *The Lice* (1967) and *The Carrier of Ladders* (1970).

We may observe the role of meter in that evolution by looking at three poems from these books. We will find, moreover, if we recognize the bacchic ($\cup$ //) as one of the essential six feet of English meter, that all three poems are in fact entirely metrical, that is, measurable by the same system.

We may also observe, in passing, several devices associated with free verse which Merwin brings to perfection in *The Carrier of Ladders*. One is the abandonment of punctuation (except for contractions like "I'm" or "it's") that is notable in the second (and later?) half of *The Moving Target*, and is thereafter uniform except in the stichomythic "The Last One" in *The Lice* (10–12). Another is the abandonment of line-capitals, which occurs only once in T*he Moving Target* (in "For the Grave of Posterity" 71), not at all in *The Lice*, and becomes uniform in *The Carrier of Ladders*. Yet another is what we may call the unpunctuated caesura, with which Merwin experiments in both earlier books, sometimes clumsily or distractingly as in this stanza of "In Autumn" (*The Lice* 41):

Moving on without memory
Without having been near turning elsewhere climbing
Nothing the wall

The device is used superbly in *The Carrier of Ladders*, however, where it rarely seems confusing or arbitrary. First, from *The Moving Target* (41), consider "The Poem":

```
x   /    ᴗ  /   ᴗ /   ᴗ
Com | ing late, | as al | ways,
ᴗ /  ᴗ  ᴗ /   ᴗ   /   ᴗ /   ᴗ    /
I try | to remem | ber what | I al | most heard.
  ᴗ   /   ᴗ /   ᴗ /
The light | avoids | my eye.
   /    /   ᴗ  /    ᴗ  ᴗ  /   ᴗ   /    /
How man | y times | have I heard | the locks close
  ᴗ   /    /   /   ᴗ  /
And the | lark take | the keys
  ᴗ   /   ᴗ  ᴗ  /   ᴗ
And hang | them in heav | en.
```

Note that, putting line 4 and its bacchic aside, the cadences of lines 1–3 and 5–6 are conventionally metrical and scan easily. All six lines are end-stopped, the sentences fully punctuated.

Twelve of the poem's twenty total feet are iambs; the pyrrhic and one of the two spondees form the familiar pyrrhic | spondee combination (as in Marvell's "To a | green thought ..."). The abrupt first foot of line 1, with its omitted initial syllable, may suggest lateness. Only four feet are trisyllabic.

This metricality is disguised by the longer lines' (one a pentameter, one a tetrameter) coming at different places and so giving an impression of stanzaic dissimilarity. But lines 1, 3, and 5 are trimeters—and line 6, an expressive diminuendo, a dimeter. The pattern of line length is *three*, five, *three*, four, *three*, two. The disguise seems too careful to be incidental.

In "For the Anniversary of My Death" (*The Lice* 58), Merwin continues to follow the convention of line-capitals, but uses no punctuation, so the poem seems freer. The stanzas differ in number of lines; and line-length visibly varies more, so one may not notice the diminution in length of lines 2, 3, 4 (reversed in 5) or the increase in length of lines 8, 9, 10, 11, 12 (reversed in the last line). A scansion:

```
x /   ᴗ   /    ᴗ  ᴗ   /    ᴗ /  ᴗ  ᴗ    /     ᴗ /
```

    Ev | ery year | without know | ing it | I have passed | the day

       ╱   ˘   ╱   ╱   ˘   ╱   ˘ ╱

    When the | last fires | will wave | to me

     ˘   ˘ ╱   ˘   ˘   ╱ ╱

    And the si | lence will | set out

x ╱   ˘   ╱   ˘ (╱)

     Tire | less trav | eller

     ˘   ˘   ╱   ˘ ˘ ╱   ˘ ╱

    Like the beam | of a light | less star

      ˘ ˘ ╱   ˘ ╱   ˘

    Then I will | no long | er

x ╱   ˘ ╱   ˘ ╱   ˘ ˘ ˘ ╱   ╱   ˘

    Find | myself | in life | as in | a strange gar | ment

      ˘ ╱   ˘ ˘ ╱

    Surprised | at the earth

      ˘ ˘ ╱   ˘ ╱ ╱   ˘

    And the love | of one wo | man

      ˘   ˘   ╱   ˘ ╱ ˘ ╱

    And then shame | less ness | of men

     ˘ ˘ ╱ ╱   ˘ ╱ ˘   ╱   ╱ ˘ ╱

    As to | day writ | ing af | ter three days | of rain

       ╱ ˘   ˘ ╱   ╱   ˘ ˘ ╱   ˘   ╱

    Hearing | the wren sing | and the fall | ing cease

      ˘ ╱   ˘ ˘ ╱   ˘ ˘ ╱

    And bow | ing not know | ing to what

Again, the poem is entirely metrical, although lines vary from one hexameter (line 1) to three dimeters (all early in stanza 2). Five of the thirteen lines are trimeters.

Among the poem's forty-five total feet, twenty-nine are disyllabic, including only eighteen iambs, although two instances (in lines 3, 11) of the pyrrhic | spondee combination occur. Notably, there are seventeen anapests and, here, four bacchics (all in stanza 2: in lines 7, 9, 11, 12). The trisyllabic feet produce the more flexible rhythm.

Except for the dovetailing enjambment in lines 6–7, the lines are again effectively end-stopped. Separating clauses and phrases in this way, Merwin keeps the sense flowing smoothly, even without punctuation. The absence of the comma we might expect after "bowing" becomes part of the play on participles in lines 11–13, which weaves together "writing," "Hearing," "falling," "bowing," "know" and perhaps even, "after three days of rain," "wren sing" (rinsing?).

   This device of unpunctuated caesura appears more frequently—and startlingly—in *The Carrier of Ladders*, which I believe is Merwin's most masterful collection in the new vein. Here is "Teachers" (4):

```
 /   ∪  ∪  /    /   /    ∪  /   ∪  /    ∪
Pain is | in this | dark room | like man | y speak | ers
∪ ∪  /   ∪ /    ∪      /
of a cost | ly set | though mute
∪   /   ∪   /   ∪  ∪   ∪   /    ∪
as here | the nee | dle and | the turn | ing
  ∪   /    /     ∪  /  ∪  /    ∪
the night length | ens it | is win | ter
 ∪  /   /
a new year


    ∪  ∪   /  /   ∪ ∪  /   ∪   ∪    /  /
what I | live for | I can sel | dom be | lieve in
  ∪  ∪  /  ∪  ∪  /    /  /
who I love | I cannot | go to
   ∪  ∪   /   ∪  /   ∪   ∪/   ∪
what I hope | is al | ways divid | ed


  ∪ ∪ /  ∪   ∪ /   ∪   ∪  /   ∪   /    /
but I say | to myself | you are not | a child now
 ∪ ∪   /    ∪  /    ∪ /    ∪   ∪   /    ∪ /    ∪
if the night | is long | remem | ber your un | impor | tance
x    /
sleep


x   /     ∪    /    ∪ ∪  /    ∪ ∪   /    /
then | toward morn | ing I dream | of the | first words
```

∪ ╱   ∪ ╱ ∪ (╱)
of books | of voy | ages

╱ ╱   ∪ ∪ ╱ ∪ ╱ ∪ ╱ ∪╱ ∪
sure tell | ings that did | not start | by jus | tify | ing

╱ ∪ ╱ ╱ ∪ ╱
yet at | one time | it seems

∪ ╱ ∪
had taught | me

Yet again, the poem is metrical if we credit bacchics. There are three, in lines 4, 5, 9. Of fifty-four total feet, thirty-six are disyllabic and include twenty-three iambs. One of two initial feet with an omitted syllable is dovetailed (lines 10–11) and there are two pyrrhic | spondee combinations (lines 6, 12). Thirteen anapests appear.

Six lines are trimeters; five, pentameters; with two tetrameters, three monometers.

Stanzas carefully modulate the pace of the narrative. Visually, three-line stanzas with a shorter middle line appear alternately with stanzas ending in diminished, one-foot lines—though the second and last of the latter are two-line stanzas, so the pattern is somewhat hidden.

The poem uses no punctuation, and only line 1 has a line-capital. A more daring unpunctuated caesura occurs in line 4—made possible, I think, by the line's metricality that smoothly carries the voice past the caesura so that both readings of "it" ("night lengthens it [the pain]" and "it [the season] is winter") coexist without competition or confusion.

Free verse was always a myth, as Eliot said (*To Criticize the Critic* 183–84). The myth succeeded because we wanted to believe. But an important contributing reason was that, if anybody was counting, the bacchic—and its natural bit of English rhythm—was not credited as a foot in our meter, although it may be found in poems from the sixteenth century on. The bacchic was concealed behind the anapest, which itself was not credited in literary meter until about 1800. (The bacchic might, thus, be called the "free-verse foot.") Another contributory reason for the myth's success was the unwarranted assumption that lines in a poem should be of equivalent length—unwarranted, given Herbert's "The Collar," Arnold's "Dover Beach," and so on. So a further muddle arose on that score, with prosodists convinced that any variation in line length made a poem free verse—and obviated counting.

Whatever the reason, in reading Merwin's three poems it was easy to over-look the twenty-seven metrical lines without bacchics—lines all readily scan-nable, lines drawing on plainly metrical cadences for their rhythm. Writing in 1967 (qtd. in Berg and Mezey 270–71), Merwin perhaps catches in two paragraphs the paradox I have been describing, which are poems "free" and yet "in meter":

> In an age when time and technique encroach hourly, or appear to, on the source itself of poetry, it seems as though what is needed for any particular nebulous unwritten hope that may become a poem is not a manipulable, more or less predictably recurring pattern, but an unduplicatable resonance, something that would be like an echo except that it is repeating no sound. Something that always belonged to it: its sense and its conformation before it entered words....
>
> At the same time I realize that I am a formalist, in the most strict and orthodox sense. For years I have had a recurring dream of finding, as it were in an attic, poems of my own that were as lyrically formal, but as limpid and essentially unliterary as those of Villon.

I, too, am a formalist. And I've had a similar recurring dream.

On Not Teaching Poetry (1966)

The problems—like the pleasures—of teaching poetry are obvious to anyone who has tried it in the classroom. Yawns from the back row, the chilly indifference from bright students who see in physics or political science the golden landscapes of the future, and—possibly most disheartening—the bumbling and myopic eagerness of the loyal few, who find symbols where there are none, who hurl jargon ahead of them like bridges, who blindly argue for the magic of l's and s's and r's that sound like running water or tiger growls, who can freely associate and see anything but the poem on the page. These last are most embarrassing, for they give us back our nonsense with a vengeance: to whom we have perhaps done the greatest disservice, since they are willing to believe us. But, I suspect, we know that we have failed them all. And, I suspect further, we know that we have somehow managed to fail ourselves.

Something seems to be wrong. Wrong despite our elaborate system of literary training—despite the courses and theories in teachers' colleges, despite the carefully contrived syllabi and textbooks (complete with meticulous questions and study hints and even, sometimes, diagrams that should set an engineering student's fears at rest). And wrong despite lectures like this one, symposia at meetings of English teachers, articles in *The English Journal* and *College English* on "'The City in the Sea': A Re-Examination" or "The 'Death Wish' in 'Stopping by Woods.'" Wrong despite Project English and the efforts of the Advanced Placement program.

I do not intend to belittle these efforts, many of which are valuable and necessary; but, despite them and although the new criticism and the art of analysis have become inescapable in our schools and in that great leveler, Freshman English, and although English departments in the colleges are thronged with majors, something is fundamentally awry. Every year we send out thousands upon thousands of products of the system ... *and they don't read poetry*. They have lost, or perhaps never acquired, the habit, the joyful skill of reading poetry. Like ourselves, they queue up for the latest movie, buy tickets months in advance for the newest play, rush out to buy the most recent novel for a perfect evening at home. But they are apt not even to know about new books of poems, much less look forward eagerly to them. A new book of poems, in a nation of nearly 200 million, is lucky to sell 200 copies. Few libraries trouble with them. A runaway best-seller may go to 10,000 copies—once or twice a decade—although the texts we require students to buy sell into the hundreds of thousands of copies each year. And I suspect the sales of Chaucer or Spenser or Donne or Pope or Wordsworth are negligible from year to year. *Is it unfair to suggest that the result is strangely disproportionate to the effort?*

And our "younger" poets turn out to be in their forties or fifties before we hear of them. I imagine that more literate Americans know the names (if not the poems!) of Yevgeny Yevtushenko and Andrei Voznesensky than of *our* thirty-year-old American poets. Wendell Berry, Larry Rubin, Donald Finkel, Sylvia Plath (now dead), Robert Sward, Frederick Seidel, David Slavitt, Tim Reynolds, Lewis Turco, Robert Bagg, Robert Mezey. The names of those nearer to forty may be more familiar: Allen Ginsberg, Theodore Holmes, Paris Leary, Kenneth Pitchford, Peter Davison, Frank O'Hara, Carolyn Kizer, George Garrett, Robert Bly, John Hollander, W.S. Merwin, James Merrill, John Ashberry, Gregory Corso, Robert Creeley, Henri Coulette, Philip Levine, Donald Peterson, James Wright, Anne Sexton, Robert Watson, David Wagoner, Philip Legler, May Swenson, X.J. Kennedy, Donald Hall, Galway Kinnell, A.R. Ammons, David Ray, Robert Pack, Maxine Kumin, Charles Gullans, George Starbuck, Adrienne Rich. Here are some in their forties—a few will begin to stand out: Edward Field, Davie Ferry, Edgar Bowers, Daniel Hoffman, Alan Dugan, Denise Levertov, Jon Swan, Jane Cooper, Philip Booth, Donald Justice, Joseph Langland, James Dickey, Arnold Kenseth, Vassar Miller, Alan Ansen, W.D. Snodgrass, Samuel French Morse, Kenneth Koch, William Jay Smith, Barbara Howes, Anthony Hecht, William Meredith, Howard Nemerov, Reed Whittemore, Robert Lowell, Robert Huff, Howard Moss, Richard Wilbur, Edwin Honig, Louis Simpson (the Pulitzer Prize last year), Jack Gilbert, John Logan, Gene Baro. And just to test you, a few in their fifties: Elizabeth Bishop, Robert Fitzgerald, Charles Olson, E.L. May, Richmond Lattimore, John Berryman, Jean Garrigue, Delmore Schwartz, Winfield Townley Scott, and Theodore Roethke and Randall Jarrell if they had lived. Stanley Kunitz and Robert Francis are in their sixties, as John Holmes would be had he lived. Our students and graduates know the names of few of these, and I doubt whether the teachers of poetry in our schools and colleges would do much better. I suspect that the reading of poetry for pleasure is pretty much a dead art, even among those who profess it. And I submit that 50¢ a line—seven dollars for a sonnet that may last as long as English does—is pretty poor pay, but represents the value our society places on poetry. I'll pass on without trying to assess the responsibility for our culture, a matter I'm probably not competent to discuss, and without trying to deal with the blame which poets certainly share, which is a bitter topic for a different audience.

This failure of the teaching of poetry is stranger still since children—the raw material fed into our machine—do trust literature, poetry, and enjoy it gaily and unsuspiciously. They are our primitives, delight in the magic of language, and even use poetry for solving the practical problems of their world: "Eeny meeny miny mo" or "One potato, two potato, three potato, four." And they employ it as name magic to protect themselves, without realizing what they are doing and without knowing that they are dealing in tetrameters or assonance: "Pudden-tane; ask me again and I'll tell you the same"; or to hurl insults: "Nancy pancy." We may well wonder what has happened to this natural impulse to use and enjoy language poetically by the time they have become the dour, resisting students we often see in Freshman English classes … and never see again.

The problems are complex and difficult, and easy blame like easy solutions will miss the mark. Generalizations are hard, since what is or should be done at any given level will in part be determined by what has been done before or what is to be done next. Always we must begin where the students are, and take them as far as we can.

When the subject, "Teaching Poetry," was suggested to me, I thought I would talk about some of the luck I've had with poems in the classroom and why I thought it happened. But as a poet, I kept bringing the Greek horse of poetry into the Trojan walls of criticism. The concomitant of teaching poetry is *studying* it, and the very word sends a chill through me. A poem is not to *study*, answer questions about, take examinations on, but to *read* or *hear* for pleasure. The experience of poetry—of any literary work—should be *joy*.

The first essential in any art is *delight*. Horace said that poetry should "teach and delight," not that it should "be taught." The *poem* will do the teaching, if any is to be done, just as it will do the delighting if it is left to its own powers and if we do not claim more for it than it does for itself. The first necessity is to read, that is, enjoy, relish, follow, lose one's self and self-consciousness in the pleasure of the poem. Only then may one ask questions, or be asked questions, without danger. If this joy is sufficient, it will support—indeed, will stimulate—any amount of learning and study. Judgment, criticism, may come after we like the work of art. But the joy must come first. Knowing that Old Whiskers is going to ask some sharp questions in class in the morning and that there will be a two-hour examination at the end of term, alas, can set up a deadly environment for understanding poems. I remember the profound relief of a girl to whom I'd been trying to teach prosody—when I accidentally said that I don't *analyze* every poem I read. Her eyes lit up to know that she hadn't been wrong about what to do with a poem. You don't ask questions of it *unless you want to*. Any work of art requires what I shall call the *necessary ignorance*—which is a little more than "willing suspension of disbelief," but not much more. We must submit ourselves to the poem or painting, ignorant as barbarians, willing to go the way it takes us, unable to go any other way; prepared to feel first and, if necessary, to think later. C.S. Lewis, in *An Experiment in Criticism* (1961), has imagined a family in which the confusions of literary activity are plain:

> As there are, or were, families and circles in which it was almost a social necessity to display an interest in hunting, or county cricket, or the Army List, so there are others where it requires great independence not to talk about, and therefore occasionally to read, the approved literature, especially the new and astonishing works, and those which have been banned or have become in some other way subjects of controversy. Readers of this sort, this "small vulgar," act in one respect exactly like those of the "great vulgar." They are entirely dominated by fashion. They drop the Georgians and begin to admire Mr. Eliot, acknowledge the "dislodgement" of Milton, and discover Hopkins, at exactly the right moment .... Yet, while this goes on downstairs, the only real literary experience in such a family may be occurring in a back bedroom where a small boy is reading *Treasure Island* under the bedclothes by the light of an electric torch. (6-7)

Beginning with the necessary ignorance will probably lead on to more sophisticated levels of reading and thinking about what we read. If we have encountered something we like, we will want to talk about it—whether at a cocktail party or in a classroom—and to listen to the best talk about it we can find; we call that criticism. But these "higher" levels of activity cannot truly exist without the foundation of ignorant joy, carelessness about why we are made to feel strange or special by a poem as long as we do—or, to change the metaphor slightly, without the intimate and unforced reading in the *cellar* of ourselves, when we are alone with the book.

I read all these signs as a *failure of joy* and, in some measure I suspect, we all are ill from it. Its clearest evidence is the sort of cultural fright which makes us *suffer* through poems or concerts or trips through a museum because we think we *should* like these things, because it is expected of us. Of all the boredoms, cultural boredom may be the worst, because it teaches us at rock bottom to feel—we would never dare say or perhaps even think it—that the classics are bores. Once burned, forever shy. I think that poems can compete with baseball and girls *on their own terms*, for there is enough of life to allow for what Cotton Mather called "a little recreation of poetry," if we can contrive not to convince our pupils—and ourselves—that poems are miserable duties. Good reading is a series of self-discoveries; we must learn to keep our hands off until they happen, if they do. We shall not be worse off if they don't happen of themselves, for we could never have forced them. We may invite, but we cannot bully.

As a poet, I sometimes feel that the job is to get poetry out of the schools and back under the bedsheet. Our students who read Donne or Pope or Frost because we make them—and so often read them badly and convince themselves they're missing nothing—in fact read Ginsberg or Ferlinghetti or Kahlil Gibran under the bedsheets after the lights are out. Or Ayn Rand. Perhaps if we forbade them to read Donne and Spenser (as being too sexy) and tried to argue that "Trees" is a finer poem than "On His Blindness," if we *taught* Call-him Gibberish and turned up our noses at Wallace Stevens, we might find we had won our battle. Cultural rebelliousness is a fact of youth; and we might get it on our side. This of course is a pipedream. But the contamination of literary joy in the classroom seems to me to be the principal fact we have to deal with. These young people discovered Salinger's *The Catcher in the Rye* and nearly wore it out under the bedsheets *until it got into the schools.*

When I first started teaching nine years ago, it brought a light into every eye. Several casebooks later, two weeks ago, talking with a class about what they'd like to read, they shrugged it off as blandly as they did *The Return of the Native. Catcher* seems to be joining *Lord Jim* and *A Passage to India* in that literary limbo we are responsible for. I think *Catcher* is a very good book, though a very different one from what our students once upon a time thought they were reading. But no matter of that: they *were reading it* and probably would have discovered somewhere along the line what its real virtues are. Now they are beginning not to read it at all.

Well, what are some of the things we—the shoe pinches me with the worst—what are some of the things we are doing to poetry in the classroom that we shouldn't be doing? The first thing seems to me to be *hurrying* the student along too fast. I see two kinds of dangerous hurry. One simply is expecting—wanting!—students to read at a level of sophistication they aren't ready for. We push our preferences backwards into the schools. What we teach in Freshman English this year will be taught in Advanced Placement courses in the schools next year and in regular courses in the year after. In one school I visited, "Sir Gawain and the Green Knight" was read in the eighth grade, and a full-scale, ten-week, all guns blazing study of Yeats was going on in the eleventh grade. This begins to leave nothing to teach in college, producing bored "we-have-been-there-before" attitudes which make any learning nearly impossible. This is part of the objection to reading snippets of things in school courses—Books I and II of *Paradise Lost*, only Lilliput from *Gulliver's Travels*—which entitle students to feel, and say, that they've *done* these things and are waiting for some still greater miracles of college. Every college English teacher looks for and can tell sad tales about those dangerous students who have already "done" it. (But of course they have never read Walter Scott or Anthony Trollope or Robert Herrick, nor enough of Dickens, and they will be surprised that anyone can take Campion or Ben Jonson seriously.) And in many cases, we know, they haven't really made much sense of *Moby-Dick* or Kafka—have in fact been burned by overexposure to Yeats and *Heart of Darkness* or "The Secret Sharer" and the critical magnifying glasses we like to use. We are all tempted to teach as we have learned, to import into a schoolroom or undergraduate classroom methods and levels of discussion we have encountered in our own classes in college or in graduate school.

Over the years I have come to think that the greatest virtue of my school education—aside from the endlessly poetic hours I was required to sit in the hall facing a clock—was that I was underexposed to the best or even good poetry. I recall being ecstatic in the fourth grade over a piece called "Somebody's Mother," and my favorite poets for years were Robert W. Service (the only poems owned in our household), James Whitcomb Riley (a 39¢ copy of which a strange lady bought me when I was staring, penniless and obviously yearning, at a department store book counter), Eugene Field, Ogden Nash, and Richard Armour, in about that order. We read "Evangeline" in the eighth grade, but I don't think I thought of it as poetry. Thanks to the glorious ineptness of Miss May Berry in the tenth and eleventh grades—I suspect she liked poetry, but couldn't bring herself to try to persuade the sarcastic football players on the back row to sample anything loftier than *The Reader's Digest*—and to a dreadful advising system which let me skip the senior lit course, I managed to reach college with a marvelous and teachable ignorance. I was ready for whatever was served up. I remember being surprised, in English I at Harvard as a freshman, that my classmates already seemed to know who Chaucer was. My achieved ignorance was even more of a triumph, as I had been writing poems of my own since the fourth grade—when "My Pup and Me" was printed in the city newspaper.[17]

A second, more dangerous kind of hurry is that automatically produced by deadlines, for quizzes or papers, or even by our expectations for class discussion. A genuine response to any poem requires a certain leisure, and, as you know, will develop naturally only through many readings over a long period of time. More perhaps depends on where *we* are in our reading skill and pleasure than on the poem. I suppose it is possible to like a poem and read it for years without ever making very much of it—"The Waste Land" might be a good case in point—enjoying its sound or the color of its imagery, without saying or having to say what it means. This is why poets and novelists so often seem to turn aside questions about what they meant or whether they meant this or that. It is perhaps more important for the reader to find *out for himself* than for him to be told. T.S. Eliot remarked:

> I know that some of the poetry to which I am most devoted is poetry which I did not understand at first reading; some is poetry which I am not sure I understand yet: for instance, Shakespeare's. (*The Use of Poetry and the Use of Criticism* 150)

And yet we create an artificial reading situation in the schools, demand of students a full, analytical account of a poem they have read once, maybe twice, the night before. Nothing is easier than to set up a kind of critical shooting gallery in the classroom and knock over, rather miraculously, on by one, rabbits the students have never seen. And by so doing, intimidate them as readers forever. It is no wonder they deliver to us so much nonsense, fail to see the poem for its symbols or techniques. It is no wonder they rush to the library for some criticism, for they know that only in that way can they find whatever it is that will satisfy us when we turn on them from the desk. In truth, perhaps we should admit, many of them never *read* the poems at all. It is not enough that we know we are not demanding more of a response than an intelligent first reading, because, whatever we say, we act in class and grade papers and exams

---

[17] "This is his favorite among the poems he has written so far," writes a local columnist in the *Springfield Daily News* of 23 February 1942: "We are a funny sight to see / Just my pup and me. / When time to go to school / I wish my pup goodby. / Gosh it's swell / To have a pup… / I wouldn't give her up, No sir!…" *-Eds.*

as if we expected the impossible. And, sweet innocents, they try to give us what they think we want.

This leads me to the second main thing we shouldn't be doing, or at least doing as we do. The use of criticism as a teaching activity is fraught with dangers. We demand analysis at a high level without being sure that the joy requires it or even makes it possible. Students lose sight of the poems, are afraid to react themselves, lope off unhappily to introductions and books of criticism because of the kind and level of response we expect. We scare them to death. And they end up seeing books through other books ... which isn't seeing them at all. Criticism, what ought to be forgotten, is too often what is remembered. There is a vast gulf between clearing away difficulties and adding them.

We are all victims of the overpowering criticism of our time. I sometimes wonder whether we haven't come to believe that books, poems, are less something to *read* than something to *say something about*. That is the clear implication of our class discussions, papers, exams. I know our students believe it. That is why overreading is their besetting sin. That is why we are buried in our own jargon about myth and form and symbols and structure. That is why they tell us meaninglessly that a poem is in iambic tetrameter or that there is an anapest in line three. That is why they say l's—nonsensically—mean something. That is why, without ever seeing the poem itself, they retail a lot of guff about Existentialism, Jungian psychology, phallic symbols, or good and evil in *Alice in Wonderland*. They don't do all this because they enjoy it; they do it because they think we expect it. Our danger isn't in bringing up readers who can't tell a hawk from a handsaw, but readers who can't tell either one from a symbol. The net effect of all the criticism in which we are immersed and in which, willy-nilly, we immerse our students, is to destroy the very *life* of the literature we value.

Let me put my point in a simple statement of C.S. Lewis's, which will be true till the end of time. *"It is always better to read Chaucer again than to read the critics"* (*Experiment* 110). I submit that will be true no matter how many times one goes through *The Canterbury Tales*. It is always better to read Chaucer again than to read the critics. If that leaves us spluttering "But" and "Still" and "On the other hand," so much the better. We need a little gravel in our craw. It is always better to read Chaucer again than to read the critics.

There are two additional dangers in criticism in our teaching. One is what I might call the *judgment fallacy*, the belief, which criticism inculcates, that we must make judgments about and among works of art. We may want to do this, but we don't have to. Perhaps we should do it as little as we can. Milton is not a better poet than Herrick because his subject is bigger or more important.

You see this judgment fallacy at its worst when our reviewers condemn John Updike or Richard Wilbur for not being Dostoyevsky or Rimbaud. The cultural, philosophical, or political importance of a work of art is the *last* thing that matters, never the first. In one of the quality reviews this fall, Robert Frost is niggled at because he lacked what the critic calls a "tragic howl." By such standards, I can't imagine how Shakespeare could ever have managed "hey nony nony" ... nor where we would be without it.

The other critical danger is that we are led to teach *difficult* poems because there is more to talk about, more to unravel and explain. It is a deal easier to make a class go on for an hour with "The Canonization" than with "Drink to me only with thine eyes." At least without falling into nonsense. And when students begin to see that difficulty is an important criterion for what we consider good poetry, I don't blame them if they vanish forever into James Bond and *The Reader's Digest* and never come back. The appropriate response to a poem is silence, not talk. We must somehow learn to teach by being *quiet* enough.

The worst villains are texts with questions and apparatus and study hints, which blight the pleasure by implying that poems are things to ask questions about, to *study*, not to enjoy, which set out to satisfy interests the student didn't know he had (and probably *didn't* have). Publishers, who know what things sell, are concerned more about the prose than about the poems it is meant to buoy up. When Mr. Taaffe and I were hunting a publisher for our anthology, *Poems on Poetry* (Dutton, 1965)—an effort, by the way, to let poetry teach itself—one publisher didn't even want to see a list of the poems, but was eager to have the prose he assumed must pad the book, ten or fifteen thousand words at least. In the end we weren't able to avoid having some little introductions, if we were to get the book published at all—which I recommend you ignore if you read it.

One generalization: Critical activity is illegitimate whenever it is answering questions the reader hasn't yet asked.

The third thing we shouldn't be doing is *enforcing taste*, which is an extension of the critical function and the judgment fallacy. To tell the student that what he likes is a bad poem may be awakening, but I suspect that more often it kills off his liking for anything. He becomes afraid to like anything, or hides it, for fear of being berated. Those analytical texts are again the worst offenders with their invidious comparisons and outright assaults. Brooks and Warren's murderous attack on "Trees" no doubt finishes off the poem, and it may also finish off the student.[18] I have gone into class armed with their dead-ly—deadening?—logic and found myself in the end facing increasingly stub-born and beleaguered partisans of "Trees," "The Little Toy Soldier," and no doubt that favorite of my own once-upon-a-time, "Somebody's Mother." It is a combat I doubt if we can win. I doubt if we should try. Bullying isn't discovery. In fact, I'm not so sure anymore that "Trees" and "The Little Toy Soldier" are bad poems. We may have outgrown them, and we may hope that our students will. But if they do not, or cannot, it would be grossest folly on our part to abuse and possibly ruin for them what they are capable of reading and liking. I don't mean that we shouldn't have preferences or make them known. The best defense against bad poems is the introduction of good poems; and I believe that in due time, however long and wasteful it may seem to us, Marvell and Yeats and even Milton will replace Kilmer and Ogden Nash and James Whit-comb Riley. But we must be willing to wait.

The folly is in expecting all readers to be like ourselves in the end. Litera-ture is not a kingdom, however wise may be the philosopher we would choose as king, but a delightful anarchy in which only fools pretend to be kings. We should be glad that this is so. It would be humorless to insist that no one can be truly a meaningful and cultured human being without a taste for Dryden. And it may be equally humorless to insist that no pupil can have our blessing unless he has abjured "The Little Toy Soldier" and proved he relishes John Donne. The classics in a sense judge us, not us them. I do not like Shelley and am no doubt the worse for it. But it will hardly do to force the issue. Any hon-est response is better than a very elaborate, even correct, but dishonest one. C.S. Lewis makes this point in *The World's Last Night* (1960):

> Suppose you had spent an evening among very young and very transparent snobs who were feigning a discriminating enjoyment of a great port, though anyone who knew could see very well that, if they had ever drunk port in their lives before, it came from a grocer's. And then suppose that on your journey home you went into a grubby little teashop and there heard an old body in a feather boa say to another old body, with a smack of her lips, "That was a nice cup o' tea, dearie, that was. Did me good." Would you not, at that moment, feel that this was like fresh mountain air? For here, at last, would

---

[18] See Cleanth Brooks and Robert Warren, *Understanding Poetry* (1960), 391. Wallace refers to Joyce Kilmer's "Trees" (1914); later in the paragraph, he cites Eugene Field's "Little Boy Blue" (1888) and "Somebody's Mother" (1878), by Mary Dow Brine. *-Eds.*

be something real. Here would be a mind really concerned about that in which it expressed concern. Here would be pleasure, here would be undebauched experience, spontaneous and compulsive, from the fountainhead.

A live dog is better than a dead lion. In the same way, after a certain sherry party, where there have been cataracts of *culture* but never one word or one glance that suggested a real enjoyment of any art, any person, or any natural object, my heart warms to the schoolboy on the bus who is reading *Fantasy and Science Fiction*, rapt and oblivious of all the world beside. For here also I should feel that I had met something real and live and unfabricated; genuine literary experience, spontaneous and compulsive, disinterested. I should have hopes of that boy. Those who have greatly cared for any book whatever may possibly come to care, someday, for good books. The organs of appreciation exist in them. They are not impotent. And even if this particular boy is never going to like anything severer than science fiction, even so,

> The child whose love is here, at least doth reap
> One precious gain, that he forgets himself.

I should still prefer the live dog to the dead lion; perhaps, even, the wild dog to the overtame poodle or Peke. (38-39)

And while I am quoting, let me call in Mr. Eliot again (*Use* 24-25):

I do not know whether little girls have a different taste in poetry from little boys, but the responses of the latter I believe to be fairly uniform. *Horatius at the Bridge, The Burial of Sir John Moore, Bannockburn*, Tennyson's *Revenge*, some of the border ballads: a liking for martial and sanguinary poetry is no more to be discouraged than engagements with lead soldiers and peashooters. The only pleasure that I got from Shakespeare was the pleasure of being commended for reading him; had I been a child of more independent mind I should have refused to read him at all. Recognizing the frequent deceptions of memory, I seem to remember that my early liking for the sort of verse that small boys do like vanished at about the age of twelve, leaving me for a couple of years with no sort of interest in poetry at all. I can recall clearly enough the moment when, at the age of fourteen or so, I happened to pick up a copy of Fitzgerald's *Omar* which was lying about, and the almost overwhelming introduction to a new world of feeling which this poem was the occasion of giving me. It was like a sudden conversion; the world appeared anew, painted with bright, delicious and painful colours. Thereupon I took the usual adolescent course with Byron, Shelley, Keats, Rossetti, Swinburne.

Eliot goes on to describe a third phase of his reading, which he dates from his twenty-second year, in which what I have called the necessary ignorance, a deliberate ignorance, can exist side by side with a critical awareness. This is very sophisticated activity, no doubt, and some readers may never reach it at all; most of us will be blocked off, as I am from Shelley, from ever achieving the necessary ignorance with certain authors or books. (This leads to a consideration of how we read at the highest level—not of real readings but of creating a kind of "ideal" reading which no actual experience can ever more than approximate—which is beyond the scope of this too short hour.)

These problems will look very different at different levels in the educational process. I suspect, for instance, that the college's expectation of a serious *interest* in its students is legitimate; the university isn't the place to evangelize for poetry—it may be way too late—although we'd be witless if we didn't take the world as we find it. We must, of course, all of us, keep separate in our minds reading (the exaltation which we value) and studying (the perception of the reading experience itself), for the main pedagogical problem seems to me to be delight. In general, let me suggest some positive ways of *not* teaching poetry.

1. I suggest a return to, or at least a major shift in emphasis toward, the *factual* in examinations and papers. Spot passages to be identified, words or phrases to be glossed, plots to be summarized, paraphrases. Research—factual, biographical—instead of critical papers. Our students are drowning in a morass of interpretive and critical activity for which they are not, and perhaps can never be, prepared. It is fair at the various levels to require them to read certain works, and to ask them to prove it, but it is neither just nor tactful to demand that they deliver us a certain kind of response, that—God help us—they prove that they *like* it. What goes on between the student and Donne or Dryden is a private matter. I suspect that we shall find that more goes on than we might believe, and certainly more than goes on when we force the student to work up a response which, most of the time, will not be his nor even genuine. And the jungle of gobbledygook in their writing will vanish overnight and the critical creepers that entangle the poems will shrink up and disappear, leaving the poems healthily and fully in the center.

2. I suggest that, instead of further educational prose, we invite real live poets into the schools, and I am thinking more even of the high schools and grades than of the colleges, where already a valid tradition is beginning to persist. There are plenty of poets around, and they would be glad to come and would cost very little. Most of them can read and talk about poetry, their own or just poems they like, with an authority and pleasure that will be infectious. A number of our best poets have even written books of poems for children. Some have already made their way into the schools—John Ciardi and William Jay Smith, whose forays into the grades are well known. I wager no third-grader, or tenth-grader, in a school Mr. Ciardi has visited will ever think poetry is sissy stuff. If a school system—or the Foundations—would put up the cash to have poets visit around in the schools for half days now and again, I suspect a lot of the problems of teaching poetry would turn out to have been solved.

3. I suggest that we all might do more in reading poetry aloud, ourselves, or having the students read to each other, since poetry is essentially an oral art. The noise a poem makes can be exciting and may be the easiest way into it. If we cannot have the poets themselves visiting the schools or teaching in them, we can have good collections of records of poets reading and use them frequently. I'm thinking of grade schools as well as high schools and colleges. We very much need a series of recordings of contemporary poets designed for use in the grades, and maybe some films.

4. I suggest not only that we resist texts with teaching aids—in which poems are harnessed into dragging sledges of numbered prose—but that we need more and better anthologies of *contemporary* poems, which publishers resist because of copyright fees. It is cheaper to use "Ozymandias" again than to get Wallace Stevens or E.E. Cummings or Richard Wilbur. It seems clear to me that we ought to begin in grade school with *contemporary* poems, since they are likely to be a lot easier to understand than poems still posturing in the manners of earlier centuries. Even grade school libraries should be flush with as many recent and uncondescending collections as can be found or milked from publishers. (An excellent anthology of sports poems, *Sprints and Distances*, just out, should be put in reach of as many hands as possible.) These books will be coming along in the next decade, and it will be up to the teachers in the grades and in the high schools to be looking for them and to insist that the money be found for them when they show up.

(I proposed to one publisher a paper anthology of really up-to-date poems for use in the schools, and was told there would be no market for it. Our publisher of *Poems on Poetry* doubts that many of the schools—for which it seems to be perfect—will be adventurous enough to pick it up for senior lit courses and advanced placement sections. They think teachers prefer the fat, old-fashioned walruses of textbooks with the endlessly reprinted "Ozymandias," but I don't believe that. If the teacher is bored, it is certain that the pupils will be. And, wherever the money or the will can be found, in schools or colleges, poetry rooms like the Woodberry Room in Lamont Library at Harvard should be set up—with books, records, comfortable chairs, smoking privileges, jack-record-players.

5. I suggest we can do more to let students *choose* the poems or poets they want to read. The burden of proof will thus be partly on them. If good enough texts are used and if libraries are vigorously up-to-date, it should be easy enough for them to come enthusiastically back to the classroom with something they *want* to talk about. And since talking about poems may be a dangerous activity, even we in colleges might think more of requiring students to memorize poems they like. It may strike us—and them—as old-fashioned and mechanical, but it may be better than a lot of things I know we are doing. Like the factual exam, it might take the pressure off in just the right places.

6. Finally, I suggest that we experiment more than we have with teaching *poetry-reading* by teaching *poetry-writing*. Students, especially in the grades, are full of artistic impulses we might take advantage of. We should find ways of encouraging and directing a playfulness with words. Writing is one way of getting technical questions asked, and getting the student to ask the questions is the art of teaching in a nutshell. Several years ago I taught a television workshop in writing verse for school children in Philadelphia, including some fifth graders. I am convinced that grade-schoolers can learn the rudiments of prosody and technical alternatives which they will need if their efforts are not to peter out into the mere repetitions of expressionism, the dullness of which they will see soon enough. A well turned couplet, they will find, is more fun to have written than a scraggly bit of free verse. And a quatrain more fun yet. We might even expect a revival of limericks! I am not promising any miracles, but I think students can be led on just as they now are in art or music in the schools. What surprises me in fact is

that when we think of teaching art or music in the schools we think of the students as *doing*, but that when we think of teaching poetry we think of them only as consumers. All this will take a lot of skill and tact on the part of teachers, and I can see the difficulties becoming more and more formidable as one goes on toward and into a high school curriculum. It may be necessary for the teachers to write poems themselves before it can be made to work. Courses in writing and in teaching writing may be wanted in our teacher training, and poets may be needed in summer institutes for English teachers.

None of this is meant as a map of where we are going, but it is at least one poet's tour folder. It is enough if I can suggest some possible directions ... and that we may find, one morning, that our ways of teaching poetry—or *not* teaching it, as I would have it—changed quite as much as the new arithmetic is altering the educational landscape.

A Wallace Bibliography

Citations of Critics and Criticism

Alden, R.M. *An Introduction to Poetry for Students of English Literature.* Henry Holt, 1909.

Attridge, Derek. *Poetic Rhythm: An Introduction.* Cambridge UP, 1996.

Baker, David. "Introduction." *Meter in English: A Critical Engagement*, edited by David Baker. U of Arkansas P, 1996, pp. ix-xxii.

Baker, David, editor. *Meter in English: A Critical Engagement.* U of Arkansas P, 1996.

Bate, W. Jackson, and David Perkins, editors. *British and American Poets: Chaucer to the Present.* Harcourt, 1986.

Bridges, Robert. *Milton's Prosody, With a Chapter on Accentual Verse and Notes.* Oxford UP, 1901.

Berg, Stephen, and Robert Mezey, editors. *Naked Poetry: Recent American Poetry in Open Forms.* Macmillan, 1969.

Brogan, T.V.F., editor. *The New Princeton Handbook of Poetic Terms.* Princeton UP, 1994.

Bysshe, Edward. *The Art of English Poetry.* 1708. Augustan Reprint Society, edited with an introduction by A. Dwight Culler. U of California P, 1958.

Chatman, Seymour. "Robert Frost's 'Mowing': An Inquiry into Prosodic Structure," *Kenyon Review*, vol. 18, 1956, pp. 421-38.

Corn, Alfred. *The Poem's Heartbeat: A Manual of Prosody.* Copper Canyon, 1997.

Cureton, Richard D. *Rhythmic Phrasing in English Verse.* Longman, 1992.

Deutsch, Babette. *Poetry Handbook: A Dictionary of Terms.* HarperCollins, 1974.

Dobyns, Stephen, *Best Words, Best Order: Essays on Poetry*. St. Martin's, 1996.

Eliot, T.S. "Introduction: 1928." *The Selected Poems of Ezra Pound*. By Ezra Pound. 1928. Faber, 1948, pp. 7-21.

——. *On Poetry and Poets*. Farrar, Straus and Giroux, 1957.

——. "Reflections on *Vers Libre*." *To Criticize the Critic and Other Writings*. 1964. U of Nebraska P, 1992, pp. 183-87.

——. *The Use of Poetry and the Use of Criticism*. Faber and Faber, 1933.

Finch, Annie. *The Ghost of Meter: Culture and Prosody in American Free Verse*. U of Michigan P, 1993.

——. "Metrical Diversity: A Defense of the Non-Iambic Meters." *Meter in English: A Critical Engagement*, edited by David Baker. U of Arkansas P, 1996, pp. 59-74.

Frye, Northrop. *Anatomy of Criticism*. Princeton UP, 1957.

——. *Sound and Poetry: English Institute Essays*, 1956. Columbia UP, 1967.

Fussell, Paul. *Poetic Meter and Poetic Form*. McGraw Hill, 1965.

Gardner, Helen. *The Art of T.S. Eliot*. Dutton, 1950.

Gascoigne, George. *Certayne Notes of Instruction Concerning the Making of Verse or Ryme in English*. London, 1575. Reprint Publications, 1977.

Gibbs, Lincoln R, editor. *Selections from Coleridge*. Ginn and Co., 1916.

Gioia, Dana. "Meter-Making Arguments." *Meter in English: A Critical Engagement*, edited by David Baker. U of Arkansas P, 1996, pp. 75-96.

Gross, Harvey. *Sound and Form in Modern Poetry: A Study of Prosody from Thomas Hardy to Robert Lowell*. U of Michigan P, 1964.

Gross, Harvey, and Robert McDowell. *Sound and Form in Modern Poetry*, 2nd edition. U of Michigan P, 1996.

Hall, Donald. *The Pleasures of Poetry*. Harper, 1971.

Halle, Morris, and Samuel Jay Keyser. *English Stress: Its Form, Its Growth, and Its Role in Verse*. Harper, 1971.

Harmon, William, editor. *The Classic Hundred Poems: All Time Favorites*. Columbia UP, 1990.

Hartman, Charles O. *Free Verse: An Essay on Prosody*. Princeton UP, 1980.

——. "Some Responses to Robert Wallace." *Meter in English: A Critical Engagement,* edited by David Baker. U of Arkansas P, 1996, pp. 109-23.

Hass, Robert. "Prosody: A New Footing." *Meter in English: A Critical Engagement*, edited by David Baker. U of Arkansas P, 1996, pp. 125-49.

——. *Twentieth Century Pleasures: Prose on Poetry.* Harper, 1984.

Hecht, Anthony. *The Hidden Law: The Poetry of W. H. Auden.* Harvard UP, 1993.

Hollander, John. *The Work of Poetry.* Columbia UP, 1997.

——. *Vision and Resonance: Two Senses of Poetic Form.* Yale UP, 1975.

Hough, Graham. *Image and Experience: Studies in a Literary Revolution.* Duckworth, 1960.

Hughes, Ted. "Myths, Metres, Rhythms." *Winter Pollen: Occasional Prose,* edited by William Scammell. Faber, 1994, pp. 310–72.

Jespersen, Otto. "Notes on Metre." 1901. *The Structure of Verse: Modern Essays on Prosody*, edited by H. Gross. Ecco, 1966, pp. 105-28.

Justice, Donald. "The Free Verse Line in Stevens." *Platonic Scripts.* U of Michigan P, 1984, pp. 176–204.

Kennedy, X. J., editor. *An Introduction to Poetry*, 7th ed. HarperCollins, 1990.

Kirby-Smith, H.T. *The Origins of Free Verse.* U of Michigan P, 1996.

Lake, Paul. "The Shape of Poetry." *Poetry after Modernism*, edited by R. McDowell. Story Line, 1998, pp. 278-306.

Lehman, David, and Jorie Graham, editors. *The Best American Poetry 1990.* Charles Scribner's Sons, 1990.

Levin, Samuel R. "A Revision of the Halle-Keyser Metrical Theory." *Language*, vol. 49, no. 3, 1973, pp. 606–611. www.jstor.org/stable/412353. Accessed 31 Aug. 2021.

Lewis, C.S. *An Experiment in Criticism.* Cambridge UP, 1961.

——. *The World's Last Night.* Harcourt, 1960.

Marvell, Andrew. *The Poems of Andrew Marvell: Printed from the unique copy in the British Museum*, edited by Hugh MacDonald. Routledge, 1952.

Myers, Jack, and Michael Simms. *Longman Dictionary and Handbook of Poetry.* Longman, 1985.

Nims, John Frederick. "Our Many Meters: Strength in Diversity." *Meter in English: A Critical Engagement*, edited by David Baker. U of Arkansas P, 1996, pp. 169-96.

——. *Western Wind: An Introduction to Poetry*, 2nd ed. Random House, 1983.

Nims, John Frederick, editor. *The Harper Anthology of Poetry*. HarperCollins, 1981.

Nitchie, George W. *Marianne Moore: An Introduction to the Poetry.* Columbia UP, 1969.

Omond. T. S. *English Metrists in the Eighteenth and Nineteenth Centuries.* H. Frowde, 1907.

Perloff, Marjorie. *The Dance of the Intellect: Studies in the Poetry of the Pound Tradition.* Cambridge UP, 1985.

Pinsky, Robert. *The Sounds of Poetry: A Brief Guide.* Farrar, Straus and Giroux, 1998.

Poetry Foundation. "Introduction." *Projective Verse, by Charles Olson.* https://www.poetryfoundation.org/articles/69406/projective-verse. Accessed 28 August 2021.

Pound, Ezra. *Pavannes and Divagations.* 1918. U of California P, 1960.

Poirier, Richard. *The Renewal of Literature: Emersonian Reflections.* U of Michigan P, 1987.

Preminger, Alex, editor. *The New Princeton Encyclopedia of Poetry and Poetics.* Princeton UP, 1993.

Puttenham, George. *The Arte of English Poesie.* 1589. Edited by Edward Arber. London, 1869.

Raffel, Burton. *From Stress to Stress.* Archon, 1992.

Ransom, John Crowe. "The Strange Music of English Verse." *Kenyon Review,* vol. 18, 1956, pp. 460-77.

Ringler, William A., Jr., editor. *The Poems of Sir Philip Sidney.* Oxford UP, 1962.

Saintsbury, George. *A History of English Prosody from the Twelfth Century to the Present Day.* 3 vols. Macmillan, 1906-1908.

Schipper, Jakob. *A History of English Versification.* Clarendon, 1910.

Shapiro, Karl, and Robert Beum. *A Prosody Handbook.* U of Michigan P, 1965.

Steele, Timothy. "On Meter." *Hellas*, vol. 1, Fall 1990, pp. 289-310.

———. *Missing Measures: Modern Poetry and the Revolt Against Meter.* U of Arkansas P, 1992.

Taylor, Henry. *Compulsory Figures: Essays on Recent American Poets.* Louisiana State UP, 1992.

Thompson, John. *The Founding of English Metre.* Routledge and Kegan Paul, 1961.

Tottel, Richard, editor. *Miscellany*, edited by Hyder Edward Rollins. 1557-1589. Harvard UP, 1928.

Trager, George L., and Henry Lee Smith, Jr. *An Outline of English Structure.* Battenburg, 1951.

Turco, Lewis. *The Public Poet: Five Lectures on the Art and Craft of Poetry.* Ashland UP, 1991.

Vendler, Helen. *Poems, Poets, Poetry: An Introduction and Anthology.* Bedford/St. Martin's, 1997.

———. *The Art of Shakespeare's Sonnets*, 4th ed. Belknap, 1997.

Wagner-Martin, Linda, editor. *Interviews with William Carlos Williams: "Speaking Straight Ahead."* New Directions, 1976.

Wallace, Emily M., and William Carlos Williams. "An Interview with William Carlos Williams." *The Massachusetts Review*, vol. 14, no. 1, 1973, pp. 130–148.

Wallace, Robert. "Completing the Circle." *Meter in English: A Critical Engagement*, edited by David Baker. U of Arkansas P, 1996, pp. 295-349.

———. "Meter in English." *Meter in English: A Critical Engagement*, edited by David Baker. U of Arkansas P, 1996, pp. 3-42.

———. *Writing Poems.* 1st ed. Little, Brown, 1982. 4th ed. with Michelle Boisseau. HarperCollins, 1996.

Wallace, Robert, and James G. Taaffe, editors. *Poems on Poetry: The Mirror's Garland.* Dutton, 1965.

Warren, Robert Penn, and Cleanth Brooks. *Understanding Poetry*, 3rd ed. Holt, Rinehart and Winston, 1960.

Weiss, David. "Rapping Scops." *Parnassus: Poetry in Review*, v. 23, no. 1, 1998, pp. 166-76.

Whitehall, Harold. "From Linguistics to Criticism." *Kenyon Review*, vol. 18, 1956, pp. 411-21.

Williams, Miller. *Patterns of Poetry: An Encyclopedia of Forms.* Louisiana State UP, 1986.

Williams, William Carlos. *The Selected Letters of William Carlos Williams*, edited by John C. Thirlwall. New Directions, 1957.

——. *Selected Essays of William Carlos Williams.* New Directions, 1969.

Williamson, Alan. *Eloquence and Mere Life: Essays on the Art of Poetry.* U of Michigan P, 1994.

——. *Introspection and Contemporary Poetry.* Harvard UP, 1984.

Wilmer, Clive. Interview with Thom Gunn. *Paris Review*, issue 135, Summer 1995. https://www.theparisreview.org/interviews/1626/the-art-of-poetry-no-72-thom-gunn. Accessed 25 August 2021.

Wimsatt, W. K. and Monroe C. Beardsley. "The Concept of Meter: An Exercise in Abstraction." *The Structure of Verse*, edited by Harvey Gross. Fawcett, 1966, pp. 150-167.

Winters, Yvor. *The Function of Criticism: Problems and Exercises.* Swallow, 1957.

Wright, George T. *The Poet in the Poem.* U of California P, 1960.

"The Smoothest Typer Ever to Come Out of Springfield"

A Treasury of Letters From the Robert Wallace Collection

James S. Baumlin

Dear Bob:

Well, how about "I've been reading the poems of Bob Wallace for thirty-five years and don't ever want to stop. A master of witty enjambment and hard-edged tenderness, he gives me back the world I live in, with a certain enhancing moonglow."
    —Postcard of John Updike (dated 7 Oct. [1987]) to Robert Wallace

Dear John,

Thanks for the sentences to run on COMMON SUMMER. I do like "moonglow." Yes, they'll say, he adds moonglow!
    —Letter of Robert Wallace (dated 15 Oct. [1987]) to John Updike

Dear Bob:

It was great to hear from you, and at such length. You still are the smoothest typer ever to come out of Springfield. I like the look of the Deciduous Review and would be happy to be a judge for the Spring issue. I think it's a wonderful thing you're doing, giving that kiss of print to these young writers....
    —Letter of John Updike (dated 4 Feb. [1978]) to Robert Wallace

Despite a life of wandering—of schooling at Harvard and a Fulbright at Cambridge, of military service (in counterintelligence), of college teaching at Bryn

Mawr, Vassar, Sweet Briar, and Case Western Reserve—Robert Wallace never forgot his Ozarks roots. As Springfield's most accomplished poet and literary editor, it's fitting that his papers are now housed in the Ozarkiana Collection, part of Missouri State University's Special Collections and Archives.

"A small-town sort of city with lots of trees, pleasant even in the Depression," Springfield surfaces throughout Wallace's writing.[19] Consider his playfully autobiographical lyric, "Melinda Lou," the first poem of his occasionally just-slightly risqué collection, *Girlfriends and Wives* (1984):

> Six, in ringlet curls,
> on Normal Street,...
> you biked, played hide
> and-seek and kick-the-can,
> played guns, played nurse
> with me and Homer Ice,
> gave me the bigger
> punch-out Valentine,
> and moved to Kansas.

"The houses are still there / On Normal Street," the poet continues,

> smaller by forty years,
> and shabbier....
> And you
> are, once a decade

---

[19] I quote from the typescript, "Robert Wallace" (1977?), a brief biography apparently composed for prospective editors. The paragraph continues:

> For a time my Uncle Clarence lived with us and I sat on the porch before the sun was up listening to his stories about Alaska or bootlegging or playing Macbeth in a traveling company with Lon Chaney, Sr., in Texas before World War I. Later, he sent me a crazy, bent up, antique typewriter from somewhere. My father wrote long, illustrated doggerel poems about people he knew, and I must have got the verse itch from him. Robert W. Service was the only poet we owned, but I found others, Poe, James Whitcomb Riley, Ogden Nash; and I was ready for Marvell and Pope and Williams when I went to Harvard in 1949....

The legendary "Uncle Clarence," to whom Wallace dedicates *This Various World* (1957), resurfaces in an appreciative letter (dated 20 Aug. [1957]) from Updike.

when I look, small, sweet
and golden in the locket of my heart,
dead, or in Kansas.

Indeed, the houses are "still there." As Wallace writes in a late letter (dated 14 Feb. 1998) to MSU archivist Jenni Boone,

> I did grow up on Normal. Lived at 456 (two doors west of Kimbrough) from 1st grade till 1946, when we moved to 1344 S. Jefferson (but I think the numbers have changed) just south of the Maple Park Cemetery. It seemed quite normal to live on a street called Normal, which of course in those days I didn't connect at all to the "Normal" school that was then STC (& is now SMSU).[20]

It should not surprise that personal experience inspires much of Wallace's poetry, as members of his literary milieu, towered over by John Updike—Wallace's college friend at Harvard and lifelong correspondent—made life the stuff of literature. So Wallace notes in a letter, again late (dated 29 Dec. 1997) to Boone, where he contemplates others reading his private correspondence:

> No, I guess I don't feel odd if people are reading old letters, etc. I'm a little surprised they find it interesting, perhaps, though it's understandable & isn't necessarily even personal curiosity. I'm not *that* person, or in that place at least, anymore. Updike is the one who is really amazing that way. I knew his folks, his first wife, etc., & almost everything of that appears just as-was in the fiction. I recall being out to dinner at a local Chinese place with him and first-wife Mary, whom I also knew in college. John was chatting with a couple in another booth and Mary said, "That's his mistress." Floored me! But I guess Mary was just used to appearing in stories & it didn't seem odd to her to tell me. They were, then, I suppose, already in some other "place."

Wallace's friend would not deny the point. "Out of soiled and restless life," Updike writes, "I have refined my books" (231). Taken from his memoirs, *Self-Consciousness* (1989), the passage continues:

---

[20] Southwest Teachers College (STC) did indeed become Southwest Missouri State University (SMSU) and would, in 2005, become Missouri State University (MSU).

... fiction, like life, is a dirty business; discretion and good taste play small part in it. Hardly a story appears in print without offending or wounding some living model who sees himself or herself reflected all too accurately and yet not accurately enough—without that deepening, mollifying element of endless pardon we bring to our own self. (231)

While Wallace's life and poetry deserve attention, my interest here, more modestly, is to illustrate the range and significance of his correspondence, which I divide (arbitrarily, given their interrelation) into several rough categories: following his *juvenilia*, I highlight his correspondence as a practicing poet, as a teacher of poetry, and as a poetry editor. Wallace's achievements in these areas find witness in the fame of those with whom he corresponded, some once or occasionally, others frequently; some professionally, others in a manner more friendly and confiding. Even a partial list of correspondents reads like a role sheet of Anglo-American literary *illustri*: Cyrilly Abels, Richard Armour, Robert Bly, John Ciardi, Robert Conquest, David Daiches, Stephen Dunn, Babette Deutsch, James Dickey, T. S. Eliot, Gavin Ewart, Robert Francis, Dana Gioia, William Golding, Edward Gorey, Donald Hall, Anthony Hecht, Ted Hughes, X. J. Kennedy, Thomas Kinsella, Maxine Kumin, Philip Larkin, Richmond Lattimore, A. L. Lazarus, Denise Levertov, d.a. levy, Peter Meinke, W. S. Merwin, Howard Moss, Mary Oliver, Howard Nemerov, John Frederick Nims, Ogden Nash, Sharon Olds, Linda Pastan, Marge Piercy, Laurence Perrine, Burton Raffel, David R. Slavitt, Elizabeth Spires, William Stafford, Lewis Turco, John Updike, David Wagoner, John Wain, Ronald Wallace, John Hall Wheelock, E. B. White, Richard Wilbur, Heathcote Williams, Miller Williams, William Carlos Williams.[21] Taken as a whole, the Wallace correspondence sketches the broad outline of a distinctive literary circle, with its mutual friendships and sharing of favors regarding editing, touring, publishing, and promotion. As such, it offers unique insights into the American literary-critical scene of the mid- to late-twentieth century.

---

[21] For brief literary biographies and item-counts of archived materials, see Appendix below.

I. Poet

As far back as fifth grade, I just wrote poems because, I guess, I'd read some I liked and that's what I wanted to do. I read a lot in college and wrote a lot—Ogden Nash and Richard Armour gave way as models to Donne and Yeats and Frost and Williams and Wilbur....

The natural thing to do with poems, when you have them, is to send them to editors. You hope they're good, that the editors buy them, and so on. But that probably doesn't matter. Good or not, poems are a way of getting something inside outside. If the transaction is roughly honest, it's valuable enough—like whittling or growing string beans. They don't have to be World Famous Golden String Beans. Pulitzer Beans. Nobel Beans.

—Letter of Robert Wallace (dated 12 Mar. 1986) to Judson Jerome

Wallace's literary talent proved precocious. A spiral-bound scrap book survives (apparently from his fifth grade), into which dozens of poems have been pasted or slipped. Boldly scrawled in red crayon is the title page,

POEM'S
These Poem's are
written by Bobby
Wallace. Wallace
Story co.
Spring field Mo.

Wallace enjoyed his first formal "kiss of print" (as Updike puts it) at age sixteen, publishing a humorous poem, "Tee Hee," in *The Rotarian*. His first major correspondent was no less than the great American humorist, Ogden Nash (see his letter dated 16 Jan. 1948). We can appreciate Nash's kindness; even as he chides the teenager for emulating Nash's own comic style, the elder poet acknowledges the youngster's "considerable sense of humor," a talent that would blossom in maturity with such children's books as *Critters* (1978) and *Charlie Joins the Circus* (1981).

While at Harvard (1949-1953), Wallace would publish in the *Lyric* and *The Christian Science Monitor*. He would remain in correspondence with several faculty, including the renowned American scholar, Douglas Bush, whose letter (dated 16 Dec. 1956) congratulates the aspiring author:

Dear Robert Wallace:

I am glad to have your biography brought up to date, since I had lost track of you. I saw the poems in the *New Yorker* and supposed they must be yours; they were very original, sensitive, and distinctive poems, and it is nice to hear of the forthcoming volume.

I shall be very happy to testify to the [Harvard] Society of Fellows.... I reminded Mr. Levin of your scholarly record here, spoke of your Cambridge degree, and of your *New Yorker* poems and I said I thought you would be a strong candidate. By the way, do you expect to teach? A candidate for a J.F. has to have some kind of scholarly project to submit. That doesn't mean that he can't write poetry, but the Society was founded as a scholarly affair, and any member is expected to put most of his energies into some biggish job. This needs, I think, to be outlined as soon as one becomes a candidate....

With all good wishes (and congratulations, however belated, on your marriage),

-Sincerely yours,
Douglas Bush

Professor Bush refers to Wallace's first major literary success upon graduating (*summa cum laude*), his publication of poems in *The New Yorker*—one of the nation's premier literary magazines (and, for a time, his friend Updike's place of employment). In noting a "forthcoming volume," Bush refers to Wallace's second great triumph: the inclusion of his collection, *This Various World*, in Scribner's literary series, *Poets of Today IV* (1957).[22] In his contract letter to Wallace (dated 14 Nov. 1956), Scribner's editor, John Hall Wheelock, ends with almost extravagant praise:

---

[22] In a second letter (dated 22 Oct. 1957), Bush congratulates Wallace for *This Various World*. A letter from Updike (dated 20 Aug. [1957]) congratulates him on the same. Donald Hall's review, hard-nosed yet even-handed, left its own strong impression: Wallace himself took time to copy it in typescript—perhaps as humbling reminder, perhaps as a teacherly example of "the art of criticism."

Dear Mr. Wallace:

I was very glad to have your letter of 6 November, which accompanied the typescript of your THIS VARIOUS WORLD. Since then I have had the chance to read these poems more than once and I have been much impressed by them, so much so in fact that we should like to include them in the next volume, POETS OF TODAY IV, scheduled for publication in August 1957.... Just as soon as I hear from you, I'll send along the usual contract....

In conclusion, I want to tell you that I haven't for a long time read any poems that seemed to me more exciting and more completely realized than yours in this collection.

-Yours sincerely,
John Hall Wheelock

Though mixed with criticism and suggestions for revision, similar praise for his poetry would come from Howard Moss, longtime poetry editor of *The New Yorker*, Denise Levertov of *The Nation*, and John Ciardi of *Saturday Review*. Typical in this regard is Ciardi's handwritten note (dated 12 Nov. 1968), on *Saturday Review* letterhead:

Thanks for the poems. I'm especially taken by 'Pantry.' The ending rings like a bell. And yet I can't conquer the feeling that it blurs (maybe in the adjective) on its way to the bong. Forgive me if it's insolent to say that, for I mean no insolence. I hope I may see more of yours soon. To my reading you're one of the few who does really vibrate at top register.

All best,
John

Of similar interest is Ciardi's earlier letter (dated 1 Sep. 1956), likely the *Saturday Review* editor's first correspondence with Wallace. One notes the complimentary opening, "Thanks for two real poems," as well as the deferential ending, "I hope these suggestions won't seem stupid. I am very much taken by these poems and hope we may have many more of yours as time turns." Ciardi's "suggestions" included his own revisions on the typescript, "The White Crayfish"—the piece for which Wallace would win the 1957 William Rose

Benet Memorial Award, given to the best poem published that year in the *Saturday Review*.

Letters of rejection arrived with equal regularity, though these, too, offered encouragement. From Levertov comes a handwritten note (undated) on *The Nation* stationary: "I like these a lot. I truthfully, at present, have no space, and at the best of times have so little that I must reject many poems I like." From Donald Hall comes a handwritten note (again undated) on *Paris Review* stationary: "You are kind to send it to us. It is charming, attractive, & consistently skillful. And I'm sending it back.... If I take a poem of this length, it prevents me from taking many shorter ones.... It's unfair to longer poems, perhaps, but I am stuck with my opinions."

Still others had formed opinions. In a letter (dated 23 July [1961?]) to Robert and his first wife, Emily, Updike offers a sweeping criticism of Wallace's work, wherein we learn as much about Updike's attitudes toward his own *persona* as toward Wallace's literary habits: "If I have any general criticism, it is of your tendency, chronic through your career, to dwell overmuch upon the poet as a dramatis persona.... It is the man that is interesting; the poet is a window." "I think that the best direction for us both," he adds, "is toward the thing to be expressed, with an intensity that burns away self-consciousness." His explanation is typical Updike:

> You and I both, coming from the middle class where the Writer was a remote rumor, are apt to marvel too much at our hard-won ability to assemble sentences, and even, God willing, get some of them published. It is marvelous, of course, and you and I know it, but we cannot expect the reader to share in our marveling, since everything he reads is by someone who has brought off the same feat.
>
> Is that clear? It seems clear to me.

Updike strikes through his next sentence, "I am tempted to tear up about a third of what I have written," and adds (in the margin), "I am not, of course." Equally striking is his gesture of identification, Wallace and he both "coming from the middle class where the Writer was a remote rumor." As if reciting the anti-Romantic stance of literary modernism, Updike declares the poet's "best direction" to be "toward the thing expressed, with an intensity that burns away self-consciousness."

Poetic victories, indeed, come scattered among defeats. In a typed letter (dated 19 Sep. 1966) on *Saturday Review* letterhead, Ciardi responds to Wallace's request for a book review. Noting the slow sales of Wallace's coedited anthology, *Poems on Poetry* (1965), Ciardi muses:

Dear Bob:

Forgive what must seem a sullen delay, please...

I am sorry to hear the anthology has done badly. I have browsed at least a dozen titles and came away with a happy sense of its unity and of your selections. It's a good job. Yet, I must say I am not surprised that it has not sold. I just wish someone at Dutton had had enough market in his head to explain to you that nothing is harder to sell than books about literature ... especially when you remember that it has to go on a shelf with any number of other titles.

Some of these others will be about Love for Sixteen-year old Boys, Erotica, The American Way, etc. When a possible customer wanders in, he is a hell of a lot more likely to buy any one of those categories than one called: "Poems on Poetry." I don't praise the world for this, but I damned well am describing it. If you want to do books for your soul's sake without considering the nature of the market, I am with you—all the way. But then, son of Man, are you entitled to feel sad when the market does not respond? Stay pure, but any man has to have some losers....

Cheer up. You will have winners, too.

All best,
John Ciardi

Wallace would, in fact, continue to "do books for [his] soul's sake," turning small-press editor in order to publish his own and others' works; and he would do so *almost* "without considering," as Ciardi puts it, "the nature of the market." But before turning to his work as editor, we might chart his transit into academia.

II. Teacher

I was lucky. Some of my poems got published, and then books of them, *Views from a Ferris Wheel* and *Ungainly Things*. I got and kept a decent teaching job, and like teaching. It is, among other things, a way of trying to pay back the teaching I had the advantage of, once upon a time. Honest, agreeable work. Even getting freshmen to bend and hammer sentences until they're true strikes me as valuable. Beats what most of us have to do for pay in our culture.

    —Letter of Robert Wallace (dated 12 Mar. 1986) to Judson Jerome

In the 1960s, when the "baby boomer" generation swelled the ranks of colleges nationwide, creative writing went to school as well, turning from the pastime of amateurs (or, for some few, a bread-winning profession) to a respectable academic discipline; most departments of English had begun to employ one or more practicing poets, and several had established whole programs in writing. Taking advantage, Wallace found a steady income in university teaching. First published in *Harper's Magazine* (1964), "In a Spring Still Not Written Of"—one of Wallace's better-known pieces—casts the poet-teacher in the quasi-pastoral setting of academia. Showing a strength of metaphor reminiscent of Dylan Thomas, the poem (as printed in *Views from a Ferris Wheel*) deserves reading in full:

This morning
with a class of girls outdoors, I saw
how frail poems are
in a world burning up with flowers,
in which, overhead,
the great elms
—green, and tall—
stood carrying leaves in their arms.

The girls listened equally
to my drone, reading, and to the bees'
ricocheting
among them for the blossom on the bone,
or gazed off at a distant mower's

astronomies of green
and clover, flashing,
threshing in the new, untarnished sunlight.

And all the while, dwindling,
tinier, the voices—Yeats, Marvell, Donne—
sank drowning
in a spring still not written of,
as only the sky
clear above the brick belltower
—blue, and white—
was shifting toward the hour.

Calm, indifferent, cross-legged
or on elbows half-lying in the grass—
how should the great dead
tell them of dying?

They will come to time for poems at last
when they have found they are no more
the beautiful and young
all poems are for.

Having escaped the "starving artist" syndrome plaguing prior generations of poets, he threw himself into the task of teaching; if, indeed, a theme runs throughout materials in the Wallace Collection, it is his care for the youthful maker of poems. Perhaps the most genteel, most "teacherly" letter in the collection comes from the great American poet and physician, William Carlos Williams, to whom Wallace—some twenty-eight years of age at the time and an instructor at Bryn Mawr—had written on a student's behalf, enclosing an essay on Williams's "Great Mullen." As Williams offers to comment on his own poem, the letter (18 Feb. 1960) has scholarly significance. A transcript (lightly edited) follows:

Dear Robert Wallace:

Thank you for sending on your student's confidence about "Great Mullen". It is a poem which technically I treasure as among one of my best though most unusual. What in the world prompted your pupil to select this poem to comment on I do not know. It must have disturbed her equilibrium I am quite ready to believe. And she no more than a Freshman!

"djer-kis" was when I wrote the poem the name of very popular perfume with which ladies used to scent their lingerie. The dialogue is correctly assumed to be between a young poet and his wife, with whom he is deeply in love, but to whom he has been unfaithful—in the way a man and woman in the modern world often are. The reference to be my witness! See my recent translation of the—my introduction to the poems of Villon which can be got from Princeton. A very rewarding book.

Sincerely yours,
William Carlos Williams

As well as "honest, agreeable work," academia offered Wallace both a public stage and an appreciative audience. While taking occasional advantage of this same stage, Wallace's Harvard housemate would never, himself, turn to teaching. In a letter (dated 12 Feb. [1965]), Updike comments on Wallace's move to Cleveland and Case Western Reserve, where he taught from 1965 to his death in 1999: "It saddens me," Updike writes, "to think of you going back to the Midwest, since your impersonation of an Easterner had almost been perfected; but as you will." Updike adds, "Brandeis asked me to teach there this next year and to my horror I hesitated before turning them down. Some sort of corruption, sapping my youthful resolve never to teach anybody anything." Much of Wallace's significant correspondence while at Case Western Reserve—with Gavin Ewart, for example, William Golding, X. J. Kennedy, Mary Oliver, and Updike—dwells on the details (payments, venues, flights, schedules) of arranging public readings and campus visits. Indeed, Wallace's networking with the *literati* of his day, bolstered by the support of university and community organizations, kept Cleveland and Case Western Reserve on the national literary circuit.

For the 1979-1980 academic year alone, speakers at Wallace's "sherry hours" included Lee Abbott, Bruce Bennett, Gerald Costanzo, Stephen Dunn, Conrad Hilberry, Mark Irwin, X. J. Kennedy, Peter Klappert, Mary Oliver, Elizabeth Spires, and John Updike. In his memoirs, Updike remembers a late visit to his mother and her Shillington, Pennsylvania home. Though they remain a "ponderous flattery," Updike confesses his "need" for such "excursions":

The drive home from the restaurant, the unseasonable sleet, and my entire life all rankle in me. I have come here from some Midwestern university where I read and talked into a microphone and was gracious to the local rich, the English faculty and college president, and the students with their clear skins and shining eyes and inviting innocence, like a blank surface one wishes to scribble obscenities on. I need these excursions, evidently: they reassure me that I don't stutter, or stutter too much. They leave me feeling dirty and disturbed, as though I have wasted this time away from my desk, posing as an author instead of being one, and it is hard to get back from the academic unreality and ponderous flattery into my own skin. (*Self-Consciousness* 237)

We might fancy that the "Midwestern university" Updike returns from is Case Western Reserve; it may well have been.

I've referred to Wallace's literary "networking." I use the term deliberately, as his later efforts at publishing drew consistently from the same circle of acquaintances. Along with several notable additions, the poets listed above are all featured in volumes of *Bits and Light Year*; they are also (with a few exceptions) authors of Bits Press chapbooks. The "Wallace circle," as we might term it, finds its gravitational center in Wallace's tabletop press (of which, more later). Consider, for example, the letter from Richard Wilbur (dated 17 June 1985), accepting two of Wallace's offers at once: a campus visit to Case Western Reserve and a Bits Press chapbook. Updike's letter (dated 7 April [1980]), does similar double-business. Having "marked October 8th ... as sherry time," he proceeds to discuss terms of the chapbook, *Five Poems* (1980). Though questioning "the price of $100," which "seems outrageously high ... as do most of the prices these collectorish things try to bring," Updike yields in a later letter (dated 20 Apr. 1980), having settled on a format and contents. It turns out that the limited, fine-edition printing sold "like ground sirloin tossed to sharks," as Wallace writes (letter dated 5 Nov. 1980):

The early flyers to [Herbert] Yellin, etc., are bringing calls from Santa Barbara to Framingham. 26 of the 43 hand-mades are spoken for, and 43 of the 116 ready-mades—and the main batch of flyers went out only Monday and the *Bookman's Weekly* ad isn't due until the issue of 10 Nov. The fiercest attack came yesterday from a dealer in NYC who wants 15 and 15. So, on the advice of a very good natured local shark (who came by Saturday and thinks the edition is too expensive, so he is presumably disinterested), we are going to limit sales to each dealer, in the hope of keeping the book available until the unfortunates who will get the flyer or see the ad have at least had a chance—maybe 20 November or so.

All this is stupifying, and instructive. People fighting over and begging for an obviously over-priced booklet. That it is a nice thing in its way seems halfway irrelevant.

I'm tempted to ask you to let us do another chapbook, when the air has had time to clear. But I don't know whether it should be in as large a printing as your contract with Knopf would allow, and as fine and expensive as we could do (I'm feeling, among other things, pity for the sharks). Or something utterly outrageous....

Wallace would, in fact, publish several more Updike pieces (though none so "outrageous" as the pornographic poem that, later in this letter, Wallace goes on to suggest).

In a letter (dated 26 Oct. 1967), poet-translator David R. Slavitt describes his touring *modus operandi*, revealing with a flourish his own famously offhand attitude toward readers, audiences, critics:

Dear Bob:

Can you set up a poetry reading for me?

Reason I ask is that I've just published a big best-seller, a pseudonymous novel called THE EXHIBITIONIST (by Henry Sutton) and I'm going around to publicize it on a nationwide tour. I hadn't expected that there'd be any carry-over from that kind of commercial feat to the real world of belle-lettrist writing in which I usually move, but there is, there is.... My publishers—Bernard Geis Associates—are amazed but delighted, because it works for them, too, getting me even more publicity. The way the game works is that I bomb into a town, do a tv interview show as Sutton, whip over to some campus, become Slavitt, do a poetry reading, and the whole thing gets covered by a newspaperman. He's got a story, I've got both of my selves some attention, so everyone is happy....

I'll be available for Western Reserve any time I'm in Cleveland—which looks to be 12/13 through 12/16. If you can work something, I'd be grateful, and pleased to have a chance to see you....

Apparently, the success of such academic, "above ground" poetry readings created occasional jealousies between "town" and "gown." One of the more curious artifacts in the Wallace Collection is a photocopied, typescript rant by the radical "underground" poet and Cleveland native, "d.a.levy." Meant to raise hackles, the spelling and style are deliberately raw—as one might expect from the author of *Cleveland: The Rectal Eye Visions* (1966) and *Comments on the Acid Landscape* (1967):

Dear Warlords of the WRU Englische Department,

I do not want to suck yr pineal glands/ or rub yr hemm rhoids the wrong way, but it has occurred to me that your excellant universe has somehow managed to continually ignor that fact that the city of cleveland has quite a few new young poets growing in its midst. perhaps you missed them because you are busily occupied turning out such fine dentists/doctors/physicists/technicians in varied fields etc.... i prefer to remain paranoid & believe that you dont like us & therefore dont see us. This method of pretending certain elements of a society do not exist often works (for a while) but in the case of cleveland poets it will not work. I highly recommend you acknowledge this cities poets & set up a series of readings for them before they all decide to ignor yr authoritarian position. Enclosed you will find a partial list of some of the new poets, some of them widely published both in & out of the U.S. I think most of them will read for a moderate fee of $10. $15, & $25 altho a few might request more.

sincerely
d.a.levy
c/o the asphodel book shop
306 W. Superior ave
cleveland ohio 44113

As a postscript, levy lists addresses for Russel Atkins ("editor of free lance"), Jeff Cook ("organizer of the Kenyon Younger Poets"), Jake Leed ("prof at kent U"), Kent Taylor, Don Thomas ("editor of The underground Quarterly"), and

R.J.S. ("editor of Free Love Press").

While Wallace did support the local literary scene as a small-press editor, his first loyalty remained with students, whose work he supported in a variety of ways. From Howard Nemerov comes a letter (dated 16 Aug. 1966) promising poems to Wallace's student editors:

> I think I can promise to send Mr Wadas something for the magazine. I've grown disgusted enough with the quality of periodicals that I've given probably a dozen of the recent poems to college magazines—because if we have a hope it is in the young, and because the editors have been kind enough to ask.

Sharing Nemerov's hope, Wallace would make similar requests of Updike. In a rather wide-ranging, nostalgic letter (dated 4 Feb. [1978?]), Updike agrees to judge submissions to the English Department magazine, *Deciduous Review*. I've quoted it in an epigraph, above; a bit more of it follows.

> I like the look of the Deciduous Review and would be happy to be a judge for the Spring issue....

> You'd probably find it easier to get your collections published if you wrote novels in between. I hope a commercial house takes your latest assortment; but self-publishing is an old and honorable tradition, from Walt Whitman to Marcel Proust.... My son David lives, or did before he took the Spring term off, on the top floor of Winthrop, and all the sensations, smells, and palpitations come back to me when I climb those five flights....

Moving smoothly from literary criticism to college-life nostalgia, Updike's letter folds numerous topics together. Again, he embraces both poetry and his friend: they are, together, "two dogged triers at this enigmatic craft." Such claims of a shared poetic identity yield only partially to Updike's earlier observation, that his old Harvard house mate "would probably find it easier to get [his] collections published if [he] wrote novels in between." Though coming from a Pulitzer Prize winning novelist, we should not entirely dismiss the implication that novels are to be written in between collections of poetry, the novel functioning as a vehicle for name-recognition, as if to help sell the poems.

Updike's advice here, as in other surviving letters, comes as if following his own sideways glance into a mirror. In the preface to his *Collected Poems*, Updike describes the role poetry played in his larger literary development:

> As a boy I wanted to be a cartoonist. Light verse (and the verse that came my way was generally light) seemed a kind of cartooning with words, and through light verse I first found my way into print. The older I have grown, the less of it I have written, but the idea of verse, of poetry, has always, during forty years spent primarily in prose, stood at my elbow, as a standing invitation to the highest kind of verbal exercise—the most satisfying, the most archaic, the most elusive of critical control. In hotel rooms and airplanes, on beaches and Sundays, at junctures of personal happiness or its opposite, poetry has comforted me with its hope of permanence, its packaging of flux. (xxiii)

Wallace did, in fact, try his hand at the novel, though without success: while often complimented by readers and editors, *Rumpelstiltskin, Go Home* (a "comedy of manners," as one agent-reviewer describes it) and the mystery-thriller, *Invitation to Silence*, remain in typescript, both abandoned projects from the late 1960s. Significant correspondence with Cyrilly Abels (literary agent of Katherine Anne Porter, who also represented Wallace) and several commercial press editors survive.

Returning to the letter cited above, we also note Updike's nod to that "old and honorable tradition," self-publishing. Wallace's "latest assortment," as Updike puts it, was likely his illustrated children's book, *Critters* (1978), for which Wallace was unable to find a trade publisher; rather than see it languish, Wallace bought and set his own type.

III. Editor

In 1974 I bought a tabletop letter press, like the one Leonard and Virginia Woolf took home and set up on the kitchen table. There's something utterly satisfactory about inky fingers and setting type and seeing the copies pile up. But there's also a potential that, once available, tempts you to use it. I was struck by A. J. Liebling's remark, "The freedom of the press belongs to the man who owns one."

—Letter of Robert Wallace (dated 12 Mar. 1986) to Judson Jerome

Following in the footsteps of Ciardi, Hall, Levertov, Slavitt, and Wheelock, Wallace turned from poet to poetry editor.[23] Whereas the poet-editors aforementioned worked for major trade presses and literary magazines, Wallace built for himself a cozier niche in small-press publication. In "Bits Press Checklist: The First Decade" (1985), Wallace describes his intentions:

The purpose of Bits Press has remained constant: to publish excellent poetry, especially the kinds or by poets neglected by trade publishers and the major literary journals and commercial magazines. Hence *Bits*, devoted to the short poem, twelve lines and under, remembering Ezra Pound's comment, "A Chinaman said long ago that if a man can't say what he has to say in twelve lines he had better keep quiet." Hence now *Light Year*, the annual of light verse and funny poems, in the conviction that laughter is the disused bridge between poetry and the general reader.

Wallace refers to *Bits* (1975-1980), a series of artfully-produced (and eminently collectible, hand-set and hand-sewn) poetry chapbooks published bi-annually, and *Light Year* (1984-1989), a well-reviewed annual featuring the light verse of some of America's foremost poets.

---

[23] I have already cited Wallace's earliest effort at editing, his anthology (coedited with James G. Taaffe), *Poems on Poetry* (1965), whose compilation led to correspondence with true luminaries of our language. On FABER AND FABER LTD stationary, an autographed letter (dated 24 July 1964) survives from T. S. Eliot, who politely declines Wallace's request to reprint selections from *Four Quartets*. From Anthony Hecht comes a letter (dated 8 Sep. 1964) allowing the reprint of his Arnoldian parody, "The Dover Bitch." Other such letters, some familiar in tone and address, survive from Robert Conquest, Ted Hughes, Philip Larkin, Sharon Olds, and John Wain. It seems mildly ironic that Ciardi and Hall (from whom Wallace received his share of rejection letters) would later submit poems to Wallace, for inclusion in *Bits* and *Light Year*.

Taking *Light Year '84* as a sample, contributors from within Wallace's circle include Bruce Bennett, Gavin Ewart, John Fandel, Albert Goldbarth, Bonnie Jacobson, X. J. Kennedy, Peter Klappert, A. L. Lazarus, Howard Nemerov, Linda Pastan, Louis Phillips, David R. Slavitt, Elizabeth Spires, John Updike, and Richard Wilbur; other contributors include Richard Armour, Roy Blount, Jr., John Ciardi, Robert Francis, Donald Hall, Edwin Honig, David Ignatow, Ted Kooser, Howard Moss, John Frederick Nims, Marge Piercy, W. D. Snodgrass, William Stafford, May Swenson, Reed Whittemore, and Miller Williams, along with lesser lights. Among others who had contributed to the previous volume, *Light Year '85* would feature Ray Bradbury, Dana Gioia, William Harmon, Anthony Hecht, Mark Irwin, Judson Jerome, Laurence Perrine, Marge Piercy, and E. B. White—author of *Charlotte's Web*, to whom the volume is dedicated. Of interest is White's brief letter to Wallace (dated 6 Nov. 1983), in which he graciously-playfully accepts the dedication: "I can't guarantee to stay alive that long, but perhaps that doesn't matter. I am pleased at the honor."

In a biographical letter (dated 12 Mar. 1986) to Judson Jerome, Wallace mentions Ogden Nash and Richard Armour as early poetic models; more than contribute to *Light Year '85*, Armour became a spiritual comrade and correspondent, whose letter (dated 6 Nov. 1985) weaves together numerous themes from Wallace's own literary career.

Dear Robert Wallace:

Today there were two memorable events for me. One was coming home from ten days in the hospital.... The other was reading your article, "Light Verse," in the December issue of THE WRITER. I do not mean to compare the two, except to say that both were memorable.

I am glad that someone at least foresees a return to the sophisticated, skillful, playful light verse, perhaps with a new label, such as "funny poetry," that once sprinkled the pages of THE NEW YORKER and other magazines.

I began writing light verse for THE NEW YORKER in 1935, fifty years ago. When THE NEW YORKER stopped taking my verse, I stopped taking THE NEW YORKER. In a copy of one of his many books I reviewed I keep a sad letter from Ogden Nash dated September 11, 1970. Here are two excerpts: "My warmest thanks for the advance copy of your review. After 4 successive rejections from the New Yorker and a fifth looming up, my spirits were in sore need of a lift, which you have assuredly given them.... I'll sell my share of this century for a nickel."

That fifth piece Nash contributed must also have been returned, because it never appeared. He died later that year. I'm not saying THE NEW YORK-ER killed Ogden Nash, but it dampened the lives of many others, both readers and writers.

I did not mean to write so much about Nash, but I owe much to him....

Armour ends with a postscript, "I'm all for John Updike. Most know him only for his prose, but his verse could lead the new wave."

Another of Armour's letters (dated 1 Feb. 1986) followed shortly thereafter, offering poems to *Light Year '87*:

Today I spent two hours with my librarian son, each of us reading from LY '85 and LY '86 to the other as we hit upon a poem we especially liked and found laugh-provoking or mind-provoking....

This brings me to the name to be given to writing verse with the variety and skill of what is found in the *Light Year* books. Here is my mention: "playful poetry." I like the alliteration. But more important is the broad but meaningful word "playful." The element of play seems to me present in what you have so well selected and brought together in your books. The playful poet has a wide range in subjects and technique. It calls on experiment and originality. And on and on....

You have started what could be a great revolution in the writing and pub-lication of a kind of poetry that might open the doors of THE NEW YORKER, THE SATURDAY EVENING POST, and many other mag-azines that have become closed to anything but prose and prosaic poetry. Playful poetry might bring them new readers and cause old readers to re-turn as subscribers. Old readers and young readers too.

"Of course I want no payment for anything of mine," Armour concludes: "With Parkinson's and entering my 80th year, nothing new of mine may be playful enough, though it might be used for contrast between the old and the new."

Since Armour discusses both *The New Yorker* and Updike, we might give Updike's view, as well. In *Self-Consciousness*, Updike describes the magazine's impact upon his own writerly self-image:

> *The New Yorker* ... was a club of sorts, from within which the rest of literary America—the many other less distinguished and fastidious magazines, the coarsely striving book trade, the tawdry best-seller lists, the sharp-tongued quarterlies and partisan reviews—could be politely disdained. Our good self-opinion ... made a useful shelter for me, a hard shell I didn't have to grow myself. While I can now almost glimpse something a bit too trusting in the sense of artistic well-being, of virtual invulnerability, that being published in *The New Yorker* gave me for over thirty years, the self who looked up into the empyrean of print from that muddy farm in Pennsylvania with its outhouse and coal-oil stove is not so remote from them that I can still think it anything less than wonderful to have become a writer. (222)

Turning back to an early letter (dated 27 Feb. [1963], on *The New Yorker* letterhead), Updike doles out a portion of this same "artistic well-being" to his friend. The letter has significance for its mention of his novel, *The Centaur* (1963), which Wallace read in manuscript; drawing attention to the "perhaps familiar stationary," Updike also acknowledges Wallace's membership in this same "empyrean," elitist literary "club."

Along with *Bits* and *Light Year*, Wallace's Bits Press published a series of chapbooks, each featuring the work of an individual poet: W. M. Aberg, Bruce Bennett, John Fandel, Elton Glaser, Albert Goldbarth, Conrad Hilberry, Mark Irwin, Bonnie Jacobson, X. J. Kennedy, Peter Klappert, Peter Meinke, Sheila Nickerson, Mary Oliver, Linda Pastan, Nicholas Ranson, James Reed, P. K. Saha, Herbert Scott, David R. Slavitt, Merry Speece, Elizabeth Spires, George Starbuck, Daniel Towner, Leonard Trawick, John Updike, Richard Wilbur, and Miller Williams. Given the extensive records surviving for each of the abovementioned volumes, one cannot do justice to Wallace's editorial correspondence; mere highlights and summary-quotation fall short. Through the remaining paragraphs, rather, I offer a checklist of projects—a sort of scholarly to-do list—for readers interested in further research.

Original, hand-corrected typescripts and uninventoried correspondence remains for each volume of *Bits* and *Light Year*; materials of considerable scholarly interest lie scattered, as it were, throughout whole boxes and files. The correspondence and manuscript records of specific authors also deserve separate inventories. For example, extensive correspondence survives concerning the publication and promotion of *The Gavin Ewart Show: Selected Poems 1939-1985* (1986), which happens to be the first American edition of this poet. In his letter (dated 12 Mar. 1986) to Jerome, Wallace writes,

> Ewart is a delightful, sexy, utterly readable English poet, who's virtually a best-seller over there and who just missed being named Poet Laureate, but who'd never been published in the States. (Remember, in New York they believe that poetry doesn't sell.) So that seemed a job for Bits Press ....

Extensive correspondence also surrounds Richard Wilbur's *A Finished Man* (1985). In his letter (dated 12 Mar. 1986) to Jerome, Wallace remembers his old Harvard professor who, along with "Donne and Yeats and Frost and Williams," served as an early poetic model: "I took a course in writing the short story from Wilbur in college—odd that's what they had him doing. That would have been about 1952. I was interested in Wilbur, of course, not the short story." (From a different college course, a portfolio of Wallace's poems survives, along with Wilbur's extensive, often wry criticisms.) Elsewhere in the collection are two letters by Wilbur on the subject of metrics, in which he scans several lines of his own poetry; these would later be published in *Meter in English* (1996), a gathering of essays focused on Wallace's own controversial article, "Meter in English." Materials of similar interest surround X. J. Kennedy's *Hangover Mass* (1984) and David R. Slavitt's *Elegies to Delia of Albius Tibullus* (1985) and *Tristia of Ovid* (1985).

Of course, such authors as these kindly lent their reputations to Bits Press; Wallace's aid to others in establishing careers, such as Bonnie Jacobson, Peter Klappert, Mary Oliver, and Elizabeth Spires deserves study, as well. In Oliver's case, Wallace's Bits Press publication of *The Night Traveler* (1977) made some small contribution to her winning of a Pulitzer Prize. As her letter of inquiry to Wallace details, Oliver had difficulty placing a first collection with New York trade presses; in preparing the same, Wallace worked closely with Oliver in cutting, revising, and shaping a coherent, thematically unified collection. Reviewed by Joyce Carol Oates in the December 19, 1978 issue of *The New Republic,* the Bits Press chapbook earned for Oliver an appreciative and influential readership (including praise from Archibald MacLeish and Stanley Kunitz, copies of whose letters to Oliver made their way into the Wallace Collection). Her *Twelve Moons* (1979) would follow shortly there after, as would *American Primitive* (1983)—for which she earned a Pulitzer. Happily, the Wallace Collection contains an apparently complete record of their work together, including tentative tables of contents, detailed criticisms and multiple drafts of separate pieces, and several poems left in typescript, unpublished by Wallace.

Oliver has firmly established her place in American letters, her poetry having become the subject of numerous scholarly articles and dissertations; her reputation, indeed, has eclipsed Wallace's. Yet an important early chapter in the poetic practice of an important American poet remains to be written, and can be written only by means of materials in the Wallace Collection. Let me expand upon this point. We've noted how John Ciardi intervened as the young Wallace's editor, helping turn "The White Crayfish" into an award-winning poem. As Ciardi did for Wallace, so Wallace would do for others, Mary Oliver included. In the unfolding correspondence between author and editor, we can watch a manuscript grow collaboratively, dialogically. By capturing the various stages of writing, revising, critiquing, selecting, rewriting, editing, publishing, reviewing, and promoting, the Wallace Collection offers an open window into the writing *process*, of interest to student and scholar alike. Composed before email and word processing became ubiquitous, the stages of their collaboration—of editing and revision—could be captured *as artifacts*. Nowadays, the "track changes" feature in word processing turns an editor's work into ephemera, rarely captured and recorded. In this respect, the Wallace correspondence gains in importance.

Doubtless the Updike materials—of which I have cited several pieces—deserve a separate inventory and interpretation. These include extensive correspondence concerning *Five Poems* (1980), for whose cover Updike (a one-time art student) supplied an original drawing; proof texts and materials relating to his chapbook essay, *Emersonianism* (1984); materials relating to the collection, *On the Move* (1988), including hand-corrected typescripts of poems; and original, corrected typescript pages marked as "An Encounter Left Out of *Rabbit Redux*." Paginated 237-241 and stamped with his name and Georgetown MA address, the five pages show two distinct layers of revision in Updike's hand. The scene recounts a bus-ride conversation between Rabbit and the Reverend Eccles. Clearly, the scene's place in the original manuscript and its thematic relation to the published novel (and to its characters) deserve study.

There is a further piece of Updikeana worth recording, a short poem in holograph—"Bliss Blanc," printed in *Bits 3* and not included in Updike's *Collected*

Poems.[24]

Laying aside the business correspondence, it's their personal letters that offer the greatest delight: among the treasures held in MSU Special Collections, these are crown jewels. This essay gives the merest hint of their quality, not to mention their considerable quantity. And anyone interested in the correspondence should start at the beginning: one of the earliest of Updike's surviving letters (dated 14 Aug. [1953]) came to Wallace typed on Sandy Island Camp stationery—a YMCA summer camp where, apparently, Updike was spending vacation. While Wallace has just graduated from Harvard and prepares for England, Updike, still the student, gossips about classes and papers and professors. The letter bears witness to the easy friendship that had grown between classmates and would continue throughout Wallace's lifetime.

We're lucky to have this correspondence. The John Updike Literary Trust has begun the laborious process of collecting, editing, and publishing Updike's letters.[25] In time, his correspondence with Wallace will need to be part of that ambitious national treasure: for Updike was, indeed, a voluminous writer whose personality reveals itself in each missive. He may well prove to be one of the last great American letter writers.[26] If so, Wallace will have contributed his share.

---

[24] The letter (dated 11 July [1976]) in which it is inscribed contains hand corrections that have removed a layer of puns: changing "blanche" to "blanc" and "blond" to "woman," the title turns more to the white wine than the bleached blonde. Here and more extensively in "An Encounter Left Out of *Rabbit Redux*," we see glimpses of writerly "process." It's hard to imagine the poet-teacher not using such classic classroom examples, given the prominence that revision receives in *Writing Poems*, whose third section, "Process: Making the Poem Happen," includes two chapters on the subject: "Revising (I): Both Ends of the Pencil" (283-314) and "Revising (II): Seven-Eighths of the Iceberg" (315-46). At the core of this second chapter are facsimiles of four drafts of Miller Williams's poem, "Politics." These "are fairly legible," write Wallace and Boisseau, "and we can follow in them all the twists and turns in the writing of the poem" (329, qtd. From the 4th ed.).

[25] See the web article by James Plath, "Updike Letters to be published."

[26] I'm speaking not just of the esthetics of letter writing but of its traditional technologies of ink or pencil on letterhead stationery in a stamped envelope. And much of the value—the collectability—of the letter as artifact rests in its author's signature. So, the shift from "snail mail" to email correspondence "taketh away" as much as it giveth. Electronic autographs are hardly collectible. Messaging is both immediate and ephemeral, composed of photons rather than ink. One might turn an email into a pdf and print it, pretending to have created something artifactually authentic. But the electron is the substance of email, of which a printed pdf reads embarrassingly like a photocopy. The informality of email may make textual communication more conversational, allowing for back-and-forth in virtual time. But, in the 21st century, both the artistry and the traditional technologies of letter writing are largely dead.

Finally, Wallace's own writing merits study. His major published collections of poetry include *This Various World* (1957), *Views from a Ferris Wheel* (1965), *Ungainly Things* (1968), *Swimmer in the Rain* (1979), *Girlfriends and Wives* (1984), and *A Common Summer* (1989). Bits Press publications of his work include *Critters* (1978), *Charlie Joins the Circus* (1981), and *The Author* (1983)—this last being a series of poems inspired by Updike's dust-jacket photographs. Early recognitions that Wallace would receive for his poetry include the William Rose Benet Memorial Award (1957), the Bragdon Prize (1967), and the Emily Clark Balch Prize (1972); numerous local awards (from Case Western Reserve, the Cleveland community, and the state of Ohio) would come in his maturity. Wallace's contributions to the teaching of poetry include his successful and influential textbook, *Writing Poems* (1st ed. 1982; 4th ed. [with Michelle Boisseau] 1996), the work for which he remains best known among students of writing.[27] *Meter in English: A Critical Engagement* (1996) is a collection of essays written in response to his own innovative, controversial article, "Meter in English," which represents Wallace's last significant publication.

Currently available in fragments, a complete bibliography of Wallace's publications (as poet, teacher, editor) is wanting. Also wanting is a detailed description of manuscripts, both of published works (many of which survive in multiple drafts and versions) and unpublished—the latter being, arguably, of more immediate interest. These include *The Lost History of Everything* (1986) and *Full Alphabet* (1993), both collections of original and revised poetry, and two novels: *Rumpelstiltskin, Go Home* (1968), and *Invitation to Silence* (1970). A fifth typescript, *Free Verse and the Orbit of Meter* (1999), was among the primary occupations of his final months. Expanding upon theories previously outlined and debated in *Meter in English*, Wallace expected *Free Verse* to "stir up still further fury in that dusty area" of English, as he notes in a letter (dated 18 Aug. 1997) to Jenni Boone. I'm pleased to have contributed to its posthumous publication.

But I should end on a lighter, more poetic note. "The Double Play" (which is reprinted here from *The Common Summer*) remains one of Wallace's most

---

[27] Wallace contributed to the 5th edition, which was published posthumously in 2000. Still popular, *Writing Poems* is currently in its 8th edition (2020), coedited by Boisseau, Hadara Bar-Nadav, and Randall Mann.

often anthologized poems; its image of the pitcher walking off the mound, "casual, / in the space where the poem has happened," offers a quiet exit for the poet and his readers.

> In his sea-lit
> distance, the pitcher winding
> like a clock about to chime comes down with
>
> the ball, hit
> sharply, under the artificial
> banks of arc-lights, bounds like a vanishing string
>
> over the green
> to the shortstop magically
> scoops to his right whirling above his invisible
>
> Shadows
> In the dust redirects
> its flight to the running poised second baseman
>
> pirouettes
> leaping, above the slide, to throw
> from mid-air, across the colored tightened interval,
> to the leaning-
> out first baseman ends the dance
> drawing it disappearing into his long brown glove
> stretches. What
> is too swift for deception
> is final, lost, among the loosened figures
>
> jogging off the field
> (the pitcher walks), casual
> in the space where the poem has happened.

Works Cited

In the following list, citations of materials unique to the Wallace Collection (WC) refer to storage box and file numbers: hence, "WC 1.5" cites box 1, file 5. MSU Special Collections publishes an online "Descriptive Inventory" of the Wallace Collection, which includes the most extensive biography of Wallace to date. The inventory and information relating to the collection can be accessed at https://libraries.missouristate.edu/Archives.htm.

Armour, Richard. Letter to Robert Wallace ("Today there were two memorable events for me"). Typescript dated 6 Nov. 1985. WC 4.194.

———. Letter to Robert Wallace ("Since you signed your letter 'Bob,'"). Typescript dated 1 Feb. 1986. WC 4.194.

Baker, David, editor. *Meter in English: A Critical Engagement.* U of Arkansas P, 1996.

Bush, Douglas. Letter to Robert Wallace ("I am glad"). Typescript dated 16 Dec. 1956. WC 1.1.

———. Letter to Robert Wallace ("I am very grateful"). Typescript dated 22 Oct. 1957. WC 1.1.

Ciardi, John. Letter to Robert Wallace ("Forgive what must seem a sullen delay"). Typescript dated 19 Sep. 1966, on *Saturday Review* stationary. WC 1.1.

———. Letter to Robert Wallace ("I hope it goes well with you"). Handwritten note dated 12 Nov. 1968, on *Saturday Review* notepad stationary. WC1.1.

———. Letter to Robert Wallace ("Thanks for two real poems"). Typescript dated 1 Sep. 1956, on *Saturday Review* stationary. WC 1.1.

Ewart, Gavin. *The Gavin Ewart Show: Selected Poems* 1939-1985. Bits, 1985.

Hall, Donald. "Donald Hall: The Western Review, Autumn 1958, pp. 88-89."

Typed transcript [by Wallace?] of Hall's review of *This Various World*. WC 7.147.

———. Letter to Robert Wallace ("You are kind to send it to us"). Undated handwritten note on *Paris Review* notepad stationary. WC 1.3.

Jacobson, Bonnie. Letter to Robert Wallace ("Sometimes I think"). Typescript dated 18 Nov. 1982. WC 1.3.

Kennedy, X. J. *Hangover Mass*. Bits, 1984.

Levertov, Denise. Letter to Robert Wallace ("I like these a lot"). Undated handwritten note on *Nation* notepad stationary. WC 1.5.

levy, d.a. Letter to "WRU Englishe Department" ("I do not want"). Undated (1966?) photocopy of typescript. WC 1.5.

Nash, Ogden. Letter to Robert Wallace ("Many thanks for your nice letter"). Typescript dated 19 Jan. 1949. WC 1.7.

Nemerov, Howard. Letter to Robert Wallace ("Again I think"). Typescript dated 16 Aug. 1966. WC Box 1.7.

———. Letter to Robert Wallace ("Poetry is itself"). Typescript dated 8 Feb. 1981. WC 1.7.

Oates, Joyce Carol. Review of Mary Oliver, *The Night Traveler* (Bits, 1977). *The New Republic* vol. 179 no. 24, 1978, pp. 28-29.

Oliver, Mary. *American Primitive*. Little, Brown, 1983.

———. Letter to Robert Wallace ("I was very happy to get your letter"). Typescript dated 11 July 1977. WC 4.94.

———. *The Night Traveler*. Bits, 1977.

———. *Twelve Moons*. Little, Brown, 1979.

Plath, James. "Updike letters to be published." *The Updike Society*, 14 Dec. 2016. https://blogs.iwu.edu/johnupdikesociety/2016/12/14/updike-letters-to-be-published/. Accessed 1 June 2022.

Slavitt, David R. *Elegies to Delia of Albius Tibullus*. Bits, 1985.

——. Letter to Robert Wallace ("Can you set up a poetry reading for me?"). Typescript dated 26 Oct. 1967. WC 1.9.

——. *Tristia of Ovid*. Bits, 1986.

Updike, John. *Collected Poems*, 1953-1993. Knopf, 1993.

——. "An Encounter Left Out of Rabbit Redux." Typescript [1971] with pen and pencil corrections in Updike's hand. WC 4.84.

——. *Emersonianism*. Bits, 1984.

——. *Five Poems*. Bits, 1980.

——. Letter to Robert and Emily Wallace ("Do come see us"). Typescript dated 23 July [1965?]. WC 4.82.

——. Letter to Robert Wallace ("Herewith"). Typescript dated 20 Apr. [1980]. WC 1.10.

——. Letter to Robert Wallace ("I so much liked seeing my poem in Bits 2"). Manuscript dated 11 July [1976]. Includes the short poem, "Bliss Blanc." WC 2.29.

——. Letter to Robert Wallace ("It was great to hear from you"). Typescript dated 4 Feb. [1978]. WC 1.10.

——. Letter to Robert Wallace ("I've marked October 8th on my calendar as sherry time"). Typescript dated 7 Apr. [1980]. WC 1.10.

——. Letter to Robert Wallace ("Jeez, am I embarrast!"). Typescript dated 14 Aug. [1953], on Sandy Island Camp stationary. WC 4.82.

——. Letter to Robert Wallace ("Permit me to bash out"). Typescript dated 27 Feb. [1963] on *New Yorker* stationary. WC 1.10.

——. Letter to Robert Wallace ("Thank you for your many informative letters"). Typescript dated 12 Feb. [1965]. WC 1.10.

——. Letter to Robert Wallace ("Thanks so much for sending us your book"). Typescript dated 20 Aug. [1957]. WC 1.10.

——. Letter to Robert Wallace ("Well, how about"). Typed postcard dated 7 Oct. [1987]. CW 12.258.

——. *On the Move.* Bits, 1988.

——. *Self-Consciousness: Memoirs.* Knopf, 1989.

Wallace, Robert. "Bits Press Checklist: The First Decade." Photocopy of a typescript dated Jan. 1985. WC case file.

——. *Charlie Joins the Circus.* Bits, 1981.

——. *The Common Summer: New and Selected Poems.* Pittsburgh: Carnegie-Mellon UP, 1981.

——. *Critters.* Bits, 1978.

——. *Free Verse and the Orbit of Meter.* Unpublished typescript. 1998. Author's private file.

——. *Full Alphabet.* Unpublished typescript dated 1993. WC uncatalogued item.

——. *Invitation to Silence.* Unpublished typescript [1970]. WC 6.140.

——. Letter to Jenni Boone ("At last, a bit of quiet!"). Typescript, dated 29 Dec. 1997 on Case Western Reserve University stationary. WC case file.

——. Letter to Jenni Boone ("Happy Valentine's Day!"). Typescript, dated 14 Feb. 1998 on Case Western Reserve University stationary. WC case file.

——. Letter to Judson Jerome. ("I'd be pleased by a 'Close-up'"). Typescript dated 12 Mar. 1986 on Case Western Reserve University stationary. WC Case file.

——. Letter to John Updike ("Thanks for the sentences"). Typescript dated 15 Oct. 1987. WC 12.258.

——. Letter to John Updike ("We are again waiting"). Carbon of typescript dated 5 Nov. 1980. WC 1.10.

——. Letter to Mary Oliver ("I'm returning the two poems"). Carbon of typescript dated 31 May 1977. WC 4.94.

——. "Meter in English." *Meter in English: A Critical Engagement,* edited by David Baker. U of Arkansas P, 1996, pp. 3-42.

——. *The Lost History of Everything.* Unpublished typescript [1986]. WC 11.223.

——. "Robert Wallace" ("I was born in 1932"). Typescript biography [1977?]. WC case file.

——. *Rumpelstiltskin, Go Home.* Unpublished typescript [1968]. WC 6.135-136.

——. *Swimmer in the Rain.* Carnegie-Mellon UP, 1979.

——. *This Various World and Other Poems.* Scribner's, 1957.

——. *Ungainly Things.* Dutton, 1968.

——. *Views from a Ferris Wheel.* Dutton, 1965.

——. *Writing Poems.* 1st ed. Little, Brown, 1982.
2nd ed. Scott Foresman, 1987.
3rd ed. HarperCollins, 1991.
4th ed. (with Michelle Boisseau). HarperCollins, 1996.
5th ed. (with Michelle Boisseau). Longman, 2000.

———. *Girlfriends and Wives.* Carnegie-Mellon UP, 1984.

Wallace, Robert, ed. *Light Year* '84. Bits, 1984.

———. *Light Year* '85. Bits, 1985.

Wallace, Robert, and James G. Taaffe, editors. *Poems on Poetry: Mirror's Garland.* Dutton, 1965.

Wheelock, John H. Letter to Robert Wallace ("I was very glad to have your letter"). Typescript dated 14 Nov. 1956, on Charles Scribner's Sons stationary. WC 1.9.

White, E. B. Letter to Robert Wallace ("Thank you for the copy"). Typescript dated 6 Nov. 1983. WC 3.55.

Wilbur, Richard. *A Finished Man.* Bits, 1985.

———. Letter to Robert Wallace ("I am back from France"). Typescript dated 17 June 1985. WC 10.202.

Williams, William Carlos. Letter to Robert Wallace ("Thank you for sending"). Typescript dated 18 Feb. 1960. WC 1.13.

The Yearbook 317. Harvard Yearbook Publications, 1953.

Appendix: Wallace's Correspondents

The following lists selected individuals with correspondence preserved in the Robert Wallace Collection. The item-counts are approximate, and a plus sign (+) indicates the presence of additional materials by or about that individual. Individuals listed with "several files" have numerous items scattered throughout the collection. Note that manuscript materials are not inventoried below.

Cyrilly Abels (1903-1975), American literary agent; managing editor of *Mademoiselle*. Several files.

Richard Armour (1906-1989), American humorist, author of *Twisted Tales from Shakespeare*. 3+ items.

Robert Bly (1926-2021), American poet, recipient of the National Book Award for *The Light Around the Body*; editor of *The Sixties*. 6+ items.

John Ciardi (1916-1986), American poet and translator, whose books include *Homeward to America* and *The Birds of Pompeii*; poetry editor for *The Saturday Review*, his recognitions include the Prix de Rome from the American Academy of Arts and Letters. Several files.

Robert Conquest (1917-2015), English poet and award-winning historian, author of *The Great Terror*; literary editor of the *London Spectator*. 8+ items.

David Daiches (1912-2005), English literary critic, author of *The Novel and the Modern World*, *A Study of Literature*, and *A Critical History of English Literature*. 1 item.

James Dickey (1923-1997), American poet and novelist, author of *Deliverance*, *Buckdancer's Choice*, and *The Whole Motion*, winner of the National Book Award for poetry; one-time poetry editor for *Esquire*. 1+ item.

Babette Deutsch (1895–1982), American poet and critic, whose collections include *Animal, Vegetable, Mineral* (1954), *Coming of Age* (1959), and *Collected Poems* (1969). 1 item.

Stephen Dunn (1939-2021), American poet, recipient of the Pulitzer Prize for *Different Hours*. 3+ items.

T. S. Eliot (1888-1965), American Nobel Prize winning poet and literary critic, author of *The Waste Land*. 1 item.

Gavin Ewart (1916-1995), British poet known for light verse, his collections include *Pleasures of the Flesh and Londoners*. Several files.

Robert Francis (1901-1987), American poet, author of *Stand with Me Here*, recipient of the Rome Prize of the American Academy of Arts and Letters. 1 item.

Dana Gioia (1950-), American poet and critic, recipient of the American Book Award for *Interrogations at Noon*. Several files.

William Golding (1911-1993), British Nobel Prize winning novelist, author of *The Lord of the Flies*. 1 item.

Edward Gorey (1925-2000), American author and illustrator, known for his animation of opening credits for the PBS television show, *Mystery!* 1 item.

Donald Hall (1928-2018), American poet and critic, recipient of the Caldecott Medal, Frost Medal, and the National Book Critics Circle Award; one-time editor of *The Paris Review*. Several files.

Antony Hecht (1923-2004), American author and Chancellor of the Academy of American Poets, recipient of the Pulitzer Prize for *The Hard Hours*. 4+ items.

Ted Hughes (1930-1998), English Poet Laureate, dramatist, and critic, author of *The Hawk in the Rain and Selected Poems* (with Thom Gunn). 3+ items.

X. J. Kennedy (1929-), American poet, recipient of the Lamont Award of the Academy of American Poets for his *Nude Descending a Staircase*; won the first Michael Braude Award for his light verse. Several files.

Thomas Kinsella (1928-2021), Irish poet and recipient of the Denis Devlin Memorial Award, his work includes *Poems from City Centre* and *Madonna and Other Poems*. 1 item.

Maxine Kumin (1925-2014), American poet, recipient of the Pulitzer Prize for *Up Country: Poems of New England*. 1 item.

Philip Larkin (1922-1985), English poet, author of *The Less Deceived, High Windows*, and *The Whitsun Weddings*. 1 item.

Richmond Lattimore (1906-1984), American poet and scholar, known for his classical translations. Several files.

A. L. Lazarus (1914-1992), American poet and scholar, co-author of *A Suit of Four*. 6+ items.

Denise Levertov (1923-1997), Anglo-American poet, her *Freeing the Dust* won the Lenore Marshall Poetry Prize; one-time poetry editor for *The Nation* and *Mother Jones*. 3 items.

d.a. levy (1942-1968), American avant garde poet of the 1960s, editor of Cleveland's first underground newsletter, *The Buddhist Third Class Junkmail Oracle*. 1 item.

Peter Meinke (1932-), American poet, recipient of the Flannery O'Connor Award for his *Piano Tuner*. 5+ items.

W. S. Merwin (1927-2019), American poet, recipient of the Pulitzer Prize for his *Carrier of Ladders*. 1 item.

Howard Moss (1922-1987), American poet, recipient of the National Book Award for his *Selected Poems*; long-time poetry editor of the *New Yorker*. 20+ items.

Ogden Nash (1902-1974), American poet and humorist, specializing in light verse; his work includes *Hard Lines* and the Broadway play, *One Touch of Venus*. 1+ item.

Howard Nemerov (1920-1991), American poet, recipient of the Pulitzer Prize for his *Collected Poems*. Several files.

John Frederick Nims (1913-1999), American poet and scholar, author of *Knowledge of the Evening*; one-time editor of *Poetry* magazine. 3+ items.

Sharon Olds (1942-), American poet, recipient of the National Book Critics Circle Award for *The Dead & the Living*. 1 item.

Mary Oliver (1935-2019), American poet, recipient of the Pulitzer Prize for her *American Primitive*. Several files.

Linda Pastan (1932-), American poet, author of *Carnival Evening*; recipient of the Pushcart Prize and Dylan Thomas Award. Several files.

Marge Piercy (1936-), American poet, novelist, and essayist, author of *Circles in the Water* and *The Moon is Always Female*. 3+ items.

Laurence Perrine (1915-1995), American scholar, author of *Sound and Sense*. 1 item.

Burton Raffel (1928-2015), American poet, critic, and translator, author of *Beethoven in Denver*; editor of *Denver Quarterly*. 2 items.

David R. Slavitt (1935-), American poet and scholar, member of the Academy of American poets, known for such classical translations as his *Complete Roman Drama*. Several files.

Elizabeth Spires (1952-), American poet, author of *Wordling*. Several files.

William Stafford (1914-1993), American Poet Laureate, recipient of the National Book Award for *Traveling Through the Dark*. 3+ items.

May Swenson (1919-1989), American poet, author of *Another Animal*, Chancellor of the Academy of American Poets. 1 item.

Lewis Turco (1934-), American poet and scholar, author of *Books of Forms*. Several files.

John Updike (1932-2009), American novelist, poet, and critic, recipient of two Pulitzer Prizes for *Rabbit is Rich and Rabbit at Rest*. Several files.

David Wagoner (1926-2021), American poet, author of *Traveling Light*; editor of *Poetry Northwest*. 3+ items.

John Wain (1925-1994), English novelist and critic, author of *The Pardoner's Tale* and *Samuel Johnson*. 1 item.

Ronald Wallace (1945-), American poet, author of *Vital Signs* and *Quick Bright Things*. 4+ items.

John Hall Wheelock (1886-1978), American poet and scholar, author of *Human Fantasy*; member of the American Academy of Arts and Letters and Chancellor of the American Academy of Poets, he was long-time senior editor of Scribner's. 15+ items.

E. B. White (1899-1985), American Pulitzer Prize-winning author of *Charlotte's Web* and other children's books; long-time staff member of *The New Yorker*. 2+ items.

Richard Wilbur (1921-2017), American poet, recipient of the Bollingen Prize and Pulitzer Prize; his works include *The Beautiful Changes* and *Things of This World*. Several files.

Heathcote Williams (1941-2017), English playwright and actor, author of *Whale Nation*; poetry editor of *Transatlantic Review*. 1 item.

Miller Williams (1930-2015), American poet, recipient of the Amy Lowell Award and Prix de Rome, author of *Some Jazz a While*. Several files.

William Carlos Williams (1883-1963), American poet, recipient of the National Book Award and Pulitzer Prize; his works include *Kora in Hell*, *Spring and All*, and *Paterson*. 1+ item.